D0867270

Up From Within

Also by George R. Metcalf
Black Profiles

Up From Within

Today's New Black Leaders

by George R. Metcalf

McGraw-Hill Book Company

New York   St. Louis   San Francisco
Düsseldorf   London   Mexico   Panama
Sydney   Toronto

*To my wife, Elizabeth, whose
constant help and devotion
strengthened this
volume immeasurably.*

Contents

Foreword

It is more than a decade now since the Negro Revolution took off in 1960 with the student sit-in in Greensboro, North Carolina. The first five years, dominated by a series of demonstrations organized by Martin Luther King, Jr., and his devoted followers, emphasized non-violence.

The climax came in 1963, on the hundredth anniversary of the Emancipation Proclamation, when the outpouring of black anguish seemed for a time irresistible.

Responding to the pressure on white America, President John F. Kennedy said: "Surely in 1963, one hundred years after emancipation, it should not be necessary for any American citizen to demonstrate in the streets for an opportunity to stop at a hotel, or eat at a lunch counter . . . on the same terms as any other American."

In February of that year he sent a special message to Congress recommending legislation that would strengthen the right of Southern blacks to vote and, after the terrifying spectacle in Birmingham of white police officers using dogs to curb black demonstrators, he broadened his appeal to bar discrimination in the use of public accommodations and to withhold federal funds from projects in which there was evidence of discrimination.

Yet Congress refused to be hurried and it took the jolt of

a presidential assassination and the consummate political touch of his successor, Lyndon B. Johnson, to enact the Civil Rights Act of 1964, generally considered the most comprehensive such bill ever enacted by a Congress of the United States.

When King witnessed the signing in the White House, he could claim that non-violence had proved the key to change and when, a year later, following the march from Selma to Montgomery—again to protest white brutality—the federal government approved a far-reaching election bill that promised an end to white supremacy in the Old South, his position appeared unassailable. As the prophet of non-violence, he had shown unbelievable skill in marshaling white support behind black aspirations.

What King could hardly sense was that a growing segment of urban blacks was already disenchanted with the cry for civil rights. They were finding no immediate improvement in either their position in society or their standard of living. What good was it, they asked, to have statutes against discrimination in employment, if the employers disregarded the law and ghetto unemployment remained two and three times higher than comparable white figures? What good was it, they went on, to have open-housing laws, amid professions of brotherhood, if white real estate agents concocted every imaginable device to keep blacks from renting or purchasing property in white neighborhoods? Moreover, the whole concept of non-violence was distasteful to this group because it reflected a philosophy of subservience, a kind of coming hat in hand to ask the master's favor, and—worst of all—submission to white violence. If you believed that black was a sign of strength, as the growing generation of blacks did, then it was impossible to achieve equality through such non-violent obsequiousness. Indeed, the situation was reminiscent of the celebrated battle that broke out between Booker T. Washington and Dr. W. E. B. DuBois a half-century before, at which time DuBois accused

Washington of giving away what it was not his to give in order to curry white favor.

Ironically, King's first rebuff occurred only weeks after his greatest triumph at Selma. Cries of "burn, baby, burn" were heard for the first time during the summer of 1965 above the raging immolation of Watts. When King tried to relieve the tensions with personal appeals to the rioting youths, he was roundly booed. The episode proved to be the watershed in the Revolution. After Watts, the directional signals pointed to militancy instead of non-violence; separation, not integration, with King's voice increasingly muted.

The *New* Revolution, born of militancy, defined itself in a number of ways. Where the non-violent revolution was primarily a product of Southern hands and Southern leadership, the violent revolution was Northern-oriented, organized largely by ghetto residents.

It wore a black raiment, lauding everything black, and in doing so gave Black America the first positive change in its psyche since Marcus Garvey stirred the masses with appeals to black pride during the early 1920s. As King had been the moral father of non-violence, so Malcolm X, of Harlem fame, now became the ghetto sire of the *New* Revolution. Ossie Davis, author and playwright, would say of his magnetism: "They all, every last, black, glory-hugging one of them, knew that Malcolm—whatever else he was or was not —*Malcolm was a man!*"

But unlike King, Malcolm X was assassinated before the forces he unleashed gathered strength. Indeed, on February 21, 1965, the day the bullets silenced Malcolm, it would have required the prescience of a prophet to reveal that a new chapter in Negro history was about to begin.

To be sure, it was not until the summer of 1966 that the curtain officially rose and then it went up, not in Harlem as one might have expected, but in far-off Mississippi—where James Meredith, the first black to graduate from Ole Miss, undertook a 220-mile walk from Memphis to Jackson, hoping to allay the Southern blacks' fear of walking the major highways of Mississippi alone.

It was a curious march. "If anyone wants to go," Meredith had said, "it's his business." Three men thought over the invitation and decided to tag along. On the second day, the leader was suddenly shot from ambush and rushed to a Memphis hospital, where his wounds were found to be minor, Meredith's march overnight became a national *cause célèbre*.

No single incident could have focused more clearly the plight of a black citizen in a white racist society. Civil rights leaders flocked to his bedside to console and to assure him that they would take up the torch and continue the march to Jackson, which Meredith was temporarily unable to do.

Yet, before long, there was evidence that the *New* Revolution was creating a serious schism in the marchers between old-line civil rightists and the new militants who had joined the column. By the time the line reached Greenwood, Mississippi, the tensions were so great that Stokely Carmichael, the twenty-five-year-old head of the Student Nonviolent Coordinating Committee (SNCC), raised the battle cry of the militants—"black power"—to the cheers of friends who, according to Stokely, had always felt it, but always "were afraid to speak it."

Out of this unexpected beginning, a river of black nationalism flowed out to cover the entire country. In October, three months after the Meredith march, Bobby Seale and Huey Newton founded the Black Panther Party in Oakland and the following summer the first Black Power summit conference was held in Newark, only days after the city had endured the worst racial riot in its history.

The thrust was twofold: the militants or black nationalists wanted (1) freedom to develop their own life styles—Afro hair, Afro dress, Afro music, and such—and (2) power to eliminate white domination even if the objective spelled separation from the white milieu. The chant was taken up in various ways. Black students on the nation's campuses began demanding separate facilities—dormitories and dining halls. They called for new courses in black history, literature, and sociology leading to a baccalaureate in black studies.

In the armed services, blacks began demonstrating an opposition to white control which seriously undermined the efficiency of units stationed abroad.

On the labor front, where unions had systematically prevented blacks from gaining power, the militants organized caucuses as a prelude to displacing part or all of the white leadership.

In the world of finance, blacks began speaking of black capitalism as the answer to ghetto poverty. Since the white-controlled banks had always downgraded real estate holdings within the black community, a demand arose for new banking institutions, supported by black savings under black management.

In the field of politics, blacks organized their urban enclaves to elect municipal, state, and federal officials. Often gerrymandered out of office in the past, they fought in court for equality within the limitations of the Warren Court's "one-man, one-vote" decision.

In the field of culture, black authors, playwrights, and artists created new dimensions, with new values quite apart from white standards. *Soul* came to have a special meaning in the black lexicon.

Objectively viewed, however, the *New* Revolution had its limitations. In its effort to achieve change, it frequently degenerated into violence and ended tearing down as much as it built up.

It was only natural, then, as more and more blacks saw this, that a third stage of the Negro Revolution would emerge. By combining the rights won in the first with the growing black pride of the second, they commenced to build a new order for the 11.2 per cent of the U.S. population that is black.

They would work within the system where black and white activities were coterminous; they would reserve the right to follow their own instincts and desires where they weren't. Sorted out, this meant that in the fields of economics and politics—the locus of power and money—blacks would compete with whites across the board.

They would demand equal rights in education to prepare for jobs in the business and political world; they would seek the preferences in corporate and governmental life that had previously been the monopoly of whites. But in their social intercourse or in the development of black culture, they felt a right to develop independently—if they wished.

Accordingly, it is worth inquiring at this point whether stage three of the Negro Revolution has been a success. In the fields where blacks compete with whites, are they receiving equal treatment within the system?

My purpose in writing this book is to permit the reader to draw his own conclusions after reading the life stories of seven men and one woman—all black. All are both non-violent and militant—non-violent because their efforts are peaceful, militant because they see in themselves evidence of the growing black image in the U.S. mirror.

Their names:

1. John Conyers, Jr. — Detroit Congressman
2. Kenneth Allen Gibson—Mayor of Newark
3. Clifton R. Wharton, Jr. — President of Michigan State University
4. Shirley Chisholm — Brooklyn Congresswoman
5. Horace Julian Bond — Georgia Legislator
6. John Mackey — Baltimore Colt Tight End
7. Alvin F. Poussant, M.D. — Harvard Psychiatrist
8. Andrew F. Brimmer — Member, Federal Reserve Board

In the process of unraveling their careers, I found certain similarities that may provide a clue for other blacks struggling to carve out meaningful lives.

First, they all had stable childhoods. During their so-called impressionable years, their families showered them with affection. Without exception, their parents encouraged them to make something of their lives.

Second, all but one graduated from college, clear evidence of the value each placed on higher education. In addition to the baccalaureate degree, two earned doctorates in economics, one took a medical degree, and one a law degree.

Third, there is no doubt that each life was touched with a bit of good fortune. If the Detroit newspapers had not been on strike during the summer of 1962, John Conyers, Jr., would most likely not have been elected to Congress. If the Warren Court had not insisted on a legislative reapportionment in New York State, Shirley Chisholm would still be a state assemblywoman. If Lyndon Johnson had not been feuding with William McChesney Martin, Jr., chairman of the Federal Reserve Board, Andrew Brimmer in all likelihood would not belong to the Board. And so it goes. As it was said of old, "There is a tide in the affairs of men,/ Which, taken at the flood, leads on to fortune. ..."

One of the most interesting results of this biographical compendium was to discover the change in black attitudes toward white people. During the era of the civil rights campaigns, it was not unusual to find black Americans sincerely grateful for any support they received from the white community that might aid the enactment of anti-bias laws affecting jobs, education, housing, and such. Black eyes were constantly turned up to the white liberal who spoke the language of equality. No one could deny, however, that a dialogue conducted on two planes was unhealthy.

With the coming of the *New* Revolution, that ceased, but in turning away from this advocate, blacks adopted a militance which made conversations between the white and the black communities equally difficult. The most cynical appellation blacks reserved for the "white liberal."

Yet it is probably true that all this was a necessary bridge to stage three of the Revolution. Blacks had to throw off the ancient chains of racial inferiority to stand equal with the whites. What is now beginning to emerge is the spirit that says "I am proud of my blackness, but I don't want the white man to remind me of it. I have succeeded and I want to be accepted for what I am and not because my skin is black."

How is it going? Can blacks compete in the public market within a system that is white-oriented? My answer is an unqualified *yes,* and the stories that follow are my best argument.

George R. Metcalf

Auburn, N. Y.
March 20, 1971

John Conyers, Jr. ═══════════

❡ "No sin rests heavier on America than the senseless treatment of the American Negro," insists John Conyers, Jr., of Detroit, forty-one-year-old member of Congress who struggles tirelessly to remove the deeply etched stains of white racism in the U.S. Articulate, intelligent, persevering, he is in the process of becoming the acknowledged leader of black congressmen on Capitol Hill. Conyers' credentials are excellent. Fashioned neither by wealth nor by poverty, he was cut from black middle-class stock which forms the backbone of Michigan's sprawling First Congressional District.

Among the 230,000 Democratic voters, the strongest economic force is organized labor in the auto industry, which has been a part of Conyers' life from birth. John's father came north from Atlanta in the twenties and took a job with Chrysler spraying auto bodies. It was a day when "blacks did the prime coat, and white workers put on the finish and got an extra dime an hour." This so angered the elder Conyers that eventually he confronted Walter P. Chrysler with the evidence of Jim Crowism and the differential was removed. For demonstrating union sympathies, he was frequently fired, but ties to the men invariably sufficed to bring him back. "It was that, or have the men go out," the son said later. In 1937 the father took part in the famous forty-seven-day sit-down strike; the following year, when the "lily-white" AFL rejected a Conyers-written paragraph in the union constitution encouraging "all workers without regard to race, creed, color, national origin or ancestry to share equally in the full benefits of union organization," Walter Reuther led the workers into John L. Lewis' embryonic industrial union—the CIO.[1]

This was the background into which John, the eldest of four brothers, was born on May 16, 1929. "And when you go through this type of life," a friend of John's remarked, "some of it is bound to rub off, and so John had the benefit, seeing the labor movement in its formative years fighting against many types of oppressions that blacks are fighting against now." The senior Conyers heartily agreed. "My sons," he observed, "got a chance early to learn about the struggle. They didn't grow up with silver spoons in their mouths. They didn't know what it was to be socially prominent. They grew up with little people and they have always staked their future with little people." [2]

Conyers' mother, Lucille, implanted the same seeds of self-reliance: to get ahead, you had to work. Accordingly, John never followed the easy road. She recalls how he liked music, wanted a cornet, but lacked the funds to buy one. Rather than plead poverty, he got a job in a neighborhood drugstore, saved, and eventually purchased one. Like her husband, Lucille insisted that John never forget his humble origin, a lesson she often had to teach alone while the senior Conyers was away as organizer for the United Auto Workers. When, years later, the son was preparing to go to Washington for the first time, she drew him aside and admonished "You're going there because so many of these little people have faith in you." [3]

As a young man, however, political service was farthest from his thinking. Conyers thought he wanted to be an engineer, but along came Korea. A month after the outbreak of war, he was called into the Michigan National Guard and eventually went to Officer Candidate School, where he was commissioned a second lieutenant in the U.S. Army Corps of Engineers. After forty-one months in the service, which included combat and a merit citation during a twelve-month stretch in Korea, he was discharged.

By then he was surfeited with engineering and had become interested in the law. Wayne State University in Detroit was offering a combined baccalaureate and law degree which fitted perfectly with his use of the Korean War GI Bill of Rights. After giving the proposition some thought, Conyers decided to jettison engineering and four years later walked out of Wayne State, with baccalaureate and law degrees in his hand.

Now began a meteoric career of six years which took him from a lowly law graduate in a fledgling partnership to membership in the House of Representatives. The start came in 1958 when he organized the firm of Conyers, Bell and Townsend. Gradually, his duties edged him toward the political flame. First he took on the additional duty of referee for Michigan's Workmen's Compensation Department. Then he became staff assistant to Detroit's Representative John Dingell, a name with historic meaning to Michigan voters, for Dingell's father had been among the first congressmen to call (unsuccessfully) for a national health insurance program sponsored by the federal government.

Meanwhile, the state of Michigan was preparing a drastic change in its congressional districts, mandated by the one man-one vote decision of the Warren Court. Its legislature had taken part of Dingell's district—a part Conyers by then knew intimately—to make the new First Congressional District. When black professional politicians had had an opportunity to study the boundaries, they were convinced a Negro could win. The question was who.

In view of the intense UAW concentration, the Democratic organization was convinced the candidate should be a mature union favorite. Accordingly, they named Richard

Austin, a wealthy accountant, overlooking Conyers as too young and inexperienced. But Conyers held several cards that could make the difference. He carefully weighed the odds of a primary contest and decided it was worth a chance. Admittedly, the UAW was strong, but at that time a power struggle was in process between Horace Sheffield, a Negro international representative, and Nelson Jack Edwards, the only black on the UAW executive board. Edwards came out for Conyers and swung into line behind him militant groups and civil rights workers, who were then riding high.

A second advantage was that the Detroit *Free Press* and Detroit *News* were shut by striking employees, a fact that militated against Austin. The customary avenues of publicity by which a candidate of the Democratic organization might expect to swallow the opposition were thus denied Conyers' opponent. In a close contest this factor could be crucial. Indeed, one of Conyers' closest allies remarked afterward, "Had the newspapers been in operation, I think John would not have been elected."

Finally, at thirty-five Conyers was bursting with the physical energy a successful campaign required. According to *Ebony* reporter Simeon Booker, Conyers "tramped, rode and drove more than 100,000 miles" in the next nine months. "He shook thousands of hands, kissed hundreds of babies, charmed clubs of housewives and single ladies, spoke at hundreds of coffee hours, ate chitterlings, ham hocks, and chicken at scores of political dinners, and visited nearly every home and shopping center."

Along the way, Conyers gathered together a gigantic volunteer organization. As many as 2000 persons offered to help him, once they understood it was a battle between David and Goliath, with the Democratic regulars supporting Austin because they thought Conyers was too young and immature. At the outset, Conyers' campaign flowed like a dry creek. Detroit's first Negro Congressman, Charles C.

Diggs, explained it this way to Booker: "He first started using the gimmick of a thinking man's friend. I told him to change that line and emphasize his youth. Folks today want a live-wire, a champion, and youth is an asset." Conyers took the advice.

Gradually, the tenor of the campaign changed. Rubbing elbows with the little people he had always known, he found he possessed other assets than a perspicacious mind. His trim 170-pound figure, spread over a five-foot-ten frame, chestnut complexion, close-cropped mustache, even rows of white teeth, and compassionate brown eyes gave him a charisma women voters found irresistible. He made no bones about its usefulness in his campaign. "Men," he would say in his mellifluous way, "talk and blow smoke in your face. Women go out and work and bring in votes." A bachelor, he practiced tossing verbal bouquets to spread his charms. "Dear," "baby," and "darling" became habitual chatter, and when it was finally finished, he had won by a few dozen votes—one of the closest primary votes in Michigan history. "What converted him into a winning candidate," explained a friend, "was his ability to make people feel important and volunteer to work for him to their maximum." [4]

The general election which followed was something of an anticlimax. Conyers swamped his Republican opponent by a 5–1 margin and took the measure of Milton Henry, founder of the Freedom Now Party, 90–1. When he left Detroit to take his seat in Washington, alongside five other black congressmen who had preceded him into the House, he could reflect (in his own words) that "politically, the Negro was just coming out of the Civil War" and that it was his primary duty to establish a standard for liberated blacks. It so happened that even before the swearing-in ceremony, the chance came for Conyers to unfurl his colors.

A dozen veterans of the House were anxious to contest the seating of the five Mississippi members on the grounds their election was illegal: Mississippi, they charged, had restricted the right of Negroes to register and vote. Conyers was one of five newly elected members asked to join the group. Their protest elicited no wide support among rank-and-file House delegates, but did serve notice that Conyers was a voice to be heard.

In fact, the House leadership which directs the assignment of freshmen Representatives to standing committees was already impressed. No single event in the life of a new congressman, apart from his original election, is nearly as significant as the committee to which he is assigned. Designation to a minor committee within the House's power establishment can mean permanent banishment to a political Siberia. On the other hand, assignment to one of the cherished committees within the House can quickly change a neophyte into a sophisticated legislator whose every action is watched. Just how one freshman is favored and another overlooked is one of the inscrutable mysteries of the House. Whether the appointive body—the Ways and Means Committee—uses its own intuition, relies on the word of other legislators, sends forth its own agents, or uses a combination of all three doesn't really matter. The fact is that by the time a newly elected member is tapped, for better or worse, a rough-hewn destiny is already at work, hence the tremendous power the Committee wields over the life of the House. It is a tribute to Conyers that he was appointed to the prestigious Judiciary Committee, for this was the simple acknowledgment that the members believed him capable of significant growth.

In their approach to legislative issues, legislators tend to display certain political philosophies. Some support the left, some the right, some cling to the middle ground. In short, they reflect the interests, desires, and ambitions of their constituents. As a representative of Detroit's black area, Conyers sought to emulate his hero, Martin Luther King, Jr., "the greatest person, the most moving human being," he said he had ever known. "Although I am hardly able to walk in the footprints of this man," he told friends, "I nevertheless study his sermons, read his speeches, and try, no matter how unsuccessfully, to live and work as he would have wanted me."

Yet such hagiographic sentiment for the man King did not prevent Conyers from seeing the limitation to the Southerner's concept of non-violence as a political weapon. "It does seem a little bit absurd," he said in his Washington office, "that this nation, the most violent, the most powerful, the most militaristic of any nation on the face of the earth, would be concerned about the concept of non-violence." This is not to draw the conclusion that he perceives in violence the cure to black ills, however. Far from it; Conyers, a friend says, "believes in the system and is going to see to it —as much as he possibly can—that it works not only for whites but for blacks also. John is not a separatist in any sense of the word. He just firmly believes that the plight of blacks is just an example of what is wrong with America as a whole."

For example, Conyers told the House just four days before the disastrous Detroit riot of July 23, 1967, that "a national unemployment rate of six per cent is considered 'dangerous' [yet] the Negro unemployment rate is estimated to be from 10 to 33 per cent. The rate of joblessness among Negro youth is estimated to be more than 30 per cent [which is] much higher than the overall rate of unemployment during the worst days of the depression in the 1930s."

A second handicap is the quality of black education. "The lifetime earning potential of a Negro male college graduate is 47 per cent that of a white college graduate," proof that educational facilities in the ghetto are "meager and inferior." More than 50 per cent of all Negro children who enter the ninth grade do not graduate from high school. And even the Negro student who does graduate receives a much poorer quality education. "In my own congressional district," Conyers points out, "I have attended high school graduations where some of the honored graduates had great trouble reading their own diplomas."

A third clinker in the Conyers lexicon is ghetto housing, which the Congressman calls a national disgrace. Is it any wonder, he asks, that millions of Americans feel frustrated when they are "trapped in this inherited poverty and degradation?"

Given these deficiencies—tragic unemployment, inferior education, and deplorable housing—Conyers is certain that nothing short of an enormous investment of public capital will reverse the trend. But no such investment is conceivable, he believes, without a change in national priorities that reduces U.S. military commitments and substitutes in their place additional appropriations for the cure of urban ills. Consequently, Conyers has become one of the most outspoken critics in Congress of the military-industrial establishment, which during the Kennedy-Johnson years was responsible (said he jointly with nine other Senators and Representatives) for "at least $500 billion sunk in military expenditures, a disastrous war in Vietnam, a senseless intervention in the Dominican Republic, more than forty-two treaty commitments to as many countries to intervene 'in case of aggression'—all this while acute poverty and distress persist within the United States itself." Their polemic went on to explain that "in the decade from 1959 to 1968, direct defense outlays of the United States came to more than $551 billion, twice the amount spent for new private and public housing in the same decade, and nearly twice as much as Federal, state and local governments allocated to education. In 1967 alone, a conservative estimate of military-related spending was $100 billion. This was more than all Federal, state, and local expenditures on health, hospitals, education, old age benefits, welfare, unemployment and agriculture.

"This order of priorities prevails at a time when twenty

million Americans live in dilapidated, rat-infested housing while the building industry cannot even keep up with the population increase and is in fact declining in productivity; when there are at least ten million victims of malnutrition and untold thousands of children with permanent brain damage because of insufficient food; when there are close to forty million people living in poverty with little access to medical or welfare care; while millions of children are doomed to lives of misery and poverty because of inadequate or non-existent school facilities." [5]

Typically Conyers wanted to know more about the reason for misplaced priorities—U.S. involvement in Vietnam. A longtime friend of the Congressman, discussing this penchant for thoroughness, says, "John will spend hours and hours documenting facts. When he speaks, he knows what he's talking about." So when a chance arose to visit that war-torn land in the spring of 1969 with a group of eight religious and civil rights leaders, he took it. The trip bore out his worst suspicions of conditions under the Thieu-Ky regime. He talked with Truong Dinh Dzu in his cell in Chi Hoa prison. Dzu, a peace candidate, had received more votes for president of the South Vietnamese Republic than any candidate, Thieu excepted. His "crime" was that he had urged the formation of a coalition government as a step toward peace, and had gone to jail with Thieu's warning ringing in his ears: "My government can die because of these pacifists, but before we die, they will have to die first." By the time the American delegation reached Paris on its way home, the members had had time to sort out their views and were boiling. They cabled President Nixon of finding "a climate of political and religious suppression" incompatible with "representative or stable government." Talk of peace or any kind of opposition to the government, they said, "easily brings the charge of Communist sympathy and subsequent arrest."

Ensuing silence at the White House aroused Conyers to a

second effort to gain anti-Vietnam support. Six weeks after returning, he held a news conference to assert his belief in the folly of supporting a "dictatorial regime while trying to bring democracy to South Vietnam. The thing that bothers me as a black man, with occasion to have observed police treatment of blacks, is that this terrible thing in Vietnam is being visited upon South Vietnamese by South Vietnamese." [6] Still the White House had no comment to make.

On October 14, just hours before the anti-war moratorium was to flood the streets of Washington, Conyers rose in the House to state his unequivocal opposition to the conflict. "I have voted against every military appropriation authorized for Vietnam since I was elected to Congress," he reminded the solons. "But I will now from this year on vote against every authorization for military appropriations until some sanity and humaneness is shown by those who now wield the power."

The reasons were compelling: nothing had happened since President Nixon was elected on a platform to end the war. "Yes, some of the names," he said, "have been changed —Vietnamization, protective reaction, honorable settlement —but it is the same shameful game and its name is war—and it has not stopped. The killing and maiming go on. Nearly 10,000 of our men have died in Vietnam since [Nixon] took office." Then he dwelt on the illegality of fighting in Southeast Asia, pointing out that the Tonkin Bay resolution, passed by Congress on August 10, 1964, did not give the President "the authority to wage a military action in Vietnam." Furthermore, there was no "obliging commitment to the Government of South Vietnam" because the action was predicated on the SEATO Treaty—an organization subordinate to the United Nations. If the U.S. wanted to land troops legally in South Vietnam, it would have to receive permission from the UN as the parent body.

In the course of his comments upon the war, Conyers

called for a new, updated foreign policy. It was time to bury the past. The name U.S. was no longer a "source of hope to the oppressed," but an easy "target for fear and hatred" throughout the world. "In my judgement," he went on, "we must terminate that double standard which in the name of anticommunism has used war to give 'peace' and repression to give 'freedom.'"

The time was past for quibbling about U.S. disengagement in Vietnam. "Any way of getting out," he argued, "is more honorable than to continue. We must stop trying to save face. Is our confidence in ourselves so imperiled that we resort to even the most transparent deceptions? The people of this country should be told the truth—our war in Vietnam has been wrong."

"Are you listening, Mr. President?" he cried.[7]

The speech came at a time when Conyers was gaining congressional stature and Washington pundits were asking if he would take over the role of Adam Clayton Powell, the New York congressman whose star as the number-one black Representative was waning. None of the other House blacks, with the exception of Conyers, was giving promise of greater achievement. As Saul Friedman, of the *New Republic*, perceived in February 1967, "the other Negroes in the House, in addition to being rather light in color, have been rather light in weight. Chicago's William L. Dawson, in his thirteenth term, is an old-fashioned Kingfish sort, the boss of a ghetto political machine; Los Angeles' Gus Hawkins, in his third term, is rarely heard from although he was elected to speak for Watts; Detroit's Charles Diggs, an undertaker by profession, now in his seventh term, has no taste for rocking boats; and Philadelphia's Robert Nix, in his sixth term, considers his seat a reward for thirty years' service as a ward leader."

Conyers' toughest competition, it turned out, was not in Washington but at home, where the UAW could not forgive his conquest of union-picked Richard Austin in the 1964 congressional primary. Prior to this, the union had always had its way in district politics. Resentment spread when the leadership found that Conyers, unlike other congressmen, was determined to get involved in local affairs. Soon the word was out from one of Conyers' close associates: "We are building the biggest and best machine in this town." Naturally, relations between the UAW and Conyers polarized, with both sides fearing a loss of power. And for Conyers, isolated in Washington a majority of the time, the prospect was unpromising. In order to speak for black America, as Adam Clayton Powell did, he needed a strong home front. He simply had to have it out with the UAW.

The first test of strength came in the fall of 1966, when Conyers' close friend George Crockett ran for Recorder's Court Justice. At the time, the First Congressional District chairman was UAW-oriented Marc Stepp, whom Conyers had originally maneuvered into the job, hoping to bridge some of the union hostility. But Crockett was an anathema to the UAW, and when Stepp proceeded to throw the weight of the district's executive board against him, Conyers saw red. He refused to accept Stepp's explanation that a white candidate was needed on the slate to attract the votes of non-black residents in the district. To Conyers this was irrefutable evidence of a UAW power play engineered at his expense. Conyers got part of his revenge when Crockett was elected in November and received full payment the following February when his candidate for district chairman, Murray Jackson, a Detroit school official, dumped Stepp.

But the next year hostilities broke out again. Early in March Conyers had solicited the aid of Martin Luther King to form an all-Negro National Committee of Inquiry to review the qualifications of the presidential candidates and to make recommendations to the black voters. By summer, the group had grown to about a thousand Negro leaders, representing thirty-nine states, ringing the political spectrum with such moderates as entertainer Harry Belafonte to such extreme militants as Stokely Carmichael of the Black Panther party and Ron Karenga, founder-chairman of US. After King's assassination in April, Conyers took over the temporary chairmanship and chief responsibility for naming the choices.

The role was a difficult one because the options were murky. Blacks generally had no use for Richard Nixon and his running mate Spiro Agnew and even less for George Wallace of Alabama, but neither did Vice-President Hubert Humphrey send them into orbits of delight. They disliked his previous association only one heartbeat removed from President Lyndon Johnson and the Vietnam war. Furthermore, they were unable to get a forthright commitment from Humphrey on ameliorating the social afflictions of the black slums. It was while Conyers was floating about in this quandary that his tormentors in the UAW saw a chance to undermine him. What if Humphrey wasn't "forthright?" they asked. Was it possible that Conyers and his National Committee of Inquiry would end up contributing to Nixon's election? "The fear was generated by Democratic campaign leaders," said a Conyers aide, "because it was the only thing they had to fight the lack of enthusiasm in the black community." [8]

The climax came in a move to upbraid Conyers during a First District meeting. In a fiery confrontation, speaker after speaker castigated their congressman's neutrality, virtually calling him a traitor to black people and warning of the consequences if Humphrey lost. There is no reason to think Conyers didn't anticipate the avalanche. He had tried unsuccessfully to lead the NCI into Humphrey's camp, but was in no position, as its leader, to disavow the majority. He understood, too, what his father, with access to UAW groundswell sentiment, had told him—that he was playing a dangerous game in not endorsing Humphrey on the premise he would eventually strengthen his stand on domestic issues to insure the black vote. But, fired at from both sides, there was nothing to do but sit and await the outcome. His future hung uncertainly after a UAW representative finally moved for a public censure, but before the motion could be put to a vote Marcellius Ivory, another UAW official, took the floor to restore calm, saying it was "vindictive and out of order," and should be tabled—which it was. Two days later, Conyers used the occasion of Humphrey's visit to Detroit to make his peace within the district. He warmly endorsed the Democratic nominee. This action cooled the UAW fever, and Conyers was returned overwhelmingly to Congress in the election that followed.

Yet, the defeat of Humphrey and the residual UAW antagonisms over the outcome had to be faced. Union president Walter Reuther was among those who saw the folly of continuing the vendetta between certain leaders in the UAW and the black congressman. Shortly after the new Congress met, he therefore searched out Conyers for a cards-up discussion. When the meeting broke up, Reuther had "promised the UAW would not dictate policy to Conyers or his largely black constituency. And Conyers promised more cooperation with the union and its leaders in the First Congressional District." [9] While Reuther's concession gained little for the UAW, it seemed a tremendous *coup* for Conyers. If all went well, he could relax for the first time since his election in 1964, secure in the knowledge that the union would not undermine him while he was in Washington. He hoped now, in his own words, to speak on the House floor "for millions of black people who were not adequately represented." [10] But the hope was one prospect in Washington, where the conference with Reuther took place, quite another in Detroit, where the agreement had to be consummated, for anti-Conyers forces in the UAW were still unable to forget the past. A week after the Reuther confab, there was struggling against Conyers' attempt to fashion a slate of district officers that would include all factions, but this time he trounced them three to one, and for punish-

ment denied them seats on the District Committee. Politically speaking, Conyers had finally mounted into the saddle.

In the midst of this political bruhaha with the UAW,
Conyers fell into a controversy with the police over the
treatment of Detroit's black residents. The spark that
touched off the feud was the Christmas-afternoon arrest of
David Lee Curry, a nineteen-year-old, who had imbibed an
excess of holiday cheer and was abusive to a municipal bus
driver. When the police intervened, he used obscene language and, according to witnesses, so infuriated the officers
that they beat him repeatedly, even while handcuffed. The
story angered Conyers, who charged "police brutality, typical of the racism that messes up the Detroit Police Department." Along with civic, religious, civil rights, business, and
labor leaders, he stormed the office of Mayor Jerry Cavanagh to protest the treatment. His charge of brutality and
racism stirred up a hornet's nest of editorial diatribes. "Balo-
ney," commented the Detroit *Free Press* on December 28.
"Brutality, yes, but not racism as far as the facts show. . . .
We imagine that a drunk abusive nineteen-year-old white
punk would hardly have fared better. Had a white youth
sworn at the police, been told to stop it or else, and cursed
them again, we imagine he, too, would have wound up with
a gash on his head." Two days later the paper rebuked Conyers a second time, saying the Congressman was "determined to hang a racist tag on the whole police department.
. . . What is evident is that Conyers is more interested in
Conyers than he is in justice. He is more interested in hurl-
ing wild charges at Cavanagh than in seeing that the few
bad apples get pulled out of the police barrel. He is more
interested in promoting Conyers than the welfare of the citizens of Detroit—white and black alike." Piqued by this personal fusillade, Conyers ripped into his accuser in a prompt
letter to the paper: "Your editorial on the David Curry case
was not only unfair to me personally, but also irresponsible
in terms of the needs of the city of Detroit. . . . I and many

others who undertake this responsibility with me are being embarrassed by your unfounded accusations that we are using police brutality cases to promote my candidacy for public office. To me, this underscores the real tragedy that this occurs after the worst racial conflagration in American history. *Free Press* is still insensitive to the very poor relations that I think characterize this city. We do not indict the entire police department. Let me repeat this for emphasis. Every policeman is not a bad policeman. We are trying to eliminate the core of racism imbedded in the police department, by making specific positive recommendations. We are not trying to incite anyone to riot. We are operating within the framework of our government by petitioning the Mayor for redress. And this supposedly liberal newspaper in Detroit has done nothing more significant about it than continue to worry about whether a black man is going to run for Mayor."

This was followed by a Conyers-led campaign to alert the Detroit community to continuing instances of police brutality since the Christmas episode. Appearing before a resolutions committee at the Democratic state convention, Conyers' administrative assistant Leon Atchison had this story to tell: "On January 24, Leroy Johnson, a Chrysler worker and the father of two, came out of a friend's house and started to get into the wrong car by mistake. The car belonged to a white policeman who lived across the street. Johnson's own auto, just purchased and identical to the policeman's, was parked only two car-lengths away. The officer saw him, tiptoed across the street, stuck his gun in his back and pulled the trigger, and the bullet went clear through his body. Johnson was later charged with resisting arrest."

Still, as demanding as Detroit was on Conyers' time, it was in Washington that his reputation was growing to national dimensions. The horns which heralded his rise played a simultaneous lament for the exit of Adam Powell, who had never recovered from his censure in 1967. It was alleged at that time that he had traveled widely for pleasure at tax-payer expense. Whites and blacks the country over were in-censed, whites because Powell appeared to act as a law unto himself and blacks because they sensed racial overtones in the congressional indictment. Hadn't white high jinks been winked at in the past, they asked?

By January of that year, the clamor had reached such a pitch that the House refused to seat Powell and sanctioned the appointment of a committee, composed of nine lawyer-members, to investigate the Congressman's qualifications. Conyers was the only Negro to be named. He was careful to express confidence in the thoroughness with which the com-mittee would function. In all likelihood, he foresaw the dan-ger of passing judgment on a fellow black with legendary appeal in the ghettos. Yet he was fascinated by the promin-ence the appointment brought. There was no valid reason, he felt, why a nimble mind could not scramble, taking the best of two worlds and landing upright. As he saw it, "it was a poor sport that is not worth the candle."

It took the special committee exactly five weeks of hear-ings and deliberations to reach an agreement. The verdict: that Powell be seated, publicly censured by the Speaker, and fined $40,000 for "drawing a salary for his wife in viola-tion of House rules and for using public funds for travel ex-penses of members of his personal staff." The harshest pen-alty, however, was the loss of committee seniority. The man who had maneuvered through the House the most far-reaching legislation on education and labor of the early Johnson years was summarily cast out, going to the lowest rung of the seniority ladder. As it was, had it not been for Conyers, the punishment would have assumed sterner lines. At his insistence, penalties were reduced to the level even-tually announced. In the early stages, during closed committee sessions, the subject of inflicting vindictive punishment had arisen. "Do that and you might as well expel him," Conyers declared.

"Will you vote to expel?" another member queried.

"No," he replied.

At the end, Conyers did sign the report but only with reservations. He declared that "punishment for Mr. Powell beyond severe censure was improper." At a news conference which followed, he stated that Powell was a "symbol to the Negro community across America—22 million people." Left at that, most blacks would have understood Conyers' predicament, but then he went on to say he was "proud to have been a member of the committee. I intend to support the conclusions, though I am not able to agree to the extent that I could refrain from additional views."

Within hours black America exploded over the treatment handed Powell. "In this nation you can be white and wrong and make it," cried Whitney M. Young, executive director of the National Urban League. "You can be black and right and perhaps be successful, but it is obvious that you cannot be both black and wrong." An "unprecedented penalty," howled Roy Wilkins, executive director of the National Association for the Advancement of Colored People. "Unless Congress metes out equal justice to all offenders regardless of their race, religion, party, regional or national origin, it will validate the charge that Mr. Powell, despite his highly irregular conduct, has been singled out personally for special treatment." Even the month before, Martin Luther King had suggested to Speaker John W. McCormack that dislodging Powell would inflame the Negro community. "They will interpret it as an attempt to take reprisals against a Negro who has risen to a position of political power," he wrote with foresight.

There is some reason to believe Conyers was surprised by the black outburst which followed the committee's findings. He undoubtedly believed that racial considerations had led to Powell's downfall, but felt that the Cellar Committee was impervious to such bigotry. He only erred in assuming his friends would see it that way too. Moreover, in all likelihood he was swayed by the heady comments that emanated from the deliberations. James C. Corman, forty, Democrat of Van Nuys, Calif., a committee member, told newsmen that "Conyers was the real hero. He was the one man who might face real political problems on this issue. But he's a stand-up guy. He never let the political situation influence him." Unfortunately for Conyers, the blacks didn't see the outcome in the same light. Powell was "their boy," and no one, least of all a black, could say he was proud to be a member of the committee that had emasculated him without incurring anger in the ghetto.

Despite this, it appeared for a time that congressional sentiment was jelling in favor of the Cellar report. The Chairman told the press on the day following that a head count by Democratic and Republican leaders had convinced him he had the votes to pass the resolution on Wednesday next. In the meantime, Conyers took the precaution of flying back to Detroit to measure the mood of his constituency in the First District. His soundings convinced him that storm clouds were gathering. He felt compelled to call another news conference to establish his position which, by then, no one had to remind him was sticky.

At the conference he reiterated his contention that the Cellar Committee acted without racial motivation and at least for the record, stated that none of his constituents were blaming him for joining in the unanimous recommendation to censure Mr. Powell. But Conyers then added prophetically, "Our agreement is patched together with Scotch tape, chicken wire and staples." To forestall black discontent in his district, he promised to seek a congressional investigation of alleged wrongdoings by white members to dispel any suspicion of racial bias against Mr. Powell.

By Monday, when House members were back in Washington, time had had its innings. There was a rising sentiment among white congressmen, particularly those from conservative Democratic and Republican districts, for Powell's expulsion. This was countered by a stiffening of black outrage that tended to polarize the thinking for and against Powell. Carried along by the dividing stream, Conyers announced in Inkster, Michigan, on his return to the capital, that he would ask the House on Wednesday to forego the fine of $40,000 and the loss of seniority and settle for censure.

On the eve of the vote, uncertainty reigned. No one was sure whether the House would expel Powell, censure him, or adopt the Committee's report. Anger was noticeable among Republicans because Conyers had disclaimed the Committee recommendations. After a four-hour meeting of the House Republican Conference, chairman Melvin Laird of Wisconsin announced that "we're about evenly split between the committee's recommendations and the position of simply not seating Mr. Powell. The party leadership favors the committee point of view, but members have been told only to vote according to their consciences. At any rate, there isn't any support for the Conyers positions."

When Representative Arch A. Moore, Jr., of West Virginia, ranking Republican member of the select committee, accused Conyers of reneging on his commitment, the Michigan congressman objected. Yes, he had signed the committee report, but he had also said after the signing that "the discipline should be censure and nothing more." Therefore he was within his rights to offer amendments to the committee report before the issue was voted. In maintaining this right, he was unsheathing a sword that cut in two directions. A defeat of the committee report would permit a flurry of amendments, opening the floodgates to those who wanted Powell expelled as well as those who, like Conyers, only wanted him censured. As one member said, "Conyers would not get into the ball game."

And that's the way it happened when the House voted on Wednesday. Before packed galleries, a motion to cut off amendments to the committee report lost 222 to 202, which opened the way for Representative Thomas B. Curtis, Missouri Republican, to offer a motion that Powell be excluded from membership, and this was adopted 248 to 176. In the meantime, the House leadership had informed Conyers that if he were to offer an amendment to censure but not exclude Powell, it could not be passed. He consequently, went back to his original position, voting with the Democratic leadership to deny amendments to the select committee report, and when this was defeated, talked and voted against the expulsion of Powell.

The struggle had awakened the worst fears of racial bigotry. With rank-and-file members given free reign to exercise their conscience by leaders fearful of riding herd, Powell was severely criticized by a number of white congressmen, among them Albert W. Watson, a South Carolina Republican, who conjectured that Powell was probably at that moment in Bimini "with a glass in one hand and a woman in the other."

Again, as with the Cellar Committee's first report, the black community erupted. "It is," said A. Philip Randolph, respected vice-president of the AFL-CIO and resident of Powell's Harlem district, "practically a universal feeling among Negroes in every section of the nation that Powell is the victim of racial discrimination by his colleagues in the House." While Powell was too sophisticated in the ways of the House not to have anticipated white bigotry, he was incensed over Conyers' part in the Cellar deliberations. He doubted Conyers' ability to speak for blacks, and during the Detroit riot five months later, when Conyers was powerless in the face of a stoning by militants, Powell called from his

self-imposed exile in the Bahamas for the Michiganer's replacement. But by then the incident was largely forgotten
and a year later, in the election of 1968, the issue was Humphrey, not Powell.

Indeed, eighteen months before the Powell incident catapulted him into the limelight, Conyers' star began to rise
when the House Judiciary Committee became deeply involved in a consideration of the open-housing provisions of
Lyndon Johnson's ill-fated civil rights legislation. Conyers
wanted this legislation passed for the benefit of black America, but he quickly saw that open housing would be mean-
ingless without teeth in the enforcement provisions. He
therefore suggested the creation of a Fair Housing Board
with powers to subpoena and command compliance from
the parties to a suit. Operationally, it would resemble the
National Labor Relations Board. The reason for this, Conyers explained, "was that if we sent everything through the
Civil Court procedure, the pile-up would be fantastic. The
backlog would make them unworkable." He said the power
to bypass the judiciary was awesome, but necessary, if the
law was to work for the aggrieved individual. Furthermore,
he pointed out, it did not "foreclose any of the complainants
to go into court." The committee listened to his plea, voted
approval 13–4, and thereafter the House went along, but a
Senate frightened by talk of a white backlash following the
Meredith march through Mississippi killed the measure.

Conyers remained convinced, however, that housing
would not become available for minorities without stronger
corrective measures by the federal government. A year
later, two incidents illustrated his concern. At the end of
June 1967, the House was discussing the advisability of
building a $200-billion electron volt accelerator (atom
smasher) in Weston, Illinois, a small community west of
Chicago with one of the most segregated housing patterns
in the U.S. Conyers knew that such a milieu would effectively prevent blacks from working on the project. He told

House colleagues that it was absurd to go ahead with a program where discrimination in housing was rampant and the local officials had no plans to cure the situation. Before the U.S. Congress invested a penny in such a project, the state of Illinois should be required to enact an open-housing law. Conyers called this "a crucial test of the government's commitment to civil rights." His motion would have held up construction by denying funds, but the legislators, anxious to start their Fourth of July respite, were in no mood for appeals to conscience. They swept by Conyers 104–7 on a non-record standing vote and five minutes later were gone.

The second occasion was when he joined eight other congressmen in charging that the Federal Housing Administration was guilty of discrimination in its administrative procedures. The agency had not, they said, implemented President Kennedy's celebrated "stroke of the pen" order of November 1962 prohibiting discrimination in housing built with FHA funds, because of a reluctance "to jeopardize its standing with the industry by aggressively implementing an equal opportunity policy." [11] By enforcing the Kennedy regulation, FHA would have made it possible, the group added, for Negroes trapped in the ghetto to move into middle-class suburbs. Its failure to do so convinced Conyers that fair housing was still mostly a dream with very little substance and that segregation "might be increasing." Speaking three years later, in the spring of 1970, following Richard Nixon's ascension to power, he was even less hopeful. "The fact that we've been unable to do much," he said, "suggests that the government, and particularly the President of the United States, have not provided leadership. Their failure to do so is the main reason why we have come such a little way."

An added tragedy, according to Conyers, is the fact that segregated housing is the pivot on which segregated education in the ghetto turns. "The quality of most schools in America is pathetic. The quality of the public education system in the ghettos is doubly pathetic. The schools are simply not in tune with the times or the children. The best evidence of this is that one-third of all the youngsters in America never achieve a high school education. In the black communities that figure goes up to about 50 per cent. In a country that has had a free public education system for 125 years, that is about the most damning indictment one can imagine, especially when we look around and find that other emerging nations have done better in a far shorter period of time. Something is wrong."

In the Conyers' view, this is only one of the problems that is rending the guts of America. Another, equally serious, is the plight of poor people. "Almost thirty million Americans, including fifteen million children," he points out, "are living below the poverty line and in this the most agriculturally productive nation in the world, malnutrition is actually increasing." [12] To reduce the crushing effect of poverty, Conyers introduced in the fall of 1967 what he called the "Full Opportunity Act," to cost a thumping $30 billion a year for the next decade, to help blacks and other poverty-stricken Americans. It would, said the Washington correspondent of the *Free Press*, "create a virtual welfare state for the nation's poor." By fixing the price tag to equal the annual cost of the Vietnam war, Conyers sought to put the public spotlight on the level of military spending, blandly adding, "this bill is aimed at what is needed, not what is possible." A conglomerate of ideas tossed together by "sociologists, educators, unionists and riot-fearing politicians," Conyers said, the measure would:

1. Guarantee employment for all Americans, Uncle Sam reeling in the slack.

2. Provide a $2-an-hour minimum for all workers.

3. Give all children under eighteen a monthly allotment of $10.

4. Provide eight million new housing units by 1977.

5. Guarantee open housing with a Fair Housing Board to enforce the law.

6. Require compensatory education by equalizing per-pupil school expenditures for blacks and whites.

The bill was deposited in the House hopper several months before the report of the National Advisory Commission on Civil Rights (the Kerner Commission)—which, Conyers points out, "was ignored by President Johnson and disbelieved by then candidate Nixon." Yet, it mirrored the findings of the Commission and was the only legislation to implement the recommendations. Because of Vietnam, the program and serious consideration of its implications languished. An angry Conyers observed, "One must only compare in dollars the national effort to bring what is claimed is 'freedom' to thirteen million people in South Vietnam with the magnitude of our effort for thirty million Americans who are living in poverty here at home." [13]

Time did little to bank his fires. Fifteen months later, on the anniversary of Martin Luther King's birth, Conyers, along with twenty other members of the House, jointly sponsored a revised Full Opportunity Act, again to cost $30 billion annually for ten years. "I do not look on this bill," he said, "as the ultimate answer to the problems of the poor and minority groups. But I do feel that by emphasizing the relationship of all the problems and aiming at the same kind of solution, the Full Opportunity Act served to educate the Congress and the American public on the magnitude of the crisis which faces us all." The time is now to progress "from legal equality on paper to social and economic opportunity in reality."

For this reason he found himself at odds with President Nixon's Family Assistance Plan, unveiled in mid-1969, because of its limited scope. The President asked that every American family of four receive a minimum of $1,600 annually. Conyers says this is too little. "I have a bill," he announced from his Washington office, "that doubles the President's figures and omits many of the very unhappy provisions which curtail the rights of recipients and imposes upon them requirements that are unbelievably restrictive. My bill essentially calls for a family of four to receive $3200 and this is still far short of the Labor Department's finding that it requires about $5500 in most places of America for a family of four to survive adequately. I think any American who will check his own income against that figure will immediately recognize that a family of four would be in trouble with an expendable income of only $5500." Conyers estimates his legislation would cost approximately $20 billion annually, based on the research of economists at Yale University.

"How is the money to be raised?" he asks, pre-empting his critics in a flanking movement designed to upstage them. "I believe it can be raised—and without adding to the inflationary spiral. I believe that the money must come from savings accruing from a drastically reduced military budget." [14]

Aside from promoting legislation to improve the socioeconomic plight of Negro citizens, Conyers has devoted a sizable part of his extraordinary energy to insuring the right of black Americans to vote. As a freshman Representative, with little more than six months in office, he voted for the Voting Rights Act of 1965, acclaimed as the most effective civil rights law in United States history by leaders of the civil rights movement. In less than five years, it made possible the registration of 897,000 Negroes in seven states of the Old Confederacy.

Two years later Conyers used his position on the House Judiciary Committee to fight emasculation of the Supreme Court's "one-man, one-vote" decision. The House was then in an angry mood, laboring to find ways to circumvent the court's ruling. A total of 279 congressmen from twenty-two states—almost 65 per cent of the House—was elected from districts that didn't comply with the Court's formula.

Largely to protect the membership, a majority on the Judiciary Committee had reported favorably a bill that would allow districts to vary as much as 35 per cent from the authorized ratio, and worse, permit the gerrymandering of white suburbs with parts of ghetto areas to weaken black voting strength. Conyers fumed, and when the House refused to budge, took his case to the Senate, where enlistment of the Kennedy brothers—Robert and Edward—succeeded in passing a companion measure that cut the variance to 10 per cent and provided that districts be compact—not gerrymandered into odd shapes. A thirteen-member House-Senate conference committee, which included Edward Kennedy and Conyers, then attempted to compose the differences between the two bodies. A compromise would normally have included bargaining over the allowable variance in districts and the proper restriction on gerrymandering. But with conservative Democratic senators Eastland, Ervin, and McClellan calling signals and Republican wheelhorses Dirksen and Hruska providing interference, the committee proceeded to write a new bill which left Kennedy and Conyers shocked. It disregarded the work of the Senate and the House and accepted a plan, proposed by Senator Ervin, which gave each state the right to redistrict if it wished to take a special federal census, or forego the effort to comply with the "one-man, one-vote" decision until after the census of 1970. The plan was worse than either the House or Senate versions, Conyers said bitterly, calling it an open and flagrant attempt to avoid the Court's edict before 1972. "The House version at least required eight states to redistrict. Under the conference bill, California with a 98 per cent variance, for example, and New York with a 34.5 per cent variance would not be required to redistrict until 1972."

This seemed to snap Conyers' efforts effectively, but no one had counted on Sam Ervin to overplay his hand. The North Carolina Senator was trying to help a congressional ally from his state whose tenure appeared jeopardized by a Court-ordered reapportionment plan. In his desire to do so, he had omitted any provision to bar at-large elections, not knowing that House members would rather wrestle a grizzly bear than run at large. Even that House fixture, octogenarian Emmanuel Cellar of Brooklyn, Judiciary chairman, moaned, "It's easy for senators to adopt a cavalier manner on how congressional districts should be drawn. But we're the ones to suffer." [15] When word of the bill's political flaw reached Conyers, he saw at once the chance to deal a death blow. Out from his office went a statement that read: "The conference report contains no standards for drawing congressional districts for the 1968 and 1970 elections, even though both the House and Senate versions did. This could mean that as many as 16 states with 275 congressmen, or possibly even more states, would be forced to hold at-large elections in 1968. For example, the Supreme Court recently declared Indiana's congressional districts to be unconstitutional and ordered the Legislature to establish new districts. Since the Constitution prohibits using the current districts and the bill prohibits establishing new districts, the only alternative for the courts, if they are to uphold this bill as constitutional, is to have no districts at all—or, in other words, to require everyone to run at large." He went on to point out that eight states—New York, Tennessee, Massachusetts, Texas, Missouri, North Carolina, New Jersey, and Illinois—were already under order to redistrict for the 1968 elections and in at least nine others, suits were pending because of the population imbalance among districts. At this Cellar paled, having opened a "can of worms," and hastily agreed to withdraw the compromise, to Conyers' delight. A succeeding compromise had, by year's end, died in the Senate.

After the Nixon administration took office in January 1969, another threat of Negro disenfranchisement rose to plague Conyers. Under heavy pressure from Southern Republicans, the President decided to send Congress legislation that would drastically revise the 1965 Voting Rights Act, a bill that originally had the support of 82 per cent of the Senate and 94 per cent of the House GOP membership. This so-called Magna Charta of Negro enfranchisement had two key provisions. It banned literacy tests in states or counties in which less than half of those eligible voted in the 1964 presidential election. Included were the six Southern states of Alabama, Mississippi, Louisiana, South Carolina, Georgia, and Virginia and thirty-nine counties of North Carolina. Second, it prevented any change in the election laws of those areas without the prior consent of the Attorney General or the Federal District Court in Washington. The Congress wanted to bar a repetition of the political chicanery that followed the adoption of the Fifteenth Amendment, when the South established such voting obstacles as the poll tax, the literacy test, and the "grandfather clause" to disenfranchise the blacks.

When hearings on the Nixon proposal got under way in late spring, one of the first to testify was Attorney General John N. Mitchell, spokesman for the administration. He called for broadening the ban on literacy tests. "It is not enough," he told the House Judicary Committee, "to continue to protect Negro voters in seven states. That consideration may have been the justification for the 1965 act. But it is unrealistic today to ignore the ghettos of Harlem, Watts, Roxbury, Seattle, Hartford and Portland, Oregon—all of which are located in states which have literacy tests. I believe the literacy test is an unreasonable physical obstruction to voting even if it is administered in an even-handed way . . . perhaps, more importantly, it is a psychological obstruction in the minds of many of our minority citizens. I don't have all the answers. But I suggest to this committee that it is the psychological barrier of the literacy test—long associated with the poll tax as a discriminatory tool to keep the Negro from the ballot box—that may be responsible for much of the low Negro voter registration in some of our

major cities. A higher percentage of Negroes voted in South
Carolina and Mississippi, where literacy tests are suspended, than in Watts or Harlem, where literacy tests are
enforced. A higher percentage of Negroes vote in Philadelphia and Chicago, where there are no literacy tests, than in
majority Negro neighborhoods in New York City and Los
Angeles."

Something about the pragmatic approach of the former
bond attorney piqued Conyers. "For this Administration,"
he countered acidly, "to discuss psychological barriers to
the Negro is the most presumptuous act I've ever heard.
Black people in the North are not being prevented from voting because of their education. But I can tell you that black
people are losing faith in large numbers every day that this
system has the promise of being what it says it is."

Mitchell's second call for change applied to the familiarly
known "prior clearance" provision. He recommended an
end to the rule requiring the Southern states to secure the
approval of the Attorney General or the Federal District
Court in Washington before adopting election law changes
and its replacement by a weaker provision requiring the
Justice Department to decide which changes were patently
discriminatory and then to apply to the federal court to en-
join the practice. The Justice role would thereby pass from
judge to prosecutor.

The ranking Republican on the Judiciary Committee,
Representative William M. McCulloch of Ohio, listened,
was turned off, told Mitchell his plan "created a remedy for
which there is no wrong and left grievous wrongs without
adequate remedy." He reminded the Attorney General that
he was calling for a change in the "prior clearance" provision in "the face of spellbinding evidence of unflagging
Southern dedication to the cause of creating an ever more
sophisticated legal machinery for discriminating against the
black voter."

For two weeks the House Judiciary Committee deliberated, finally voting overwhelmingly to recommend a five-year extension of the original law and rejecting all administration proposals. Presidential forces were not to be dissuaded, however, and when it came time in mid-December to take a vote of the full House membership, the contest was between an extension of the 1965 law and the Mitchell amendments. Conyers was particularly bitter about the proposed repeal of the "prior clearance" provision. "If accepted," he warned the House, "the administration substitute, most obviously, would be a clear impediment to the enforcement of our constitutionally guaranteed right to the vote, and would obstruct access to the ballot for those millions of Americans who are still disenfranchised." Anyone backing the administration would have to believe, said Conyers, "that Southern public officials would not make every effort to disenfranchise those black people already on the voting rolls and to hinder in every way those still attempting to become listed."

"We must look at the facts, regard the evidence," he continued, noting that a hundred-year history of voter discrimination and racial injustice could hardly be reversed in four years. Despite the Voting Rights Act of 1965, "there are still 185 counties where less than 50 per cent of the eligible black Americans have been registered to vote. In the entire State of Alabama the percentage is only slightly above a majority, 51 per cent; in Georgia, 52.6 per cent; in South Carolina, 51.2 per cent. In Mississippi, the percentage is 59.8 per cent; in Louisiana, it is 58.9 per cent; in Virginia, it is 55.6 per cent. In the 6½ states covered by the 1965 act, only 57 per cent of the black voting-age population is registered. This must be compared to the 79 per cent of the white voting-age population that is registered, a difference of 22 per cent.

"But there are those in this body who are saying that enough progress has been made. My colleague from Michigan [Gerald R. Ford, Republican Majority Leader in the

House] is the sponsor of the administration substitute. He says that black people have been included in the Southern political process to such an extent that the State Legislatures will not reverse the trend. Let me remind Mr. Ford that there is only one black legislator in Louisiana. There is only one black legislator in Mississippi. There is only one black legislator in North Carolina. There is only one black legislator in Virginia. There are none in Alabama or South Carolina.

"The democratic process in the South is well described by the former Assistant Attorney General in charge of the Civil Rights Division, Mr. Burke Marshall, who said:

> When the will to keep Negro registration to a minimum is strong, and the routine of determining whose applications are acceptable is within the discretion of local officials, the latitude for discrimination is almost endless. The practices that can be used are virtually infinite.

"If the U.S. House of Representatives today accepts the Nixon Administration substitute amendment, it will see tomorrow the injustices it has perpetrated. All America will suffer. For when freedom is denied for some, no one is truly free to enjoy it." [16]

Despite this plea, when the voting began on the Ford measure, a shift in sentiment was quickly detected. Between July and December the administration had done its homework. Republican ranks held firm and, supported by Southern Democrats, the substitute bill squeaked through 208 to 203. The result was a severe blow to the leaders of the civil rights cause. "What happened to the party of Lincoln?" a Republican congressional aide was asked by a reporter, trying to make sense out of the turn about. "It has put on a Confederate uniform," he snapped dejectedly. Speaking with greater passion, the legislative director of the NAACP,

Clarence M. Mitchell, Jr., cried a "cataclysmic defeat. The Nixon Administration has sold us out in order to get the segregation vote in the South." [17]

For Conyers as well as for Mitchell, the spectacle of Southern intransigence against the Negro was something that invariably raised hackles. A perfect example was the case of Private First Class William Henry Terry, Jr., of Birmingham. A twenty-year-old black, Terry had volunteered for military service in September 1968 and was shipped to Vietnam the following spring. Somehow he had a premonition of being killed and had written his wife to inter the body in Elmwood Cemetery, a white burial ground near his boyhood home, in case he didn't return. When word came that he had fallen during a search-and-destroy mission on July 3, she did her best to comply with his request, but the cemetery authorities refused on racial grounds to allow his burial and he was laid to rest in one of Birmingham's black plots.

To his colleagues in the House, Conyers eulogized, "Bill Terry did not think of the slave ships, the auction blocks, Jim Crow or Judge Lynch. He thought only of what he conceived to be his duty to his country. He fought for what he thought right, and he died for it. His family asked that he be buried in Birmingham, in a place called the Elmwood Cemetery. But the Elmwood Cemetery said no, only white people could be buried there. So, because he was black, Bill Terry was buried in another cemetery outside of Birmingham, where only blacks were interred. And he was buried in an unmarked grave."

Meanwhile, Terry's family filed suit in Birmingham's District Federal Court to force Elmwood Cemetery to open its plots to Negroes. Judge Seybourn Lynne studied the testimony carefully and, a scant two days before Christmas, handed down a seventeen-page ruling that ordered Elmwood to accept Terry's remains. Cemetery officials, the jurist said, could not operate under a restrictive racial covenant that was outlawed by the century-old Civil Rights Act of 1866.

In the same month that Lynne was rapping Alabamans across their racial knuckles, Conyers got wind of another discriminatory act—a $265,000 federal grant for building a segregated golf club in Tupelo, Mississippi, right in the backyard of Republican Jamie Whitten, notorious in Congress, according to the Washington *Post,* for "withholding food stamps from poor Negroes, feeding subsidies to fat cotton men and laughing off civil rights laws," and for being boss of the agriculture subcommittee of the House Appropriations Committee. It happened that under Section VI of the Civil Rights Law of 1964 it was illegal to use federal funds for projects where discrimination exists. To get around this limitation, officers of the Natchez Trace Golf Club had trumped up a bogus membership roster that included three blacks—one a television repairman employed by the chairman of the membership committee, one a mechanic, an employee of the applications chairman, and one, a milk delivery man, employee of the club's president.

Conyers scheduled a meeting with Secretary of Agriculture Clifford M. Hardin and took along Charles C. Diggs (D-Mich.) and William Clay (D-Mo.), two House blacks, to condemn the allotment in the strongest terms, and reported the results in a news release on December 9, 1969: "I question the basic competence, honesty and sincerity of your investigation" upon which the loan was granted. "In truth, there has been absolutely no good-faith participation of black people in that club," he told an embarrassed Secretary, who awkwardly proceeded to field bureaucratic excuses. Conyers was unimpressed and told Hardin so. "After your Department told me the loan had been given a so-called 'civil rights clearance' and would be closed, I set up this appointment," the Congressman went on. "No date was given me on when this loan would be granted. Now, after we present our case, you say it is too late." He demanded a reinvestigation of the loan. Hopping mad, he growled at Hardin, "There are millions of Americans across our country who go to bed every night hungry or undernourished . . . of all colors and beliefs. We lack the Federal money to take care of utterly essential projects across the land, ranging from housing and pollution control to education and medical research. Human rights and human needs cry out for fulfillment. Yet, this kind of money can be given out to this type of organization by an organ of the Federal government . . . with an attempt at silence. No more perfect illustration can be offered of what is wrong with our country than this case."

Ordinarily Conyers is too even-tempered to raise his voice in the face of racial badgering, but there is a limit to his patience. One such time was the visit of Lester Maddox, Governor of Georgia, to the House restaurant during the winter of 1970. Conyers and Diggs discovered the Georgian was passing out autographed pick and axe handles—souvenirs of the days Maddox rose to public notice by wielding a pick handle in Atlanta to bar Negroes from entering his Pickwick Chicken House restaurant. Diggs acted first. He summoned the restaurant manager, grabbed Representative John C. Kluczynski of Illinois, chairman of the House Restaurant Committee, and together they walked over to the table where Maddox was eating. Words passed, and in seconds the Governor was as heated as the broiled salmon steak before him. He told Diggs he was acting "more like an ass and a baboon than a member of Congress," according to the report published in *The New York Times*. Diggs shouted that he was a member of Congress, and Maddox wasn't. Fortunately, a District of Columbia plainclothes policeman moved between them to prevent either antagonist from throwing punches. Within minutes, Conyers was on the floor of the House, calling the incident totally disgraceful. "I hear some of my colleagues laughing about it. They think it is funny. I say it is a tragic mockery of law and order to have Lester Maddox bring axe handles to the Capitol, assisted by the Capitol Police. Some think it a shame but will not say anything about it. And I suppose there are others who think it is fine. They know too well that the axe handle is that symbolic instrument encouraging violence in the South. And yet there are members in this body who condone this conduct and at the same time, hypocritically call for law and order." [18]

This was bold, unqualified, the kind of statement that friends have come to expect from John Conyers. There is nothing schizoid in his approach to politics. "He doesn't play the kind of game," says a close associate, "that a number of people play where they have one face in the legislative body and try to hide it if it is too liberal and put on a political front for their constituency back home." Quite the contrary, he is, says another friend, "willing to take a chance, willing to do things, willing to go to the wall on many issues." Talking to Conyers, one has the feeling that here is a man of great integrity who can be counted on to do the honorable thing as on the occasion he heard that Rosa Parks, of Montgomery and civil rights fame, was in Detroit without a job. Immediately Conyers ordered her on his staff. "I don't care whether she can type or what she can do," he said.

In the eyes of some people, the fact that Conyers is unmarried tends to type him as one with only time to work. His answer to a reporter's question about this is that "I definitely hope to marry eventually. I think a wife can be a tremendous asset to a man." In the meantime, says one associate, he finds it "hard to let go." Another acquaintance reports the same: "John loves a good time, he's no stick in the mud, but he foregoes many of those things in order to achieve his ambitions." One reason why his popularity continues to rise is his willingness to forget the slings and arrows of past battles. A close intimate tells of being in his Detroit office one day when a call came through from a young man who had just been appointed to an office in the city government and needed help. The person had been a political enemy of Conyers, but now he just had to talk to the Congressman. "I'll take care of it," said Conyers, picking up the phone. Two or three calls and the problem was quickly solved. "The guy needs some help," he explained, "and, okay, so I'll help him."

In a broad sense, Conyers stands today at the interstice between white and black, trying to view the responsibilities of each in a biracial nation. Whites, he believes, "must stop being racist in their attitudes, and in their actions, by promoting integration and supporting the causes of black people, by understanding the nature of their biased relationship toward black people, and by understanding that the future of America is tied up in how they react to the problem. After all, America's problem is not a black problem at all, it is a white problem, white attitudes, white will, white government, white decisions, white military, white police, white legislators, white everything that determines what it is we will do, how far we will go and whether we will succeed or not. So, if whites want to know what they should do, it is to stop being racist." That the White House has not yet received the message depresses Conyers. "The simple truth," he declares, "is that Nixon doesn't comprehend the dimensions of the race problem in America. He just hasn't seen that white racism—as the Kerner Commission showed—is at the gut root of our nation's urban ills." [19]

Speaking of the black role in a white-dominated America, Conyers has this to say: "Our own intelligence about the oppressiveness of the kind of society which would like to forget us along with other historical 'mistakes' should give black people a unique force in effecting change in America. An infusion of blacks into the political arena might provide the moral force of 'soul' which America either lost or never had." In the Conyers' view, "Government makes, interprets and enforces the laws that set the limits of our lives. It determines the extent to which we will be educated, the kinds of jobs we may have, where we may live, the kind of health care we may receive. It selects which of us shall fight and, if necessary, die, in its name. It even defines our personal freedoms and dictates in large measure the quality of life that each of us, every single American shall have." Accordingly, blacks should be raising their cudgels, not in dreams about revolution, which "the white power structure would not permit," but in the political mainstream. Blacks should have "twelve senators and fifty-five congressmen—their minimum fair share—rather than the present count of one senator and nine representatives." But this will not happen, Conyers points out, short of dedicated involvement on the part of black America.

"Some see," he adds, "the black American's choice as between withdrawing from this 'hopeless' government or overthrowing the entire system. I see our choice as between political involvement or political apathy. America is the black man's battleground. It is here where it will be decided whether or not we will make America what it says it is. For me, at least, the choice is clear." [20]

Kenneth Allen Gibson ═══════

¶ It was only two years after the British had driven the Dutch out of New Netherland in 1664 and renamed the province New York that a Connecticut Yankee named Robert Trent led a band of New England adventurers down the Atlantic coast and into New Jersey, there to raise a settlement on the west bank of the Passaic River which they named Newark.

To be sure, three centuries have produced great changes in demography and geography. Only the topography of the land remains immutable, the bend in the Passaic unchanged. Today, Newark is the largest city in New Jersey, covering 23.6 square miles, its population a tiny dip under 400,000, with huge problems to wrestle down.

These have primarily arisen from ethnic face-lifting, the kind confronting every metropolitan center in the U.S. as efforts proceed to melt diverse radical ingredients into an even black-white mix. Only with Newark, the lumps are more stubborn on account of the speed with which the facial contours are changing.

Sixty years ago, the black percentage was slightly in excess of 3 per cent. The city's population of 350,000 consisted mainly of native-born Americans with heavy sprinklings of Irish, German, Italian, Polish, and Jewish immigrants. On the eve of World War II, Newark had become known as a city of the foreign-born, with three-fifths of the city's population either immigrant or first-generation American. But by then, a revolution had begun in the Old Confederacy, farm jobs were disappearing, and the report of semiskilled and unskilled jobs in the Newark complex was drawing blacks northward. From a modest trickle it suddenly became a mighty migration. By 1950, the black count had risen to 17 per cent; a decade later it was more than one-third of the total population. Before the end of the sixties, Newark was the second American city (after Washington, D.C.) to have a black majority, a growth in less than twenty years of more than 300 per cent.

The effect of this wave on the white population was awesome. Not only did one white depart for every black arriving in Newark, but the city's population actually declined from 438,776 in 1950 to 398,000 in 1970. Incoming blacks took over the inner core area, which was dubbed "the rotten casket destined for the burial of the living dead." [1] Of the five ghetto wards, the worst by far was the notorious Central Ward, Newark's version of Watts, Hough, or Harlem. As this overflowed, blacks poured into the central business district to the east, South Broad Street and Clinton Hill to the south, and the West Ward. Within this area the city built the largest per capita public-housing program in the U.S., hoping to contain the flood. When it was complete, approximately 12 per cent of Newark's population existed "in semisanitary dungeons." [2]

No wonder that all the social ills indigenous to urban decay thrived in this milieu. As Nathan Wright, Jr., pointed out, "Newark's life in recent years was distinguished by an unexcelled list of firsts in urban pathology:

"1. The highest crime rate, 1967.

"2. The highest tuberculosis rate.

"3. The highest syphilis rate.

"4. The highest gonorrhea rate.

"5. The highest maternal mortality rate.

"6. The highest population density (adjusted to usable land).

"7. The highest proportion of land set aside for urban renewal clearance." [3]

All these deficiencies had their locus in the Central Ward. Almost a third of the city's houses were substandard or dilapidated; the largest proportion, scheduled for demolition, belonged to Central. From the air the abandoned structures in Central looked "as if they had been smashed by a giant fist." The result was to crowd the inhabitants into a declining housing supply, where the "owners of slum property gouge the tenants mercilessly." Added to this grinding pressure was the knowledge that urban renewal was aiding "Negro removal" by gobbling fifty acres of choice Central land for a medical-dental college complex sponsored by Rutgers University.

Inside this racial inferno there obviously were blacks who could afford mortgage payments for the purchase of homes. The trouble, as one distraught resident told *Atlantic* writer Thomas R. Brooks, was that "fixing one house in a block was a waste of time. Maintenance men wouldn't come into the neighborhood for fear of being mugged, or losing their tools. You couldn't get fire insurance. The only people willing to live here were problem tenants, and they steal the fixtures and strip out the plumbing. The buildings were not built to carry the traffic of large families."

Moreover, housing was not the only measure of Central's headlong deterioration. Another equally revealing yardstick was the vast welfare drain. In Central, the remaining whites are elderly and the blacks overwhelmingly young. Professor George Sternlieb, director of the Center for Urban Social Science Research at Rutgers University, found in a study of Newark's tenement population that the elderly were the "remnants of previous white immigrant groups. The elderly Italian widow, and her equivalent, whether Jewish, German or Irish, dominate this group." At the same time, demographic studies showed fifteen-year-olds and younger to be almost 25 per cent of the city's population. Result: in the elderly category, about 20 per cent of New Jersey's payments for old-age assistance went to residents of Newark, and at the other end of the scale, more than 35 per cent of the state's payments for aid to dependent children were spent in the city of Newark, although the city's population was only 7 per cent of the state's.

Another sign of Central's slide from grace was the increasing level of serious crime in Newark—up 26.6 per cent in 1969. There is, however, nothing particularly startling in this. Newark had seethed with crime for years—indeed, a half-century ago, during Prohibition days, it was virtually the bootleg capital of the Eastern seaboard, and the pall of illegality had hung over the city much as the air pollution and the stench from the polluted Passaic River. It had seeped into the government and the police hierarchy. Ex-Governor Hughes' Select Commission on Civil Disorder reported, after interrogating city residents, a widespread belief that Newark's government was corrupt. Contact between New Jersey's Mafia and the Newark police was reportedly strong. An Essex County grand jury indicted Dominick A. Spina, Newark's former Police Director, for not enforcing the gambling laws, saying he was "either incapable or unwilling to perform his duties," but such legal efforts got nowhere. As Thomas Brooks put it, "busting up gambling in Newark is rather like sweeping back the sea into a tidal wave." Consequently, fear of corruption and violence was a continuing ghetto syndrome, especially in the Central Ward.

Lamentable as were these deficiencies, probably the worst element of the Central Ward was the discouraging output of the school system. The dropout problem was particularly severe. More than 50 per cent of the class of 1965 at Central High School had departed prior to graduation. Of the 344 who did graduate, only 79—23 per cent of the total—went on to higher education. The loss could be due to the poverty permeation of black youngsters, nearly half of whom were the offshoots of homes permanently on public welfare. Or they might have been victims of an educational system that failed to give adequate instruction. "In the City of Newark," writes Nathan Wright, "the average black student in 1963 was 1.5 years below national standards in reading. The then Acting Director Newark Human Rights Commission explained: 'Taking the sixth grade level as our medium, this means that thousands of Negro youths are still reading at a third and fourth grade level, but are in sixth grade due to so-called 'social promotions.' This can only lead to an inadequately prepared adult, most likely, one who has joined the increasing ranks of school drop-outs.'" Despite this, despite the fact that Central's dropout rate was the worst in the city, Central High received during the 1964–1965 school year less than the average reimbursement per pupil for the city's eight public high schools. The census figures demonstrate what happened. In 1960, Central Ward residents twenty-five and over had completed an average of 8.4 years of schooling. Following the Biblical admonition that heart and treasure dwell together, the Newark City Council during the winter of 1970 was at the point of cutting its $2.8 million appropriation to the Newark Museum and the Newark Public Library, the city's twin cultural gems, in order to save money. Only the awakening of an angry public prevented officialdom from tripping the fiscal guillotine, but the likelihood of such action serves only to emphasize the city's meagre concern about issues that affect public learning.

City Hall was more interested in the subject of property taxes, which tripled between 1945 and 1967 and are still rising, giving Newark the dubious distinction of being second only to Boston among the nation's large cities in tax rate. Computing this in dollars and cents means that a person in

Newark who pays $2100 on a house valued at $25,000 is contributing about $600 more than he would on property assessed at $50,000 in nearby Short Hills—one of the cogent reasons why Newark is low on home ownership and high on the exodus to the suburbs. No less an expert than former Mayor Hugh Joseph Addonizio claimed that taxes were the first cause for the flight. Whether true or not in the face of Newark's rising black population, taxes have had a tremendous impact upon white thinking. The facts speak starkly.

Around the city's core area were once wards that housed Newark's wealthy and great. To the south was Weequahic, a Jewish center made famous by the complaints of Roth's Portnoy. At the corner of High Street and Waverly Avenue stood Temple B'nai Jeshurn, built in 1848, heritage of the oldest and largest reform congregation in New Jersey. Other temples dotted the area, but today, fifteen years after the rush began, only two or three survive. The same story holds for Vailsburg to the west and Forest Hill to the north, inhabited primarily by the Italians and a sprinkling of "first families." Forest Hills for years contained "the bulk of the traditional leadership potential." But the tidal wave of city escapism rolled through these areas, taking with it "the rising young and already arrived executives of IBM, Western Electric, Prudential, the successful lawyers and doctors, and the growing number of professors teaching at Newark-based colleges" and dumping them in the suburbs.

It is not hard to understand the impact of the daily migration in and out of Newark. "The daytime population is well over 800,000, double the resident population," says the Division of City Planning. "About 480,000 people travel into Newark every day to work." For the most part they are white, educated, capable of holding professional jobs, working in the banks and the insurance companies, filling in the need for service employees. These are the very positions that blacks—the city's majority—are not prepared by training to fill. The latter are even denied work in the construc-

tion industry because jobs in the white-dominated craft unions are closely guarded. Their brightest prospects are jobs
with Ford or GM, but these require an eighteen-mile drive
to the suburbs. Consequently, Newark's work pattern is
askew, with suburb-based whites working in the city and
city-based blacks going outside.

The fact that Newark has the greatest proportionate daytime population turnover of any major U.S. city has prompted
one critic to complain of the "symptomatic exploitation." One
of the first casualties is a lack of police protection. So great
are the demands on the police when the city expands to twice
its normal population that residents go unprotected at night.
Out of fear of the rising crime rate, streets tend to be deserted
after dark. LeRoi Jones, the militant black playwright, who
lives in the Central Ward, calls Newark a ghost town after
dark, adding it has to become a city to live in as well as to
work in. In his view, change can only come from Newark's industrial leaders. The downtown deficiencies are "a couple of
movies in sad shape, nothing in the way of sophisticated
mind-revolving activities—no bookstores, no theaters, nothing
to suggest intellectual activity." [4] But there seems little
chance of business adding an intellectual diet to its formula
for Newark unless attitudes change. Newark's industrial leaders pride themselves on the construction of a new $50-million
Gateway complex of offices in the downtown area and on a
$150-million expansion of Newark's port and airport, but the
official spokesman, the Chamber of Commerce, says nothing
about the culture of the city. Prudential board chairman Donald MacNaughton calls Newark a "most viable metropolitan
center. It has a reason for existing. It's a good place, a very
good place, to base business," but it hardly follows that what's
good for Newark's white business leaders is necessarily good
for Newark's blacks.

The black who knows this best is a thirty-nine-year-old
Central Ward resident Kenneth Allen Gibson Southern origin,
Northern mold, who was born on May 15, 1932, to Willie Foy

and Daisy Gibson in the small southeast Alabama community
of Enterprise (population 7288). Along with Harold, two
years younger than Kenneth, the Gibson family was a closely
woven entity. Described as warm, religious and patriarchal, it
had experienced none of the grinding poverty that touched the
lives of most Southern black sharecroppers caught up in the
attack of the boll weevil on the cotton crop prior to World War
I. Although the elder Gibson earned only twelve dollars a
week as a meat cutter in a local grocery store, he went ahead
with the construction of a new home and was able to meet the
mortgage payments on the family's first home with a bath-
room and electric lights. But the fiscal strain was unsettling
and when his wages were reduced to ten dollars in the summer
of 1940, he concluded it was too much.

"I told my wife," he recalls, " 'I'm going to leave here.' I
caught a ride out of Enterprise. The first stop was Washington.
Then I went on to Baltimore, but I couldn't find work there. I
had some relatives in Newark, so I went up there and finally
got a job with Swift & Co., for $25 a week." He fully ex-
pected to return to Alabama within a year, believing—as
many European immigrants before him—that he would save
enough to liquidate his obligations.

It didn't happen that way. Northern prices were higher, and
he found life unbearable apart from his family in a one-room
apartment in the Central Ward. Even when his wife and two
sons joined him five weeks later, in answer to his call, the
family was far from happy. "I didn't know a soul," Mrs. Gibson says, remembering: "My husband's relatives were here,
but I had left all mine down there. Until I became active in
the church, I really didn't know anyone. I cried for a whole
year." [5]

Life for Kenneth Gibson, however, was relatively stable. In
fact, a quality of pragmatism began to emerge, encouraged no
doubt by his father who was, Gibson admits, the greatest influence on his life. "You can do anything you want to, if you
try hard enough," he told the son. With undisguised pride, the

son relates how his father "never got beyond the fourth grade elementary school, but he taught me the kind of things they're writing books on now, this whole thing of positive thinking. That was my father's philosophy, you know; he'd do anything he wanted to do. All you had to do was to go and do it. It would take me longer than other people to do certain things. I would try to play football—the slowest guy in school—I would try to play football. I was no star, but I played. So, I always felt because of this early training that I could do anything I wanted to do. I developed a great deal of confidence. If I wanted to do it, I'd do it. I guess you call it determination."

With such self-command, it was relatively easy for Gibson to remain apart, objective, to look on or to join the action as he and he alone saw fit—in a word, to be independent. "My mother always said that I was a quiet kid. When everyone else was jumping off fences and getting broken bones and scratches, I never did. I didn't think it was important to get scratched up." And he didn't—not out of fear, but simply because he saw no advantage in doing so. Actually, his brother engineered their boyhood scuffles. "I'd pick the fights," Harold remembers, "and he'd settle them. On the way to school, we used to have to pass a bunch of kids on the corner down from our house. They'd try to take our lunch money, but Ken could take care of them." [6]

Work was as natural to the Gibson household as eating apple pie. Not only did both parents have jobs, but by the time Kenneth was twelve he was employed by a Weequahic diner, rushing food to passing motorists. The wages were small—only six dollars a week—but the tips added up. In school he discovered an ability for mathematics and science. "I had a natural inquisitiveness about science, the practical aspects of education," he says. "I would spend a great deal of time, for instance, in solving mathematical problems, but I wouldn't spend a lot of time reading books or writing essays and that kind of thing. I knew, based on that, that my area was in math and science, and not in the arts. I personally believe that every child has some natural ability, some God-given natural ability. The question is one of finding and developing it. I came to realize my own talent. I would get A's in mathematics and D's in English. So it didn't make any sense for me to study English. My direction was in math and science."

According to Harold, "He just sat down one day when he was twelve and planned what he was going to do, what courses he'd have to take in school, what college would be best." This calm, unruffled quality became a Gibson trademark. A close boyhood friend had this trait indelibly scratched on his memory. "It was Easter Sunday," he says. "I guess we were about fourteen or fifteen, and had decided to go to one of our friend's churches. Well, it was very hot, we were all dressed up, naturally, and there were no seats left downstairs. So we went up to the balcony and there we sat, right along the railing. The minister was real fire-and-brimstone, and the church kept getting hotter and hotter. Finally, at one point the minister said to the congregation 'All you sinners come up front and be prayed for.' Everyone started trooping down, except us. But then the minister happened to look up to the balcony, and who does he see but us four sitting there. 'You, too,' he says. 'You sinners up in the balcony, you come down here and be prayed for.' So we marched downstairs and knelt down—all except Ken. And when we got him outside when it was all over and asked him why he didn't move he told us, 'That man never saw me before and he just looked at me and called me a sinner. I could have been Jesus Christ sitting there, for all he knew.' " [7]

In June 1950, Gibson walked out of Central High School, a diploma in hand, one of the lucky 5 per cent destined for college. He had acceptances from the Massachusetts Institute of Technology, Stevens Institute, and the Newark College of Engineering, but few funds with which to pay tuition and support the wife he had married after graduation. Faced with this responsibility, NCE seemed the best solution, but when two months of school ate up all his reserves, he quit. For the first and only time, Gibson's father became nettled over the thought his son had given in. Still, he scratched about and found Ken a job in the Swift plant, hoping the son would yet earn a degree in civil engineering. He waited and prayed. Boredom did the rest. "Ken used to come home," his mother remembers, "and just collapse on the bed exhausted." For two years he stuck it out, taking various factory jobs, adding a few dollars on week-ends with saxophone parts in a dance band. But by the fall of 1951, he had had enough. Back he went to NCE, this time as a night student after working all day in a new job at the New Jersey Highway Department.

Ahead of him lay eight years of study and, with two years of military service intervening (with the 65th Engineer Battalion in Hawaii from 1956 to 1958), matriculation lasted ten years. At graduation he was acclaimed as the only black majoring in civil engineering during the decade.

There was never a question this time about his perseverance or intellectual curiosity. Two of his superiors remember him as a "real man who always did his share, but wouldn't let himself be abused or misused," and a "man with an analytical mind, who liked math. He never took anything at face value, but slowly and methodically would try to reason it out. At times he would appear so deep in thought that you couldn't actually force a conversation." [8] He had started at a salary of $2040. When he left in November 1960 to accept a position with the Newark Housing Authority, he was earning $6684.

Henceforth Gibson was to be molded by new forces. He saw firsthand the frayed sleeve of municipal government, and began questioning the reasons. Second, he joined the black battle for liberation through civil rights. Their convergence produced a man with new visions. In summarizing his developing attitude about City Hall, he said, "I found that they were very slow, but they could become flexible in certain situations. It's a question of how much pressure is applied." In the case of urban renewal, for instance, he discovered that delays which usually took a period of years could be shortened to months if the public only found the correct pressure point.

In this light, it is not surprising to find Gibson in the early sixties involving himself in the traditional civil rights campaigns. Here was a chance to exert pressure on government. And there were no classes to interfere. "What do you do after you've been to school for ten years at night, and you've got all that free time on your hands?" he asked rhetorically. What he found was "that the people who were really making the decisions were the people who were elected to office and all we were doing was picketing those guys. I decided if you've got to picket that guy to make the decision, why don't you be that guy? This is the engineering approach, the logical one. So I decided I'd be mayor." Just like that. Only don't forget this is the man who has said "Just to have confidence and be able to succeed with no opposition—that's no problem. But to be able to have confidence in yourself as an individual against all kinds of odds, regardless of the numbers or regardless of the economics of the situation, how much money's against you or how much power's against you—now that's real confidence."

Thus turned, Gibson decided to attack in two directions: vertically up the ladder at the Housing Authority to gain expertise in city government and horizontally into community affairs to gain exposure. In both efforts he succeeded. At the Authority, he "took one step at a time and knew where he was going. He didn't buck the system. He made it work." [9] In four years, he reached the top of the staff charged with basic engineering on Newark's urban renewal projects. Alongside this achievement, Gibson became co-chairman of the Business and Industrial Coordinating Council, an agency designed to improve employment among blacks and Puerto Ricans. Although Newark's largest business was the chemical and pharmaceutical industry, only 6.7 per cent of the employees were then black, only 10.3 per cent of the electrical industry work force, and 5.4 of the insurance business—a figure that had remained static for the previous eighteen years.

In addition, he was named vice-president of the United Community Corporation, Newark's anti-poverty program, which attacked on three fronts—education, manpower, and special services intended to limit exploitation of the poor, and to draw black businesses into the Central District. Encouraging as the plan seemed, it failed to dislodge the gloom that increasingly shrouded Newark. Within City Hall, the government was coming unstuck. Mayor Addonizio, a resident of Vailsburg, owed his election in 1962 to a coalition of Italians, Jews, and blacks. But by 1966, when he was preparing to run a second time, the alliance was breaking down. As Addonizio's aide Donald Malafronte observed, "First, the liberal Jews were moving out rapidly; second, black responsiveness was coming on strong; and third, the Italians were never that liberal." [10]

Obviously, an opporunity was unfolding for an ambitious black to challenge the mayor, who up to then had seemed invulnerable. He was, he said, born in the heart of the Central Ward, and liked to tell friends that "in a sense all of us come from the ghetto. Some make it and some don't," inferring he had. Addonizio was the offspring of Italian immigrants, had copped football honors in high school, and at Fordham University an athletic scholarship enabled him to play quarterback behind the famed "Seven Blocks of Granite." He could point to an exemplary World War II record —private to captain, plus a "fruit salad" display of medals for bravery in action. Barrel-chested, lusty, outgoing, he had caught the attention of Dennis Carey, the Essex County Democratic leader, who elected him to Congress in 1948 from the 11th District, which covered the Oranges and Newark's Central, West, and South wards. His record in

Congress from 1948 to 1962 was typically urban liberal. He voted affirmatively on everything that would help the downtrodden and the poor—civil rights, Medicare, higher minimum wages, and increased Social Security benefits.

Still, none of this prevented Gibson's friends from thinking the time had come to throw his hat into the ring. Six weeks before the primary election, he agreed to give it a try. There was little money and less professional staff. Altogether the campaign cost about $3000, but it did serve as a beginning. "Things were pretty rough," one intimate recalls. "I remember one night a couple of us were spreading some campaign posters throughout the City. When we finished, we decided we should drop off the ones we had left at the campaign headquarters. Except that we didn't know where it was. So we went over to Ken's. He was loading some stuff into the trunk of his car, and we asked him where the headquarters was. 'You're looking at it,' he said, pointing to the trunk. 'Well, where's the inner, select circle of advisers?' 'You're looking at them,' he grinned."

When the returns were in, however, he had collected a surprising 16,200 votes to 45,817 for Addonizio, good for third and sufficient to compel the Mayor to enter a runoff election to win a second term. Far from crestfallen, Gibson reacted in typical fashion. "If I could come in third in six weeks," he said, "I can certainly become Mayor in four years." He began campaigning immediately for 1970—not an easy objective, no matter how optimistic he seemed about the outcome. Whites still held the upper hand, and they were unlikely to let go without a struggle if the contest were racial, which inevitably it would be.

Several areas of conflict were already developing, among them the actions of the police, the Planning Board, and the Board of Education. In each confrontation the blacks charged Addonizio with favoritism. In the case of the police, as the Kerner Commission later pointed out, the officers "were largely Italian, the persons they arrested largely

Negro." Hundreds of affidavits charging police brutality were gathering dust in the files of the Newark Commission on Human Rights. To mounting criticism, Addonizio had replied "It is vital to establish once and for all, in the minds of the public, that charges of police brutality will be thoroughly investigated and the appropriate legal or punitive action be taken if the charges are found to be substantiated," but this spelled wasted rhetoric. Pulled between setting up a Police Board of Review by angry blacks and doing nothing to please the police, Addonizio gave the charges to the FBI and "no complaint was ever heard of again."

A second *cause célèbre* was the Mayor's new proposal to take over one hundred fifty acres of the predominantly black Central Ward for a state medical-dental college. Involved was the forced removal of 22,000 residents, which the community saw as a political ploy to reduce black power in the area. The Mayor was charged with high-handed disregard for Ward opinion. When the Planning Board finally listened to the people's voice, the hearing lasted until 4 A.M. as speaker after speaker blasted the administration.

But perhaps the worst slight to Newark blacks was the Mayor's refusal to countenance a black candidate for the prestigious position of Secretary to the Board of Education. The latter serves as accounting officer for the school budget and chief administrator for the Board. When word leaked out that the incumbent was preparing to resign, black militants put forward the name of a young black certified public accountant with a master's degree in business administration from Cornell University. What could be more natural than to appoint such an individual to this powerful post in a school system that was 80 per cent black? But Addonizio was unimpressed by the argument; he wanted one of his cronies, James Callaghan, whose educational qualifications added up to a high school equivalency certificate. The issue was joined when blacks in large numbers swarmed to the

Board meetings and threatened to disrupt the proceedings. On one occasion, a former black state assemblyman delivered a four-hour filibuster, and on another occasion blacks kept the Board in session from 5 P.M. to 3:23 A.M. the following day. The city was warned that "if the mayor persisted in naming a white man as Secretary to the Board of Education, and in moving ahead with plans for the medical site, violence would ensue." The first inkling of what lay ahead occurred on the evening of June 27 when an aggressive Congress of Racial Equality chapter descended on the Board to take over the meeting. Addonizio began to see he was stalemated. But he only reacted with a left-handed concession when the Secretary, who was prepared to resign, agreed to remain on the job another year, thereby temporarily defusing the issue.

But a fortnight later, the circle of conflict was whirling again. It began when the police arrested a forty-year-old cab driver, John Smith, on a charge of tailgating a prowl car and dragged him into the Fourth Precinct Police Station for questioning. Rumors spread that he was being beaten by the police. A crowd gathered, hurled angry epithets at the officers, but then dispersed. The next day the Mayor stepped in with promises to appoint the first Negro police captain and a civilian panel to investigate the charge of brutality. But the damage was irreparable. Negro radicals were already gathering at Spirit House to discuss the incident; angry cads were circulating among the Fourth Precinct streets; it was even said that Smith had died. All that remained was the spark to ignite Newark's tinder.

This the black youths willingly donated as they paraded up and down Springfield Avenue in the Central Ward that night, smashing windows and looting. It was only a step for the police to unsheath their guns and another stride for Addonizio to ask the Governor to send in the state police and the National Guard. When the violence finally subsided four days later, twenty-six people lay dead amid destruction by fire and theft of some $10 million. The riot blew the lid off the fragile coalition Addonizio had hoped to preserve and changed his image almost overnight. The Negroes and the Italians began withdrawing into their own enclaves as the process of polarization accelerated. New figures arose, more militant by far than those they hoped to replace. High on the list was Anthony Imperiale, a racist bully boy, schooled in karate, who vowed his band of vigilantes would restore law and order, an obvious reference to the blacks. The promise was good enough to elect Imperiale to the City Council in 1968, where he immediately locked horns with Gibson as the latter stepped up his campaign to replace Addonizio.

On paper, Imperiale talked equality. He wasn't against electing a black mayor—"If there is a good one, you can bet your bottom dollar, I'll jump on his bandwagon, but I don't think they got a strong black candidate. Too many of the good Negro leaders are still in the woodwork and are afraid to come out." The fact was that Gibson was not a "good one." His appearance at Council meetings sent Imperiale into a rage. When Gibson quietly queried the membership about its proclivity for fiscal mismanagement, a practical question as well as an image-booster, the Councilman turned and roared, "I'm sure—bein' as you're running for Mayor—you're concerned about taxes. . . . Now, we're paying $14,000 for a structural engineer—that's you—so as we don't go outside. We still have to go outside the city, bring in people to do the work you're unable to perform. . . ." To Imperiale, Gibson was nothing but "a liar and a hypocrite." Which didn't disturb Gibson, knowing that every blow from Imperiale was a boost in the black heartland. His one apprehension was the effect such attacks might have in the white community. Fully suspecting the trap, he countered, "The job really is not to be a black candidate, but to be a people's candidate and not get hung up on the racial thing. What I think I could do is create a climate of respect and honesty." [11] By the summer of 1969, Gibson was becoming shrewdly aware that "honesty" was his number-one issue. The Hughes Select Commission on Civil Rights had quoted a former state official, a former city official, and an incumbent official as saying "There's a price tag on everything at City Hall." [12] "You can't expect the state and federal governments," Gibson emphasized, "to allocate money to an administration they feel is corrupt. They gave Addonizio over $11 million in state aid, and they haven't got a proper accounting of what happened to that $11 million. Pickets and demonstrations are not going to make those guys shake loose with more money." [13]

With the 1970 mayoralty campaign some months away, the contour of the conflict was finally taking shape. Gibson was running on a platform that promised a housecleaning and emphasis on the elimination of governmental waste. Imperiale, with one eye on law and order and the other on Addonizio, had jumped into the contest in May, taking pains to time his announcement with a minor riot in the South Ward. "I feel that in the early part of the outbreak," he declared, tossing a verbal incendiary at the Mayor, "Addonizio did not use the force to quell the problem. I feel we've been kneeling too much to the perpetrators of arson, looting and physical assault on decent citizens." Told what Imperiale had said, the Mayor grunted, "There are more serious problems confronting the city at the moment. We will get to the politics at the appropriate time." Gibson, never at a loss to put two and two together, could now see that Imperiale was no threat to the Mayor.

There was every reason, however, to secure his rear flank. He had to have this bloc even though it would take white votes to win. Accordingly, when a number of minority groups met in mid-November in the Clinton Place Junior High School to nominate candidates for the following year's primary, he sought their brass ring for mayor. The Black and Puerto Rican Convention was tremendous—three delegates from each of 397 organizations and about 900 spectators. As predicted, Gibson was their choice and promptly moved to stake his claim before any edgy competitors decided to disregard his selection. "Black people select their own leaders and their own political candidates," he warned, "and they won't be happy about other groups' trying to put up puppets and carpetbaggers and Uncle Toms." [14]

But within a month everything political had turned topsy-turvy. Federal and state investigators who descended on Newark following the revelations of the Hughes' report had found "a city of impacted rackets," and were ready to hand up their first indictments. On December 17, Mayor Addonizio and nine past and current officials were charged with extorting $253,000 on contracts totaling $2.7 million and failing to pay income taxes. The Mayor remained impassive in the face of the allegation. To the question "Will business go on as usual?" he replied, "We will continue with an efficient and effective governing of Newark." Less impassive was the *Star-Ledger*, Newark's daily, which advised those "under a cloud of suspicion" to "remove themselves from office."

Three weeks before the bomb dropped, the key figure for the prosecution, forty-eight-year-old Frederick Lacey, a long-time Newark attorney, had said, "Organized crime is taking us over. For a few rotten dollars, mobsters have been able to corrupt officials in various governments. Organized crime will not even go into a community unless and until it has brought it protection against raids and arrests." In what was a classic example of American municipal corruption, Addonizio had grabbed the lead part, by ingratiating himself with members of the Italian Mafia and eventually allowing the mob to move in. Residents could recall his presence at a 1950 bash when "Tony Boy" Boiardo, Newark's most notorious racketeer, threw a party at the Essex House for some two thousand guests to celebrate his marriage. Young Tony was a protege of Richie "the Boot"—short for bootlegger—Democratic leader of the city's old First Ward

during the forties. Father Boiardo, now seventy-eight, lived
on a forty-acre estate in neighboring Livingston, famous as
the spot where a human incinerator immolated the victims
of mafioso atrocities.

Addonizio and his co-defendants denied the charges of
extortion and income evasion, but when the court ordered
twelve hundred pages of FBI transcripts released in the trial
of Angelo ("Gyp") De Carlo, the Mayor's association with
the underworld appeared undeniable. De Carlo was reputedly a high figure in the New Jersey Mafia who boasted of
helping to move Addonizio from Congress to City Hall in
1962. He had been a financial procurer and afterward spoke
confidently of Addonizio handing over the city to the Mafia.
"He'll give it to us," he said, knowing the Mayor was in his
grip.

Gibson's reaction to the latest development was to treat it
low-key. "I hope this will mean a new look by the electorate
at the candidates," he said matter-of-factly, but others in the
black community were more skeptical. Their chief worry
was over the encouragement Addonizio's plight would give
other blacks ambitious to be mayor. Already, one group was
promoting George C. Richardson, a three-term state assemblyman. Others talked up Willie Wright, president of the
United Afro-American Association, and Albert Black, former
chairman of Newark's Human Rights Commission. A fifth
possibility was Harry L. Wheeler, a former schoolteacher,
who said he was a candidate. As it turned out, only three finally filed petitions for the primary—Gibson, Richardson, and
Wheeler.

The latter two adopted the view that Gibson had already
lost the election by alienating the white vote. As Albert
Black, a Richardson supporter, put it, the Black and Puerto
Rican Convention that nominated Gibson during November
was "based on extremism, racism and segregation." It was
not likely the whites would forget this. In addition he
charged LeRoi Jones, a Gibson supporter, with using his po-

sition as a national figure to mislead the "nation's black, Puerto Rican and liberal white communities into thinking that there was only one black candidate of stature in Newark." Jones had previously established a New Ark Fund to aid Gibson and during a meeting of the organization in February had prevailed upon well-known black figures, none from Newark, to endorse Gibson. In March he had gone a step further by persuading a group of seven prominent Negroes and one Puerto Rican to ask Assemblyman Richardson to step aside "in the interests of black and Puerto Rican unity." Signing the wire were Representative Shirley Chisholm of Brooklyn; Representative Herman Badillo of the Bronx; Representative John Conyers of Michigan; Mayor Richard Hatcher of Gary, Ind.; Dr. Nathan Wright, formerly associated with the Episcopal Diocese of Newark; Mayor William S. Hart of neighboring East Orange; Ossie Davis, the actor; and John O. Killens, author and playwright. Knowing that any black candidate would need from 10 to 12 per cent of the city's white votes to win, Richardson turned down the request. "The appeal to quit the race was based on black racism, which," he said, "is no better than white racism."

What worried Gibson's supporters was not Richardson's strength at the polls. A survey of about twelve hundred voters taken by Oliver Quayle and Co. showed Gibson outpolling Richardson three and a half to one. What did upset them was the rift it caused in the black community when cooperation, not dislocation, was needed. Gibson tried to meet the racial charge by setting up a compaign staff that was half white.

Meanwhile, back at City Hall the rubric was as normal as though nothing had transpired. The Mayor's deputy Paul H. Reilly voiced the optimism that extortion and tax evasion would have no effect on the coming primary. "I have great faith in the people of Newark," he said. There could be no doubt that Addonizio was "Newark's best hope for a sound

future." Time—that miraculous narcotic—was even tranquil-
izing the Mayor's judgment. On January 29, a bare forty
days after the indictment, he calmly repeated for a group of
newspapermen that "he had acted at all times with a sense
of respect and honor. . . . I swear to each of you today that I
have never committed a single act in public life to betray
that trust. . . . I could not, and I would not, face my children
if I had." And forthwith announced his candidacy for a
third term. Asked what he thought of City Hall's latest
move, Gibson decided on discretion. The time not to kick an
opponent, he knew, was when he was down. In Addonizio's
case it would lose white votes that Gibson needed. "It is up
to the legal system and the courts," he understated, "to determine the Mayor's future."

In the market place, though, other pots were commencing
to boil. Newark's Fire Director, John P. Caufield, had been
sacked for not supporting Addonizio's mayoralty ambitions.
He said he could not support a candidate who, in his opinion, had "lost the confidence of the people." Ten days later,
he announced that he would run for mayor, adding a sixth
to those already in the race. Before the month of February
was out, a seventh had joined up for the duration of the primary, State Senator Alexander J. Matturri, the race's lone
Republican, who entered the fray, he said, because the city
needed "a new administration and a new image."

Campaign rhetoric was unchanged. Corruption and racism remained the leading issues. Despite Addonizio's dis-
claimer, the indictment of the city's top official was an undeniable persuader. Gibson simply pointed out it was a matter of
public record, and as such something to be examined. Fortunately, even in the heat of the campaign, he refused the
temptation of personal buffeting. He left it to others to unsheath the stiletto—to stab it, for instance, into the body of
racial conflict. Assemblyman Richardson gave mouth to municipal apprehension when he said, "Newark could not afford either 'the all-black politics of a LeRoi Jones-oriented

government' headed by Mr. Gibson nor a 'white racist government' headed by Mr. Imperiale." So the campaign raced
on toward the tape. Gibson placed his chief hope in the per-
son-to-person approach, sidewalk appearances, coffee parties, any forum where he would reach the greatest number
of blacks and whites. He had established a Broad Street
headquarters in the business area and five other offices in
the surrounding wards where hundreds of workers aided his
cause. Dennis Sullivan, white assistant, Princeton 1970, opti-
mistically predicted on the eve of the election, "We are confident. We have the scent of the smell of victory." The only
worry of the Gibson forces was the low registration of
133,502—off 20,350 from four years before. Particularly disappointing was the knowledge that LeRoi Jones' New Ark
Fund had made a special effort inside the black ghetto to
boost the registration. This was somewhat offset by Harry
Wheeler's withdrawal, two days before, with a plea to his
followers to vote for Gibson.

On Tuesday evening, May 12, Gibson supporters jam-
med the Georgian Room of the Robert Treat Hotel. The
polls closed at 8 P.M., and within minutes the results were
pouring in from the city's 207 election districts. Gibson went
into an immediate lead and the black crowd, sensing victory, began to cheer. "We gonna win. My God, we gonna
win," an unbeliever cried. But the primary winner needed
50 per cent of the vote plus one, and while Gibson outpolled
his nearest competitor (Addonizio) two to one, he had not
reached the magic figure. The final count was:

Candidate	Votes	Percentage
Gibson	37,859	43
Addonizio	18,212	21
Imperiale	13,978	16
Caufield	11,950	13
Matturri	4,734	5
Richardson	2,038	2

A runoff election, June 12, between Gibson and Addonizio was now necessary. As the political pundits surveyed the
figures, they saw that despite the efforts of Jones' New Ark
organization, less than 70 per cent of the city's registered
voters had bothered to vote. Of these, 40 per cent were
black and Puerto Rican, 60 per cent white. The four white
candidates had outpolled the two blacks by nearly 9000
votes—55 to 45 per cent. Gibson's chances therefore depended in large part on what happened to Imperiale and
Caufield's supporters, assuming that Addonizio's votes clung
to the Mayor. As to Imperiale, the die appeared cast. Given
the animosity between Gibson and the North Ward white
militant, Addonizio would pick up the votes to put him
within striking distance of Gibson. It would then depend
upon what Caufield and Matturri decided. On the day after
the primary they intimated a switch to Gibson.

Addonizio fought back. According to Caufield, he immediately dispatched a personal envoy who promised "anything" in City Hall if Caufield would only return to the Addonizio reservation. Caufield fumed. He had only wanted,
he retorted, "honesty, integrity, efficiency and a fair deal for
all citizens of Newark." With this final straw, he cut his ties
to the administration and vowed full support of Gibson.
Whether his supporters would march with him into the Gibson camp was now the sixty-four-dollar question. "I doubt
it," said a member of the Addonizio organization. "The
whole thing rests with the Caufield vote, and I can't see him
being able to deliver his vote from the white Vailsburg districts, for instance. I think a lot of those voters are going to
stay home. Of course, this would help Gibson. But those
who vote, when they get in that booth, it's going to come
down to a question of white and black—and no 'ifs' and
'ands' about it." Just to make the prognostication more difficult, a racial breakdown of the May 12 returns showed that
15 per cent of Mayor Addonizio's vote was black compared
with 8 per cent of Gibson's vote that was white. Mathemati-

cally, if the mix of black and white votes remained fixed, Addonizio could win on June 16. Moreover, it was well known that whites had outvoted blacks in the primary. The only sure antidote was to arouse the black community as never before.

As a hedge on this predictable onslaught, the Addonizio forces took up the race issue. The first rumble came the day after the primary election when the Mayor blandly remarked he would not use the issue. "I have never raised the issue of race in my twenty-two years of public life," said he with a political wink, while pointing out that Gibson had vied for black militant support. Like a flight of homing pigeons, each rumor set aloft was designed to light in the white community. First it was alleged that LeRoi Jones, the white-baiter, would get a job in City Hall if Gibson won. Then Rhody McCoy, the militant Brooklyn educator, was said to have the edge on running the schools. What did it matter to the administration that Gibson should brand these tales "very dirty and low, an appeal to fear," or that Jones should say "I have no connection whatsoever with the Gibson campaign machinery; no policy or advisory position. I've known Ken since we were little boys, but actually, I've given more advice to Addonizio—only he's never listened." The objective was clearly to put Gibson on the defensive and smugly to deny any racial motive. Addonizio backers were convinced that white fear of a black-power usurpation was the one way to shield the Mayor from the publicity of his pending trial. From the moment the primary figures were in, lawyers for the Mayor had attempted to delay the lawsuit. But federal judge George H. Barlow refused the request. He said Addonizio would have to stand trial in Trenton, beginning June 2, and return to Newark at night if he wished to campaign for a third term. Checkmated by this legal restraint, the Mayor tossed discretion aside. He now realized the only chance of staying alive politically was to project white supremacy.

Accordingly, the last two weeks of the mayoralty campaign turned into one of the bitterest race-infected campaigns in American politics. Since Gibson was a black moderate, Addonizio found him a poor target. But he still charged him with being part of a raw and violent conspiracy to turn Newark over "to LeRoi Jones and his extremist followers." The Mayor saw in Jones the perfect *bête noir*. He was the man, he told white audiences, who had said of white police "waylay them in an alley, cut out their tongues and send them back to Ireland."

Unsigned hate literature began to flow from Addonizio headquarters into white neighborhoods. Again, on the printed page as on the stump, the Jones name overshadowed the entire election. One sample recalled an alleged remark of two years before when he pressed Elizabeth Negroes to "slit the white man's throat" and "rape his daughter." Another cast a picture of the militant playwright under the heading *Gibson's Chief Aide Says 'Kill whites right now.'* Nor was this all of Addonizio's "yummies." Goon squads tried to frighten Gibson and his followers. These gangs of white youths were determined to provoke street fights which would pander to the Mayor's expressed fear. Gibson gave strict orders not to listen to such threats, but on occasion it required great control not to react, like the day he visited a supermarket in the heavily Italian North Ward. His bodyguard—a black Newark plainclothesman—had to stand erect while tormentors called him "baboon" and "nigger ." After the incident, he confessed, "I don't know what I would have done if he had as much as touched me." Whatever composure the blacks might muster, it was by now obvious that Addonizio's racist approach was bearing fruit. Four days before the election, a reporter for *The New York Times* found a typical white voter who informed him, "Look, I'm Italian. I don't like Addonizio. He set us back 30 years with all this scandal. But I'm voting for him, because it's white against black now."

As the two candidates came down to the wire, Gibson had two things going for him. The big names in the black world descended upon Newark to lend a hand. Bill Cosby, Julian Bond, Sammy Davis, Jr., Leontyne Price, Harry Belafonte, Mayors Carl Stokes of Cleveland and Richard Hatcher of Gary were there. Just three days before election, the Reverend Ralph D. Abernathy, civil rights leader, escorted Gibson through every ward in the city, caravan style, with black members of the New York Mets, Jets, and Knicks. It was like a tidal wave of Negro enthusiasm sweeping blacks to the polls. The other advantage was the increasing number of thoughtful whites flocking to his banner. As he talked in the white wards of improving the quality of life in Newark, better education, new housing, additional state revenues to keep the city out of bankruptcy, the white enclaves saw a short, stocky, confident, close-cropped black, knowledgeable on municipal affairs, quite the person they wanted for mayor after eight years of sloppy government, broken promises, topped by an indictment of the Mayor and several of his close associates. There was also the work of John Caufield, who bore the brunt of the deep anti-black sentiment. Caufield was roughed up, spat upon, and called "nigger lover," but he continued to campaign for Gibson. Some said he was still the key to victory. If his followers backed Gibson, the latter was certain to win. Finally, the white establishment was in his corner, pledging thousands to his campaign fund and providing an air-conditioned Lincoln Continental in which he rode to the political gatherings. The turnout on June 16 was the largest in Newark's runoff history. A total of 98,231 voters—73 per cent of those registered—cast ballots.

With victory in the air, a tremendous crowd gathered in Gibson's headquarters and began to chant "Power to the people!" and "We want Gibson!" A big man with a powerful voice sang out, "We *want* Gibson? Hell, we *got* Gibson!" And the woman on the dais said, "Hold onto your hats.

Here's the final count": Gibson 55,097 votes and Addonizio 43,086.[15] The man who had said "no one can rule a divided city" had scored a victory of more than 11,000 votes, better than his most sanguine supporters thought possible. Pushing his way to the podium, the Mayor-elect cried, "Right on! Robert Treat never realized that someday Newark would have *soul*. This is an important victory for all the people of Newark. This will be an administration of all the people— black, white, Puerto Rican, and all colors. We will work for everyone, and we will work on and on—right on, as we say!" One of the first to offer congratulations on a "splendid victory" was Addonizio, beaten and contrite but telling his supporters Gibson must be given "every opportunity to succeed." Two weeks later, Gibson was inaugurated the first black mayor of a metropolitan city. From the steps of City Hall, he raised a clenched fist, the black power symbol, and called for mending Newark's good name. Success, he said, depended in part upon the question of whether "men and women of all faiths, races and backgrounds could find the good that I sincerely believe exists in every man."

The initial days at City Hall were fraught with the stock frustrations that invariably accompany the changing of the municipal guard. It was one thing to turn out Addonizio, quite another to unravel the civil service bureaucracy that surrounded him. "You get in a rut, I guess, after thirty years of doing things the same way," Gibson lamented. His first job was to fashion priorities on a broad front. "The greatest thing," he concluded, "would be to revamp the City's public school system." To find high school graduates reading at an eighth grade level in the richest country on earth was criminal, he said. More money would be needed to reverse the trend, and to his dismay, aides found the Addonizio administration had buried a $21-million school operating deficit out of fear that raising taxes in an election year would prove fatal. Despite this setback, Gibson wanted Newark's industrial establishment to recognize the need for training its future labor force. "It's like an insurance policy," he declared. "You pay the premium, and the cash value comes later." [16] Yet, as enthusiastic as Gibson was to improve the school system, it was not, he hinted in his inaugural address, to be accomplished overnight. His one immediate step would be to increase black representation on the school board—giving it an equal black-white cast.

In other areas there were the heads of the police and fire departments to replace. The latter presented no problem. John Caufield was the natural selection to fill the job Addonizio had taken from him in January. But finding someone to fill the post of Police Director was something else. Dominick Spina, Addonizio's chief, had infuriated the black community before and during the election. It was not only that he had gained a reputation similar to Birmingham's notorious "Bull" Connor, but also that he had spoken over and over during the mayoralty campaign of a "black and white situation" that could spell out "Whether we [whites] survive or cease to exist." But should his replacement be white or black? From one side the Mayor was told that a white Director would tend to quiet white fears aroused by the election. Conversely, such adherents as LeRoi Jones adamantly called for a black choice. "This is a racist nation," Jones reminded Gibson. "A lot of white people have a social attitude that will permit racist practices simply because they are not as sensitive to racism as black people." In deference to Jones, Gibson asked him to sound out a list of black candidates outside Newark. Not a nibble. Gibson himself then talked to blacks, but followed a more pragmatic approach. "Whether you were black or white," he said, "was not really the factor. The question was whether the guy could do the job." Despite Jones' fear of white racism, the Mayor finally appointed John L. Redden, an experienced white police officer with a reputation for being "a tough, honest cop." Within days of Redden's appointment, two hundred policemen had been moved up or down or trans-

ferred. "Scores of detectives were reduced to uniformed policemen pounding beats, and scores of patrolmen elevated
to plain-clothes detective work." [17]

The fact that his brother Howard was a member of the
police force undeniably affected Gibson's idea of the officer's
role. He talked of a "two-way street" in which the individual
patrolman and the individual citizen needed to understand
each other. "You see," he said, "a policeman is still a human
being and he doesn't stop being one just because you put
the uniform on him. He's going to react like anyone if he's
pushed hard enough. You have to make him understand
what his role is at the same time you make people understand what their role is and then try to eliminate incidents
which can blow things out of proportion in a city like Newark. I think police attitudes are not that bad. There are individuals who have to be re-educated, but take the average
policeman on our 1400-man force; he is going to feel dis-
criminated against if you send him to class to learn how to
be nice to citizens. It's hard to teach a guy how to be nice
to someone who calls you 'pig.' After all the training, a policeman might get a little annoyed so it really has to be a
two-way street."

Gibson sees the complicated subject of racism in objective
terms: "We all have faults, all of us, whether we are black or
white, and the real question is how best we can work together in our society. We have whites that don't get along
with other whites, we have blacks that don't get along with
other blacks, and, of course, we have blacks that don't get
along with whites and vice versa, so the question is how
best we can work with each other and that includes getting
the Catholic to work with the Jew, and the Jew to work
with the Protestant, and blacks to work with whites and
vice versa. Blacks have some very difficult times with blacks
in other countries who only have each other to get angry
with—so it's a much larger question than just dealing with
white racism," a caveat he reserves for the findings of the

National Advisory Commission on Civil Rights—the so-called Kerner Commission.

Asked if he thought the Commission, in blaming the riots of 1967 on white racism, overstretched the point, Gibson answers, "No. I think it did not. I think, however, it was only dealing with a very narrow area of violence and reaction to violence. We're in the seventies now and the report was dealing with actions in 1967. Moreover, we're not talking an exact science. I'm pretty sure that if someone were going to analyze me objectively, I would probably have some 'hang-ups' and prejudices, some kind of strange views, too, if I were pushed.

"Frankly, we are dealing with human beings and human nature and the fact the world is not what it should be. What we should be doing is not so much just trying to eliminate white racism which exists and which is probably going to exist as long as we have people in the world, or black racism which exists and which is probably going to exist as long as we have people, but making people understand that their interest is unalterably entwined in the interests of other groups. We should make people respect each other and respect each other's positions and work with each other for the common good. I mean this is what our goals should be rather than the Utopian idea that we're going to eliminate racism—I just think we're not prepared for that."

A primary result of Gibson's election was to lift the curtain from organized crime. He said, on taking office, "One thing my election has done already is to serve notice on organized crime that their license has been revoked. Crooks hate the spotlight. They want the freedom to operate with the official sanction of city administrators. Now that I'm the mayor they won't be able to have that." But responsibility for cleaning up the mess was far more encompassing and frustrating than Gibson had imagined. The indictment of Addonizio and his co-defendants on sixty-four counts of conspiracy and extortion, their conviction and eventual sen-

tencing (ten years and a $25,000 fine for Addonizio) had
seemed a blow aimed at the heart of municipal chicanery,
but as it turned out, the guilty were no more than a sapling
in a forest of evil. Gibson's sleuths discovered that "virtually
every contract signed by the city in recent years was
inflated by 10 per cent to allow for kickbacks to city officials." Moreover, the Mayor revealed after seventy-five
days in office that he could have already pocketed $31,000
in under-the-table transactions. Indeed, he told a large gathering of the Greater Newark Chamber of Commerce of
hearing that someone was willing to put up $15,000 if he
could appoint the Police Director. Was this the case of another business-political deal? Gibson could only challenge
his audience "not to offer any money to anyone in the city
administration." But admittedly, in a city so long permeated
with crime, so infested with Mafia roots, his plea was as
likely to bear immediate redress as a snowfall on the Fourth
of July. Far more promising was the Mayor's pledge to establish a city investigations bureau that would comb over
the operation of each department—including the mayor's—
for evidence of malfeasance. This would shore up a bad situation in the Department of Public Works, where not a single licensed engineer was employed under the Addonizio
administration to scrutinize contracts involving millions of
dollars. In the background was still the fear that hostile elements in the police force would join hands to thwart his
plans for law and decency. In all probability he had hoped
that some of them would resign as Dominick Spina had predicted in the event of a Gibson victory. But Spina "was the
first one to ask for his old job back," the Mayor said in reporting his return under civil service status to deputy
Chief.[18]

Unquestionably, as the newly elected chief executive,
Gibson's chief task was to lift Newark from its economic
abyss. As he saw it, this consisted of a two-prong attack, one
launched in the private sector by a joining hands of business

and City Hall to attract new firms, the other in the public sector, to develop sufficient cash inflow through municipal taxes, state and federal grants and subsidies plus administrative efficiencies to keep the city from bankruptcy. Getting capital improvements for Newark, in the Mayor's view, "had to be done in the same way that business is attracted to any other city. You have to have reasons for their coming. They're not going to come for social reasons. The business of business is business. Businessmen are not in business to get involved in social sciences, in social services. They're in business to make a *profit*. We have to give them the means to make a profit." Then, ticking off the incentives, he could point proudly to tax abatement, an ample labor supply, one of the best transportation systems in the world (New Jersey Turnpike, Garden State Parkway, Newark Airport), the center of the largest metropolitan market in the world. "The basic need," he added, "was to get more jobs, not special programs, but more actual jobs where people work for a salary. And the best way to get more jobs was to make the area attractive; that's the first step. The next step was to make sure the hiring patterns are equitable for the entire community. The solution to the unemployment problem for blacks and Puerto Ricans and other minority groups in this country was to have them prepared for the jobs that are available. Some people estimate that in the last decade Newark lost more than 10,000 unskilled factory labor jobs. Moreover, top-level jobs, the available insurance and banking jobs, didn't fit the labor supply. So what we're doing through special training programs is to change that kind of imbalance."

The first visible success of Gibson's campaign was an announcement on August 12 that Ideal Toy Corporation, the industry's third largest independent, had paid $1,254,000 for a thirty-eight-acre site on Newark's Meadowland on which to erect a 600,000 square-foot manufacturing plant. It would be the largest plant to settle in Newark since the end of

World War II and would provide an estimated 8000 jobs by 1980, primarily in the unskilled-labor category. It would give the city, according to Gibson, a chance to "recoup the deficit in jobs for the unskilled."

Beyond the question of jobs and income, the Mayor had known he could expect support from the industrial establishment. The white power structure's most influential spokesman, the head of Prudential, had announced after the election, "I am sure that Mayor Gibson will be calling upon business and industry for assistance and I am certain that he will find them responsive." This open sesame shook out a half-dozen of Newark's brightest young executives from the corporate rooms of the city's elite—on loan for ninety days —to "assist in making departments function more efficiently." What they found was devastating. "I was almost in a state of shock for the first two weeks," a Prudential vice-president remarked after looking at the records. A city contract for towing away cars had expired with no attempt to renew it. Noncompliance with state and federal restrictions had canceled valuable programs. The administration was permitting overruns on public works contracts to add huge sums to the cost of government. And a feeling persisted that the city had lost $10 million the previous year in federal aid "simply because the city administration didn't know the money was available." [19]

It was this loss of revenue, tied to fiscal dishonesty and plain ineptitude, which gave Gibson his greatest worry as he tried to gather in the reins of office. With Newark's property tax already one of the nation's highest, he was forced to initiate steps, some immediate, some long-range, to avert bankruptcy. The former consisted of a package request to the New Jersey state legislature for permission to impose a 2 per cent payroll tax on residents and non-residents who work in Newark, a tax on jet fuels sold at Newark Airport, a state takeover of municipal Martland Hospital, and a lump-sum grant of urban aid designed to raise $56 million. Leaders of the Republican-controlled legislature blanched at the thought of making the GOP-enrolled suburbanites dig deeper and instead suggested that the employer pay the tax. This would raise an estimated $36 million, allowing the Mayor to scratch for the rest, naked proof of the reason U.S. municipalities are locked in financial trouble.

In Newark, where the property tax is the primary revenue source, the result is tragic, for only a third of the land actually contributes to the support of government. The airport occupies a third of the terrain and the huge college complex in downtown Newark takes up a hundred acres. As a matter of principle, Gibson thinks "these institutions should make payments to the city in lieu of taxes." But to do so requires state permission. "The City of Newark," he says heatedly, "cannot afford to take continually fifty acres and fifty acres and fifty acres and remove them from the tax rolls." The airport situation is equally painful; it is protected by a long lease which pays the city a million dollars a year (on a budget of $160 to $170 million), based on whether the Port of New York Authority spends money on capital improvements. Currently, it is spending at the rate of $500,000 a year, thus providing the city with a half-million dollars from about one-third of the property. "This, in my opinion," says the Mayor, "is inequitable." The total effect of such paucity spreads its fingers through the city apparatus, restricting the employment of top-grade personnel to a maximum of $20,000 for most departments. Under prodding, the City Council did approve a salary of $35,000 for the post of Business Administrator, but when Gibson named a Midwestern city manager with eighteen years experience, he refused to come until the city's business community added a $2500 supplement. The result of such penny-ante maneuvers has the Mayor riding in a former vintage city-owned Cadillac because the city cannot afford to update the ownership.

The sense of urban poverty which this reflects originally

prompted Rutgers Professor Sternlieb to say "When the blacks get Newark, they're getting it on a bankruptcy scale. There will have to be billions spent to repair sewers, bad schools, welfare and so forth." But the lamentation slides off an impervious Gibson. "It's not a question of blacks getting Newark," he argues. "It wouldn't be any different if there were a white mayor. I think we have to spend a great deal of money in cities like Newark. The city itself cannot afford to spend that money. Unless we get state aid, massive state aid, massive federal aid, we'll never be able to spend those billions that Dr. Sternlieb was talking about. But we do have to deal with the basic necessities and the crisis situations in a very short period of time. In the long run, we in America have to reorder our priorities to deal with the needs of people, people in cities, people on farms, people all over the country. Caring for human needs is more important than caring for property rights and we're a long way from that, but when we start moving in that direction, we'll spend those billions."

Asked whether the suburbs might receive the "billions" in preference to the cities in view of the changing power structure of the state and federal legislatures, the Mayor again appears unimpressed. "I think they'll vote to spend the money in the regions and in the states, not just in the cities. The problems of Newark have spread to the surrounding area so Newark is not isolated, surrounded and walled in. I think our state legislators will be voting to deal with education in the state of New Jersey, which means, of course, they will be dealing with education in the city of Newark. I think they will be dealing with health problems in regional areas, which means they will be dealing with problems in Newark. We have to solve these problems from the top down rather than from the city up. What I'm saying is that Newark's crisis is going to be looked on sooner or later as if the bubonic plague had struck New York City. No one would wait to see whether or not we were going to deal with it. We would deal with it because it's going to spread to us. The problems of Newark are going to spread to the suburbs, so people are going to say 'We'd better deal with that quick before it gets to us.' That's not going to happen this month, it's not going to happen this year, but it's going to happen." Among the first signs of the new day is the Mayor's revelation that "federal authorities were thinking about making the city, the entire city, a model city. We'll probably be one of five or six cities that will have this kind of designation."

In the meantime, much depends upon the public's attitude, white and black, toward the government and toward each other. A greater voter sophistication would undoubtedly change the posture of elected officials and alert them to ghetto sentiment. Gibson thinks this is already happening. "The citizenry is a great deal more informed, a great deal more intelligent and knowledgeable than most traditional politicians give them credit for being," he maintains. "I think the recent election pointed that out. People tried to run fear tactics, run all kinds of crazy campaigns. And people just didn't fall for it." Because of this, any effort on the part of blacks to withdraw or separate themselves from the community, out of frustration or disenchantment, draws the Mayor's ire. "I don't think that many black leaders are really talking about separatism. I think a few people are. But leadership is a very tenuous thing. You've got to find out who is following those folks. And you don't find too many following people that are talking about separatism, because that's not where it's at. You're not going to gain better education, better housing, better economic conditions with separatism. Two and two are four; it doesn't make any difference what school you get that in. The only way to get these things is to struggle very hard for them, the same route that any other ethnic group has used throughout our society."

The Gibson saga is fascinating, perhaps a foreword to the rebirth of municipal leadership in the U.S. Unlike the familiar ward personality of old, who had his eye on the person ahead of the hand he was shaking, Gibson is a direct man, with a direct gaze. His credo for success is: "I think the Mayor should work for the benefit of the community rather than for the benefit of someone's pocketbook or personal ambition. I didn't go to school for eight years to become an engineer to switch to politics, so my ambition really doesn't lie in the area of politics." He can say and do things other politicians wouldn't because he doesn't "look to be Governor or something else down the road." What Gibson wants is solid accomplishment in a city plagued by bad performances. "In order for me to do something, since my basic nature of physical activity is slow, I have to know exactly how I'm going to get there the same time as a guy who's very fast. It's a matter of planning and also of understanding what your own abilities and limitations are, and dealing with them. I know that I'm never going to win a hundred-yard dash—there's no way in the world I would ever win—but I'll probably win all the marathons."

Clifton Reginald Wharton, Jr. ═══

¶ Digging about, trying to discover what contributes most to the seeds of eminence is a frustrating pursuit. No one knows, for instance, whether heredity or environment is the dominant factor or whether the mix of the two changes from individual to individual so that in one heredity is the more important and in another, environment.

One thing, however, is certain. In black America, the success stories, the tales of those who "made it" within the system flow from a pattern of stability. The Kings, the Youngs, the Brookes share a common identity—they came from black middle-class families and thought enough of the American way to give it a try. Their cry was evolution, not revolution.

One of the best examples is Clifton Reginald Wharton, Jr., born September 13, 1926, in Boston. The elder Wharton was a scholastic marvel. A native of Baltimore, he emigrated north to Boston, attended English High School, skipped college, went directly to Boston University Law School, and graduated at twenty-one. He fell in love with Virginia-born Harriet Banks, an undergraduate at the university, took a master's degree, their son hints, in order to remain near her—and eventually the two married. For a short span, he practiced law, then turned to the Foreign Service.

In the twenties, a black American with striped pants and cutaway credentials was an oddity of major dimensions. Yet, beginning with service in Monrovia, Liberia, the senior Clifton Wharton climbed nimbly upward, serving eventually as minister to Rumania and finally ambassador to Norway. When he retired in 1964 after forty years in the Department, he was the highest-ranking Negro in the diplomatic service.

Traveling abroad to foreign outposts, mixed with occasional leaves at home, left an unusual imprint on the Wharton family. Young Clifton was born in the U.S., a second son in Spain, a third son in the U.S., and a fourth child, a daughter, in Spain. Clifton began his education while his father was still assigned to the Canary Islands, a Spanish possession. Since there were no American schools, his mother taught him with books and instruction from a Baltimore correspondence school. "She was a superb teacher," Wharton says, fondly recalling those days. "She took me certain afternoons to a French school, operated by White Russians, where I had my first exposure to French. I picked up Spanish at the same time I learned English so I was trilingual from the beginning." But this was no substitute for a formal education.

Urged on by the fact that the Canary Islands were seething with dangerous intrigue on the eve of the Spanish Civil War and that Clifton had already spent six years abroad, the Whartons decided to return to the U.S. and deposit their son with his maternal grandmother, where he could attend the prestigious Boston Latin School, oldest public school in America.

Besides living in an atmosphere which he found "fascinating," Clifton was immediately struck by the quality of education and the democratic instincts of the school. "They were real teachers with a talent for encouragement. I think they affected me a great deal, although at the time I was unaware of their influence." What perhaps impressed him most was to discover that "innate abilities are randomly distributed through society," and not on the basis of color. Boys attended the school because of their demonstrated intellectual ability, not simply their parents' pedigree or inherited bundle. He saw how a student who was excellent in Latin might be the son of a poor wage-earner; the student who was good in Greek might be the scion of wealth or the one outstanding in mathematics might have a middle-income background, or he might be Jewish or black or Irish or Italian. It was the student, not the family, that counted, a biological lesson that gave him a peer feeling in competition with whites.

Moreover, this was not the only lesson Clifton Wharton received at Boston Latin. He might be part of the educational elite, but his father made certain of his indoctrination as a worker by hand as well. He took a job in a spool factory in Boston because the elder Wharton said it would do him "good." Besides, Wharton reminisces, his father told him "he'd cut off my allowance if I didn't." On the extracurricular side, Wharton developed an enviable record as a track star, a talent he further pursued at Harvard, the predictable objective of most Latin School graduates.

Explaining his cinder record at the university, he intimates modestly enough that his prowess was his own undoing. "The coach used me quite frequently in a number of different events, the 120 high hurdles, the 220 dash, the 440, and the high jump. In my junior year, I entered the high hurdles, pulled a muscle badly at the first hurdle, and never ran again." As the saying goes, what he lost on the bananas, he more than made up on the peanuts. Denied a burgeoning track career, he countered by piling up "firsts" in other fields. He was the first Negro to be connected with the Harvard radio station, the first black to become secretary of the National Student Association, a group he worked hard to fashion. In the midst of such strenuous activity, he still found time to concentrate on history and graduate *cum laude* in June.

1946—the year that Secretary of State George C. Marshall, Harvard's commencement speaker, electrified the world with a U.S. offer to aid the bereaved nations of World War II.

Wharton had always thought he would follow his father's footsteps in the Foreign Service. It seemed the natural thing to do. Not yet twenty, he applied to the School of Advanced International Studies of Johns Hopkins University in Washington, D.C., to gain additional training. His acceptance was another first. "I was the first black student," he recalls. All the facilities—rooms, the dining hall, the library, the classrooms—were in the same building. It was a white world, a challenging world to one who had been a part of the white establishment at Boston Latin and Harvard. He would show them that he could succeed within the system. "I decided that I should give up all of my extracurricular activities and perform to the utmost of my abiility to insure the chance of other blacks being admitted. I was the youngest of my class and when I finished, I stood second."

One day his father returned from abroad to consult with officials in the State Department and invited Clifton to meet his associates there. As the son remembered the occasion, "They all said, 'Oh, you're Cliff's son. When are you coming in the Service?'" Something in the tone of the voices, the posture of inevitability they conveyed, got under the student's skin. "I stewed about this. I said to myself, 'Well, now, if I do go in, and I begin to move along, I will never know whether it's because I'm his son or because I really have the ability.'" So time passed, and finally he said, "I'll try something on my own," and after reviewing the various choices, he hit upon the idea of technical assistance. Wharton was increasingly intrigued by the blossoming of the Marshall Plan and the State Department's Point 4 programs. Their success, he could see, would hang upon individual expertise in the field. Finally, he went to his father and told him he "wasn't going into the foreign service after all, he was going to try his hand at technical assistance." As young

Wharton remembers the conversation, the elder Wharton looked condescendingly at him and said, "Well, that's a sort of do-goodism. That has nothing to do with foreign policy." So they disagreed.

The son set out to prove his point by applying for a job with Nelson Rockefeller's American International Association for Economic and Social Development, an organization primarily interested in Latin America. "I was a young 'pumpkin'—twenty-one—going to be interviewed by one of Rockefeller's associates. I rode the elevator to the fifty-sixth floor in Rockefeller Center and was ushered into his office. Behind the desk sat a precise man who calmly intoned, 'I understand you're looking for a job.'"

"Yes, sir," answered Wharton.

"What can you do?" asked the man disarmingly.

Wharton moved uncomfortably, his mind revolving like a ship's screw. "What on earth can I do?" he finally asked himself. "I've been to Harvard for four years, I'm finishing my master's at Johns Hopkins, what can I do?" He looked up and blurted out, "I can think."

"Well," smiled the precise man, "there will be a job here for you in public relations in June if you'd like it," but he added cryptically, "I wouldn't advise you to take it. It will just be a pigeonhole without progress prospects."

"Thank you very much," Wharton replied dejectedly and rose to go.

"No," the man said hurriedly, reading Wharton's mind and wanting to know more about him. "Sit down." And with that they sat and chatted for a half-hour.

Their conversation could well have been the turning point in Wharton's career, for several months later when the Rockefeller group was preparing a program to train executives, Wharton was among the bright young men selected. "The fascinating thing about this for me," he remembers, "was that during those first years I had the opportunity to move from one unit or division to another and in the process learn a great deal about the operation of each at the top level at an age when I could really begin to grasp what was going on—I spent time with the public relations people, I spent time with the accounting division, I spent time with the programing division at the level where I could see how this interaction worked and conclude which part appealed to me most—it was a marvelous experience." With one step he, a black, had crossed the threshold of the white establishment. He had become a part of the system.

Meanwhile there were other irons in the Wharton fire besides an interest in foreign affairs. The most incandescent one was a young woman, Dolores Duncan, petite (5 foot 3½), attractive, whom Clifton had met on a blind date during his sophomore year at Harvard. Miss Duncan was the daughter of a Harlem undertaker and had lived in upper Manhattan for eleven years. After attending the Little Red Schoolhouse, a modern institution in Greenwich Village, she had moved to Danbury, Connecticut, attended the local teachers' college, and transferred to Chicago Teachers College to finish her baccalaureate. She had intended to be a high school English teacher, but found her plans gradually coming unseamed.

Dolores' first meeting with Clifton was a comic heirloom for the family album. She was visiting a cousin at Radcliffe who knew Clifton and decided to match them. What made it funny, he said, remembering the incident, was that he had a policy then of never accepting a blind date. So did Dolores. Her recollection of their first date is that they didn't "click," but somehow their paths kept crossing. In the end, the denouement involved her cousin as it had at the beginning. The two had dates with West Point cadets one evening and were awaiting their arrival when Clifton chanced by. The threat of losing out was all Clifton needed. Thereafter, Dolores would only admit weakly that the poor cadet didn't have a chance! Clifton and Dolores were married in 1950 in her mother's Danbury home.

By now one could see that Wharton's greatest asset was

his fixation on work. He drove himself unsparingly, and found little or no time for vacation. While given to humor, levity, and the quip, underneath lay the iron purpose. He would circle the objective, look at it from every direction, assess the difficulties, but he knew what he wanted and where he was going. This determination and preciseness convinced him after five years with the Rockefeller group that, to excel in economic development, he had to know more about the financial system.

Accordingly, in 1953 he enrolled in the graduate school of economics at the University of Chicago. Since he needed to support a wife and their year-old son Clifton 3rd, he was delighted to discover that the Ford Foundation had given Professor Theodore W. Schultz money to evaluate U.S. technical assistance in Latin America. Who could be more valuable in such a project than one who spoke Spanish fluently and had analyzed such problems for the Rockefeller organization? Schultz readily agreed to Wharton's persuasion, and for the next four years while Wharton was collecting first a master's degree and second a doctor's degree (another Negro first), he served as research associate to Schultz. With each day, his potential increased, making him a high-priority item. Even before Wharton had finished his doctoral dissertation, Arthur T. Mosher, Executive Director of the Agricultural Development Council, was at his doorstep with an offer to join ADC. Five years before, John D. Rockefeller III had established this non-profit organization to work in the field of agrarian reform, especially in Asia. Population explosions were threatening mass starvation in the Orient and no one in the U.S. seemed concerned about the outcome. Rockefeller saw the need and quietly set out to train local manpower, bringing Asians to the U.S. under a comprehensive fellowship program and returning them to their own countries. This was the kind of agricultural economics—a kind of private Marshall Plan—that Wharton liked and he signed on.

ADC immediately assigned him to Malaysia and for the

next six years he directed council programs in Vietnam, Thailand, and Cambodia, as well as teaching economics at the universities of Malaysia and Singapore. Although his days were filled, it did provide an opportunity for firsthand study of the Asian personality and his rural environment. In this setting of relative tranquility, Wharton was able to comb the ricefields and talk openly with peasants about agricultural development, which he felt was "at the heart of many of the world's most basic social and economic problems, since agriculture remained the dominant occupation of three fourths of mankind." [1]

Within a decade of Wharton's arrival in Malaysia, developments in agrarian science and technology had so advanced production that a "Green Revolution" was being heralded in Asia's developing world. "Startling developments," wrote Wharton, "had been accomplished in wheat, rice and corn. . . . Traditional food-importing nations like the Philippines and Pakistan were becoming self-sufficient and had the prospect of becoming net food exporters." Much would depend upon the adequacy of water, fertilizer, pesticides, and modern equipment. Taming the massive Mekong River, for example, to provide irrigation for Laos, Cambodia, Vietnam, and Thailand, Wharton estimated, would "require a capital investment over the next twenty years of about $2 billion, roughly 35 per cent of the annual national income of the four countries involved." [2] Why not a U.S. Marshall Plan for Asia, he asked. "The need in Asia is to assist in building dynamic, modern economics where they do not exist, while simultaneously encouraging the necessary political strengths to allow these developments to take place." Out of his experience, Wharton called for a three-pronged advance that would emphasize the plight of the small farmer, give priority to Asian leadership, and alter U.S. foreign policies in that part of the world.

In order to aid the masses of subsistence farmers, Wharton said the U.S. must learn to work at the "rice-roots" level, not exert pressure from "the top down." Also, the U.S. is in error, he charged, thinking it has *the* "message" for the peoples of Asia. This must come from their own leaders. Finally, he said, a drastic overhaul in our foreign priorities is badly needed. "We have been slow to realize that the military solution is no longer viable for small scale wars and internal subversion. What is worse, we have let our foreign policy toward less developed countries become little more than a simple-minded policy of force. Military policy has virtually become our sole foreign policy." Yet the United States cannot avoid being a part of that world. It "must help to provide developing countries with a sound agrarian policy which gives the people hope—a policy which gives them ideas but not necessarily our ideals. We should no longer seek to direct or to dominate the future of Asia. But the challenge which history will not allow us to ignore is our human responsibility to help Asians build a better life for Asian peoples." [3]

Part of our trouble, Wharton stresses, is in not knowing "there are differences in the way they deal with each other and treat each other compared with the American way. Many Asian cultures seem indirect to a westerner. Let me illustrate with Indonesia and Java. If there is to be a solution to a problem or a dispute or an issue, among the members in one of their communities, everyone must eventually agree. It's what they call 'mushwara.' The head man, the village chief, calls the people together. They sit there and attempt to compose their differences. If this is impossible, do they take a vote? No. If they feel a difference exists, then the head will say, 'Well, we must do more thinking on this,' and the meeting breaks up. Then the chief sits down with the recalcitrant and talks to him until he has convinced him the majority is right and that he should make amends. A second meeting is held and everything goes smoothly. Now that doesn't mean there are no eruptions—sure, there are eruptions, but this is the normal procedure. Now here is an-

other example of how an Asian works: suppose an Indone-
sian felt he wasn't getting an adequate salary and wanted to
find out whether or not to ask for a higher one. Indirectly,
he would ask me the question of whether he was being adequately paid and I would know that he was asking even
though he didn't quite say it, and I would answer him without really saying I was answering him. Now, to a westerner,
this sounds involved, long-winded and complicated, but if
you are Asian, you know the system. It would be just as
quick as saying, 'My, I've been having a hard time making
ends meet, Boss, don't you think I should get a raise?' What
the Asian does not like is a situation in which you suddenly
say, 'no' because then he is hurt. You have, in effect, rejected him. In the same circumstance, an Asian would be
apt to approach me and say, 'I feel very gratified that you
have seen fit to provide me with increased responsibilities in
my position and I feel very honored that you have done so.
Of course, I have, as you know, children who are becoming
older.' And I would know exactly what he's asking and as
soon as he starts down that track, say, 'Yes, I realize that
they are getting older, they are getting ready to go to college, aren't they? That must be very difficult for you and I
can see it's a very serious problem.' I've already said, 'yes.'"

Learning to recognize these differences between Eastern
and Western cultures gave Wharton a new insight. When
he finally returned to the U.S. in 1964 to spend a sabbatical
year at Stanford teaching economic development, he could
say "Mankind is heterogeneous in race, religion and culture,
and that's the beauty of it. The problem is to find ways of
living with his heterogeneity, and of not letting it destroy
us." [4] His stint at Stanford ended, he became director of the
American Universities Research Program back at the Council's New York headquarters; to advance the heterogeneous
theory, he worked simultaneously in two areas—abroad and
at home building interest and action in the problems of
third world agriculture. Aided by a foreign staff of twelve,

he combed Asia for fellowship prospects, sending back an average of fifty to sixty for instruction in the U.S. each year. "We wanted Asians who would be trained to work on the agrarian problems, not experts from the outside who would help for a couple of years and then leave." The cumulative effect of this was demonstrated once in Korea when a visiting American professor, attached to the Council, was asked to introduce himself during a conference, and to describe the ADC. "Well, I can," said the man, "but I don't think I need to as I look around the room, and see the number of Council fellows and grantees." The chairman, who was unfamiliar with ADC, literally wilted after his guest said, "Will all the people who have received ADC fellowships and grants please stand," and something like two-thirds stood up. At home, Wharton administered a $1.5-million program of research grants to U.S. universities in order to stimulate domestic concern for the problems of the third world. The workshops and seminars attracted about five hundred professors and professionals from all over the United States. "Very few of the universities," Wharton observed, "had any people trained in these fields and yet such instruction was vital if they were going to have sound economic plans for agriculture."

The Rockefeller organization liked the way Wharton operated—low-key—and when ADC needed an executive director in 1966, he got the job. A year later he was named vice-president. He had now become a full partner in the white establishment. Based in upper Manhattan, his two boys (a second son, Bruce, was born in 1959 in Singapore) in the Dalton School, he enjoyed the work and prestige of association with John D. Rockefeller III. He found him a very warm, thoughtful, considerate person, extremely able, one he respected tremendously as a human being. According to Wharton his contributions were little appreciated or understood. Lincoln Center "was really his, he pushed it from the beginning while others simply talked."

Recognition of Wharton's rising eminence in the system was his admission to America's corporate board room. On February 26, 1969, the Equitable Life Assurance Society of the United States, one of the ten largest U.S. corporations, named him a director, making him the first Negro so honored. The speed with which Wharton was expanding his influence inevitably foreshadowed new developments. For a man of his talents, greater responsibilities seemed just around the corner.

In the spring of 1969, he organized a seminar at Michigan State University to discuss African development. Invitations, as usual, went to intellectual luminaries throughout the country, expenses paid by ADC. For Wharton, the choice of MSU as conference site was *ne plus ultra.* A world-renowned agrarian economist coming to a world-renowned agricultural school could draw both into the same orbit. MSU was the imprimatur for sixty-nine land-grant colleges and universities that sprang up under the Merrill Act after the Civil War. Each one depended heavily upon the "graduates, the educational innovations and intellectual philosophy developed at Michigan State University." In fact, MSU was so patently agronomic that students from neighboring Michigan University referred to it for years as the "cow college." Quietly filling its role, after six decades, MSU had less than fifteen hundred students. As late as 1920, it was one-sixth the size of neighboring Michigan University. Then things began to happen following the outbreak of World War II. Dr. John A. Hannah took over as president and under his regime, lasting twenty-eight years, MSU grew to one of the ten largest universities in America, with an enrollment of 43,983. In the decade of the sixties, student population doubled, placing MSU enrollment 5000 above Michigan University. This gigantic growth spilled into eight square miles, adding 134 new structures.

Moreover, the expansion was not limited to bricks and mortar and larger student bodies. Since 1963, MSU's freshman class had enrolled more National Merit Scholars than any other university in the United States. Its standing was also reflected in the number of National Science Foundation Scholarships won. In 1969 MIT was first, Harvard second, and MSU third. Box score: MIT (48), Harvard (31), MSU (25), followed by Princeton (19), Cornell (16), Stanford (15), Berkeley (15), Yale (14), Illinois (14), and Michigan (14). While students came from all fifty states and ninety foreign nations, four out of five were Michigan residents, who paid half the tuitional costs outsiders did. MSU was widely known for its "unique creative capacity, its flexibility and willingness to risk, to experiment, to take up the new, the unusual." The story was told that when a British visitor recently set out to visit the university, an eminent Harvard social scientist informed him "he was going to probably the most exciting campus in the United States today." [5]

A second reason why Wharton's appearance on the MSU campus came at a remarkably fortunate time was the fact that a search was commencing for a new president. Hannah had left the university in March to become head of the Agency for International Development, an appointee of the Nixon administration. The Board of Trustees voted to fill his place from a list submitted by a seventeen-member Search and Selection Committee composed of students, faculty, and representatives of the university administration. Among the three hundred names in the suggestion hat was Dr. Clifford R. Wharton, Jr., tossed in by Nicholas Luykx, a professor of agricultural economics at MSU, who had met Wharton on one of his frequent visits to Vietnam. Wharton, he said, was creative, energetic, resourceful, and resolute. "He can gather information, reach a decision and stick to it, once his mind is made up." The committee was so impressed by Wharton's credentials that representatives went to New York City during July to interview him.

"All of us in the delegation," purred Michael Hudson, MSU's black deputy on the committee, "were thrilled to see

Dr. Wharton's credentials measured up to those of any white candidate. After talking to him, I could tell that he would be sympathetic to the black student movement and that he had an extensive knowledge of problems facing the black community." But the meeting went badly. Wharton mentioned the fact that he had turned down presidential offers from four other universities, giving the impression he wanted some other job, perhaps under-secretary of state. The committee departed, unconvinced Wharton was a candidate, and had its premonition confirmed when a few days later he departed with Governor Nelson Rockefeller on the latter's ill-fated trip to Latin America, undertaken at the White House's urging. If Wharton were interested, they concluded, he might at least remain in the country to be available, as did Wharton's friends, who said he was naïve not to stay and compete for such a job. Happily, Hudson persuaded the committee to send back another delegation, and this time the reception was mutually warm. "They came back bubbling with enthusiasm." [6] When a reporter for the campus *State Journal* called August 29 to ask Wharton if he knew he was on the list of finalists for the presidency, it was his first inkling of their positive reaction. Three other candidates besides Wharton were on the Selection Committee's final list: Stephen K. Bailey, fifty-three, professor of political science, Syracuse University dean, and member of the State Board of Regents; Dr. Edmund Pellegrino, forty-nine, chairman of the department of medicine at State University of New York, Stony Brook, L.I.; and William Bevan, forty-seven, vice-president and provost of Johns Hopkins, who withdrew a week later, according to the Detroit *News*, narrowing the field to three.

The work of the Search and Selection Committee now finished, the ultimate selection lay with the trustees. Initially, they appeared happy with the choices. Trustee Chairman Don Stevens, an Okemos Democrat, after two days of interviews in New York with the finalists, returned Thursday evening, September 4, and issued an airport statement in behalf of all the trustees, saying, "We interviewed some very fine candidates." It seemed clear from this that Wharton, Bailey, or Pellegrino would become MSU's thirteenth president. Stevens' handout, while purposely vague, had predicted the selection "sometime during the fall."

Then the political mills began grinding in behalf of former Governor G. Mennen Williams, Michigan boy wonder of the Democratic Party whose star had been falling steadily since John Kennedy sent him to Africa in the early sixties as roving ambassador. Michigan labor, a longtime Williams advocate, reportedly suggested to Stevens, state AFL-CIO education director, that he be named MSU president. Since the Board had a five-to-three Democratic majority, the possibility of Williams' selection was the weekend talk. As rumor of the impending crisis circulated through the campus, reaction from faculty and students alike was bitterly antagonistic. They were not only critical of the possible selection of an ex-governor for a purely academic post, but they also charged the Board with trying to abrogate an agreement unanimously adopted when Dr. Hannah retired, that the new president would come from a list supplied by the Search and Selection Committee. After conferring for six hours on Monday, the Committee issued a statement which said in part "it is obvious that the intervention by partisan political groups can only assure this campus a long and costly conflict." Any president chosen "in a high-handed manner would be totally unacceptable to the faculty and students of Michigan State University." [7] A total of 5000 MSU students joined the opposition by signing petitions to block Williams' appointment.

Throughout the week of September 7 the battle raged. The trustees were deadlocked. Reportedly, four of the five Democrats, responding to political heat, were prepared to name Williams president despite prior commitments and despite public denials, but the fifth balked. He was Blanche

Martin, a Lansing dentist, former MSU football star, and the only black board member. Although he owed his selection to the Democratic Party, he refused to put politics above his alma mater. By joining the three Republicans, he split the Board four to four and thereby killed Williams' hopes. Presumably, he was also motivated by the knowledge that of the three candidates on the Committee list, only Wharton now stood any chance. There was little support on the Board for either Dr. Pellegrino or Dean Bailey. And if it came to a test on Wharton, there was always the chance that Chairman Stevens, who appeared to like the Negro, would join Martin and the three Republicans on the Board in supporting him.

The tip-off that Williams' nomination was dead came at the end of the week when Trustee Warren Huff, one of the Democratic regulars, announced that the Committee selections rated no more than 60 out of a possible 100 in his book of criteria. Accordingly, when the Board called for additional names beyond those already recommended by the Search and Selection Committee, the inference of Democratic face-saving was apparent.

The Committee obliged by adding the name of Dr. James Dixon, president of Antioch College in Ohio, but refused to add others in protest to the Board's action. A month went by. Students tossed in their own compromise; a petition with 17,000 names asked that Walter Adams, popular acting president, be permanently elevated. But this effort came to nothing when Adams took himself out. Haunted by the necessity for some decision, the trustees eventually gathered behind closed doors and caucused three times to sort out their differences. On the first trial, Williams was rejected by a five-to-three margin, Stevens and Martin joining the three Republicans. Then, in a peculiar twist of political logic, the name of Jack Breslin, Republican Board Secretary and former MSU football star, was put in nomination. Presumably, this sent Stevens scurrying for Democratic cover, but Martin didn't want to alienate his Republican allies, and this time the vote split four to four. The impasse cleared the way for Wharton. With Stevens and Martin joining the Republicans, he won five to three. A black had finally made it possible for a brother to become the first president of a major American university.

Victory, however, was not without friction. As soon as the vote was openly arrived at the following day, October 17, the minority complained of outside pressure and inside emasculation. Clair White, schoolteacher and Wharton opponent, accused Dr. Hannah and New York's Governor Rockefeller of interference. He alleged that "Mr. Rockefeller had used his influence in repayment for preconvention support that Dr. Hannah gave him in 1968 for the Republican Presidential nomination." This was stoutly denied by a spokesman for the Governor, who termed the charge "utter nonsense." And this was followed by a personal statement from the Chief Executive, calling Dr. Wharton "an able administrator and a talented innovator. He has demonstrated," the message went on, "a deep commitment to achieving the kind of understanding needed so badly between young and old, between persons of different cultures, religions and nationalities. He was an invaluable member of the recent Presidential mission to Latin America. I hold him in the highest esteem." [8] Wharton was equally mystified by White's outburst. There simply was no truth, he said, to the charge that Dr. Hannah and Rockefeller had influenced the choice: "I met Dr. Hannah years ago and spoke to him only a few minutes and it wasn't until after I was appointed that I talked to him at any length. We spent an hour together discussing MSU. And Gov. Rockefeller certainly had nothing to do with it." What irritated Frank Hartman of Flint, a second Democrat to vote against Wharton, was the feeling that the Search and Selection Committee had masterminded the selection and that the Board had actually had to play second fiddle despite its role as the university's governing body. He accused the Committee of having "ramrodded" the selection. Only Warren Huff, the third opposition Democrat, agreed to back the choice. After the decision was reached, the only comic relief to a selection engineered by politicians was that Wharton, an enrolled Democrat, could not have won without unanimous Republican support.

As soon as the wires leading from East Lansing announced the appointment, Wharton was deluged with congratulatory messages from all over the world. "These are touching," he said, eyeing the pile in his New York office, "but I suspect there is some other reason than race which prompted this choice. It could not be the exclusive criterion any more than the fact that I am six feet tall or stand a little higher or lower than someone else. It is just that this aspect gets a tremendous amount of public attention." [9] Indeed, Wharton would not have accepted the presidency if he thought the offer were couched in racial overtones. "I have never in my career knowingly accepted a position or job where race was the primary consideration. I like to express my militancy by meeting the competition totally on their own ground without any special consideration. Meeting white competition and racism on these terms—and beating it—is what I call positive militancy." [10] Still, he could not be unaware of the effect his appointment would have on black America. One of the letters that touched him deeply was a note from the fifth Negro graduate of MSU. "I am proud and happy," penned Delbert Prillerman, of Columbus, Ohio, then seventy-five. The sentiment was extremely gratifying, not only because it elated Wharton, but because it symbolized a new era of rising expectations for black Americans. When one of his friends tried to strip away the euphoric curtain by reminding him that he was not the first black to become a university president in the U.S., that "one of the presidents of Georgetown, starting in 1872, was a black American," Wharton laughed and quipped back, in "Avisese": "You're right, I'm not. Since I'm 'No. 2,' I'm going to have to try harder."

A week after his election, Wharton flew in to East Lansing to lay the groundwork for taking over the presidency. In an interview with Gail Morris, assistant director of the MSU News Bureau, he had previously outlined his definition of leadership. No hard hat, he would "adhere to a policy that it is *not* the president who decrees or directs. I look upon this task as an opportunity for me to provide the necessary support to the individuals in the university who have ideas or programs or projects or activities in which they are interested." Going further, he added: "There's nothing more exciting than the person who's suddenly got an idea or a program or a project; he's got the ball and he wants to run with it. I get a big bang out of this. I like to encourage people." If, on the other hand, one "proceeds to delimit, delineate the strictures and limits of an activity, this is a very stifling environment. I like a situation in which people are able, in the common parlance, to 'do their thing.'" [11] As to MSU, he insisted, its greatest attraction was its "reputation for dealing with the problems of the world around it rather than being just an ivory tower." This fitted in perfectly with Wharton's idea of community service. He subscribed to the historic philosophy of the land-grant school which combined teaching, research, and extension service in a meaningful whole and he was prepared to use this formula in the solution of other problems confronting Michigan residents —for instance, the problems of urban living. The University, he was determined, would become "more relevant for the teacher who will work in the inner city and the urban centers."

The first visit was something of an ordeal to Wharton and his wife. The name of Clifton R. Wharton, Jr., might be a name to consider inside the financial corridors of the Rockefeller empire, but in East Lansing he was just another name to the thousands of students on campus. When he and his wife appeared, they came in the wake of a campus effort that had unsuccessfully tried to lift Walter Adams into the presidency. Its abortive failure only increased apprehensions, and the news conference which followed their arrival did not relieve the anxiety. He was asked by James Crate, editor-in-chief of the *State News,* campus daily, if he would have taken part in the October 15 moratorium against the Vietnam war. Wharton saw the curve coming and stepped back. "It would be inappropriate for me to make any comment at this time," he answered. Then he was asked to comment upon a statement by Sam Riddle, MSU Black Liberation Front leader, who had remarked: "We hope Wharton does not make the mistake of most black administrators and try to be fair. We think it is time the blacks around here received preferential treatment." It was a tough question to throw a black, not yet president. Wharton had suffered discrimination, humiliation at the hands of white men. "Show me a Negro who hasn't," he had remarked. "But I'm not one to chew on bitter bones. I've forgotten the incidents." He was sure if justice reigned, blacks would receive "preferential treatment." But to say as much blatantly would involve him in bitter controversy even before taking the oath of office. Accordingly, Wharton replied, "To start talking about what is fair and fairness is to get bogged down in semantics." [12]

Fortunately, his initial appearance on campus had its brighter moment. The students in Landon Hall, a women's dormitory across the street from the president's house, had draped a "welcome" sign across the door for his arrival and at eleven o'clock that evening, they serenaded Wharton and his wife with Michigan State songs. "About a hundred of the girls were there," Wharton said afterward. "I had to put on my pants over my pajamas before we invited the girls in. They gave me an 'instant kit'" to be used in case of crisis. "It was a marvelous occasion. Mrs. Wharton and I were very deeply touched."

A month later Wharton returned, this time to consult with his new boss, the Board of Trustees. According to the Detroit *News* for November 22, 1969, he succeeded in "deftly defusing a politically explosive problem." After an

argument arose within the Board over his salary and perquisites, Board member White, who had accused Dr. Hannah
and Governor Rockefeller of influencing the choice, wanted
to know what part of the perquisites was taxable. As tempers waxed, Wharton grew uneasy. Finally, he sought permission to speak. "I know I probably should not speak now,"
he said modestly, "but I will. On January 1 and thereafter, I
will make public—both to the trustees and to the press—my
income tax returns and the sources of my income. I have no
intention of any chicanery or trying to hide any income. My
actions, whether we like it or not, will reflect on the university and I want to make it irrevocably clear that I will operate in a public manner and in a public forum." White was
shocked. This was a side of Wharton he had not previously
sensed, and it won his acclaim immediately. Indeed, when
the Board met in December to conclude its discussion on
Wharton's salary, it authorized without ripple a salary of
$47,500 plus residential maintenance, an entertainment ex-
pense account, retirement allowance, and the expense of
moving from New York to Michigan. The only stir followed
Wharton's announcement that he wanted to remain a director of Equitable. Huff objected to this, said he "would like
to see his proposed salary increased to make up for whatever he gets from the society so he could devote more time
to the university." This contention struck Kenneth W.
Thompson, a Grand Rapids Republican, as pointedly "narrow." He understood that Equitable was "interested in the
problems of the urban area, particularly the disadvantaged.
The university could well afford to have its president know
what is going on in the business world." When the confrontation of the two appeared headed for a minor skirmish,
Wharton stepped in to halt further acrimony. He offered to
place any renumeration from Equitable in a scholarship
fund and to ask the state's attorney general if there was a
conflict of interest in holding an insurance directorship and
the presidency of MSU at the same time, and clinched his

point by saying, "It is my intention to proceed with the fullest honesty and candor." [13] The trustees sustained him with a six-to-two vote of confidence.

As the day approached for assuming the presidency, he told writer William T. Noble that he was not contemplating "any radical changes. Only a fool would think he could take over a large university and immediately change it to his will. I've learned that you have to work through existing framework. I will guide and make suggestions." Wharton harked back to his first appearance on campus when Jim Crate, of the *Michigan State News,* asked him about the moratorium, hoping for an off-the-top-of-the-head opinion that would grab a banner headline. Wharton was on to this and told Noble how he had learned a lesson in Malaysia from an astute newspaperman whose assignment, Wharton said, "was to scan the incoming passenger lists and find leading dignitaries for interviews. The newsman was well versed on hot local issues. He would find a dignitary and ask what he thought about certain things only minutes after he had his feet on Malaysian soil." There came a day when "he asked an American official whether or not he thought it would be wiser to teach the sciences in English or the Malaysian language. The official did not know that Malaysian nationalists were demanding a return to the Malaysian language in schools. He said he thought teaching should be in English and it almost caused an international incident. So before I make any comment about what I plan to do or suggest at MSU, I'm going to study carefully the situation." In only one area would Wharton make an exception—relating to fifteen hundred black students. "One of the things I will be able to do," he informed Noble, "is interpret for whites what the black students are thinking and why." [14] No doubt about it, the presidential role would require understanding and patience, but Wharton assured him he could do it. He would not practice a get-tough policy to impress whites when what the blacks needed was a sympathetic ear to hear their grievances.

On January 2, 1970, Dr. Wharton took charge, precisely eleven weeks from the day he received news of his selection. True to his commitment, he softly, quietly picked up the official reins. Nineteen days passed before he made a public pronouncement. Then, in a thoughtfully phrased address to the Faculty Club, he outlined in broad terms his concept of the university and its place in the community. He declared he would not "advance any new or startling views" about his hopes for MSU. Instead, he would use a generic brush to paint educational horizons. First, he believed that a human focus should take precedence over all other dimensions of a university. "We need to remind ourselves that we are individuals, not merely blacks, whites, Chinese, Nisei, Chicanos." Second, he reminded the overflow audience that "every man is entitled to an equal opportunity to accomplish his fullest inherent potential," and that education has the responsibility to provide the tools. This led to his third point, that "the heart of education is scholarly creativity." Universities can no longer adopt an "ivory tower" approach to life. Modern forces are bearing down on institutions of higher learning and the only question is whether they will be changed from within or without. This prompted his final theme, that the university should become a "central agency for change," using its intellectual resources to accomplish the goal.

In short, it was a first-rate presentation of what one should expect from a modern university like MSU, but hardly the sort of copy to make twenty-seven-year-old Jim Crate of the *Michigan State News* throw his hat in the air. Crate was editor-in-chief of the campus publication, largest college daily in the world, with a circulation of 50,000 and an annual advertising income of $575,000. It took big feet to fill the editorial shoes of such a behemoth, Crate confided to *Editor and Publisher*. "The *State News* is not a laboratory toy or extra-curricular activity with which to tinker on the environment. Neither is it an interesting hobby, demanding little, giving much. The damned thing is, and has been for quite some time, the fifth largest daily newspaper in Michigan. The *State News* is big business." Listening now to what seemed an educational bromide instead of a call to action, Crate decided he would make news himself. Under an editorial headlined WHAT ELSE IS NEW, PRES? Crate charged that Wharton had served up a "disinteresting rehash" of adages and clichés without substance. It was "equal to zero" or less, "at best, a disappointment and, at worst, an abysmal failure." He went on to say that Wharton had "copped-out" where "new and startling" actions were needed. He found the rhetoric "soothing," but "purely irrelevant to any realistic and pragmatic application." [15]

The arrows caught Dr. Wharton unaware, since he had anticipated greater leeway to enjoy the protective cloak of a new president. "My reaction," he told Valerie Jo Bradley of *Jet* magazine with some warmth, "was what would the editorial look like if I had come out with a program without consulting the students or faculty? I'm used to working with developing countries that have a gross national income less than the budget of this whole university [$171 million] and they get five years to develop five-year plans. They expect me to have a five-year plan in twenty days." This was Wharton's outward stance, but inwardly he realized, being a highly sensitive person, that he was dealing with a different type of problem than he had had in Southeast Asia. Campus youths were unwilling to await gradual change as the Asians were. They saw "major world problems solved on 'Mission Impossible' in sixty minutes or less and wondered why the same couldn't apply to real life." [16] His best chance of softening such unrest, he wisely reasoned, was to dig in, approach students, talk to as many as possible to demonstrate his respect for their idealism, and to do it without fanfare. "I wanted to proceed in a very low-profile way, but with a very strong involvement," he said. Accordingly, Wharton and his wife began a round of dormitories, sororities, and fraternities two or three nights a week, and the president used his office to consult with members of the student body. "If the typical adult were to follow the path of our youth," he explained to a Detroit audience, in praise of young people, "it would be equivalent to applying 7½ per cent of our personal income to nation-building activities. They have become, in many areas, our national conscience—and we in the older generation respond with guilt feelings. What is wrong with building a better world?" [17] he inquired. Twenty-five per cent of the 40,000 MSU students, he added, are committed to "positive activism as student leaders, tutors for the blind, ghetto workers and the like." The students who worried Wharton were the 2 per cent he called "nihilists," those who were ready to tear up everything and start over.

All this 2 per cent of the student body needed to revolt was an incident to trigger their violent yearnings. They found such a cause in mid-February, following Justice Hoffman's famed decision in the trial of the "Chicago 7," and rampaged through the streets of East Lansing throwing rocks and breaking windows in the business district and confronting the police. This was Wharton's baptism to student unrest. As soon as the rioters headed for the Student Union, he appeared with pleas to "cool it." He could understand their anger, he said, but violence had to be denounced as "appalling, senseless and counterproductive." Unfortunately, appeal had no noticeable effect on the unruly mob that was bent on destruction. It was a bitter night and perhaps the greatest impression on the student body was not the sight of Wharton, but of his wife standing alongside, as much as to say, "I believe in my husband and I know he will survive the crisis." She knew too well what would happen to Clifton if he cracked under pressure. There would be no tomorrow. The trustees would see to that.

In her quiet, effective way, Dolores Wharton had already made her presence on campus known. A vicarious artist, she liked to learn about the personality of a community. By observing the work of its artists, she had already ingratiated herself in East Lansing by finding the local contributions "most impressive." She liked to relate how she responded to the Malaysians in the same way. Of their art, she said, "It was a distinctive form, but it was not to be confused with the art of other Eastern countries. Malaysian culture was a combination of the contributions of three separate peoples, Malays, Chinese and Indians, and they brought diverse elements into their art." The subject so intrigued her that she had accompanied her husband in 1966 on one of his frequent trips to the Orient to collect material for a book on contemporary Malaysian artists. After coming to East Lansing, one of her first accomplishments was to schedule a showing of faculty paintings and sculpture in Cowles House, the president's campus residence. "It will be exciting to live with these works," she smiled. "Art belongs in homes as well as in museums." In addition to the college art works, Mrs. Wharton proudly displayed some of her own possessions, gathered from distant points. A special prize was the large Japanese screen stretching across their living room wall. "That slit in the bottom of the screen," she told visitors unconcernedly, "got there when my maid killed a cobra snake."

Few would question either the fact that Mrs. Wharton has considerable influence on her husband's thinking or that she may be a chief factor in his having done more for women students at MSU than any president in the university's history. He empirically understands the discrimination under which women labor. "Just as racism is woven into society, sex discrimination is equally endemic," he said, pointing out that inequality has led many women to give up their educational training. Tragically, because of this, they "receive partial or full college educations and never put them toward work in society." [18] As for MSU, he was determined to end the practice, by adding the word *sex* to the antidiscriminatory policy adopted by the university. In other areas, too, Wharton discovered signs of class discrimination, as for instance in the "inaccessibility and exclusivity of the University." He rejected the idea that students should be selected only "from the most culturally advantaged in society. We can no longer treat any human being as if he were waste material to be extruded from society." Speaking to the Detroit Economic Club in March 1970, he laid his unvarnished conviction before the city's top establishment: "Universities must honestly face society's pressures to provide *universal access to higher education*." All persons, not alone the economically and educationally disadvantaged, are coming to know the value of higher education. "These men and women realize that to be uneducated is to be disenfranchised from a full life." It is no longer possible, Wharton went on, to think of education as "a privilege"; that concept is being replaced by "the concept of education as a right." There was no mistaking the direction of the pressure. It was coming from the black community "because of its new spirit of unity and self-determination," but, said Wharton, "I predict we will shortly see an equal, if not greater, pressure not only from other minority groups—the Mexican-Americans, American Indians, Puerto Ricans—but from similarly disadvantaged white Americans who comprise the largest of these groups." The way to meet such pressure, he emphasized, was to act prior to the crisis. Accordingly, he told the audience, he had asked for and been granted authority by the university trustees to appoint a twenty-five member Presidential Commission on Admissions and Student Body Composition, composed of administrators, faculty, students, and outsiders. Their charge was to talk to PTA groups, union officials, businessmen, and politicians to inquire about such questions as student body composition, the proportion of resident to non-resident students, of full to part-time students, of graduates to undergraduates, the total university enrollment, and above all, the number of high-risk students the university should admit.

This final criterion, "the number of high-risk students," was soon to become a subject of fierce debate. Vice President Spiro T. Agnew donned the hard hat to attack. "New socialism," he quipped caustically. "College, at one time considered a privilege," he informed a Republican audience in Iowa, "is considered to be a right today—and is valued less because of that." It was time to restore the Jeffersonian concept of "natural aristocracy" by applying the "rigorous demands of intellectual competition" to all university applicants. Wharton found such polemics distasteful. "Attacking the concept of universal higher education in terms of a 'natural aristocracy,'" he said, "is an argument of unbecoming arrogance." His objections to Agnew were twofold: "No one is arguing," he heatedly maintained, "for the admission of individuals who are innately below standard, but of those persons with real academic potential. We all recognize that original innate intelligence is randomly distributed in society regardless of race, creed, income level or color. The difficulty is that our societal structures and institutional imperfections have frequently inhibited or prevented the full development of that potential. The problem then becomes one of identifying the individual who has the potential, yet who for economic or social reasons has received a disadvantaged education. And second, the real measure of excellence in the university is not how the person measures up at entry into the educational process in the freshman class, but what he or she is like upon graduation." [19] Finding that person with the "innate ability to perform" is an exciting challenge. "To me," he declared, "a truly great university is *not* one which can *only* work with and nurture the minds of those who have already proven their intellectual excellence before arrival, but the university which can work with *both*. If this were not so the Ivy League would have been reduced to ruin decades ago by the thousands of less than brilliant sons of the wealthy who have passed and continue to pass through their doors."

Wharton's sole caveat on the principle of universal higher education was the reminder of student responsibility. "The student," he declared, "incurs an obligation to himself as a serious student and to the institution of which he becomes a part. Those who view college as simply an opportunity for disruption and violence, those nihilists who seek to destroy our institutions rather than improve them, forfeit their right to higher education." [20] As he spoke these words to the graduating class of Michigan University on Saturday, May 2, violence was already erupting on the MSU campus. The previous evening, students allied with the Committee against ROTC had assembled in front of the Administration building, seeking an answer to the demand that ROTC be abolished. A spokesman for Wharton came out to inform the group that ROTC was being continued but with certain restrictions. The protesters were also reminded that a majority of MSU students had voted to retain ROTC on campus the year before and that two faculty committees working separately had reached the same conclusion.

The mob drifted away, reassembled again in International Center to listen to its leaders. At about 10:30 P.M., an estimated crowd of 500 demonstrators, their mood now honed to a cutting edge, attacked Demonstration Hall, ROTC headquarters. It reminded one Pacific veteran, at least, of a *kamikaze* attack as he watched them storm the structure with stones. Windows were broken and the office of Col. Jean Burner, chairman of the political science department, was set afire with a Molotov cocktail. The arrival of police reinforcements prevented further destruction and tear gas dispersed the students, who then broke up into small bands and roamed the campus, causing further destruction. Surveying the estimated $40,000 damage next day, President Wharton said it was "obviously a prior decision to precipitate acts of violence." He asked the 98 per cent of the student body that hadn't rioted to "isolate the destructive elements that have no goals but the ruin of a great university."

Calm quickly returned to the campus and the odds were against further violence. But unnoticed in Saturday's news media was a short paragraph reporting "500 Kent State University students had broken windows, set fire and damaged cars during a mile-long march from the center of Kent, Ohio, to the 19,000-student campus." Along the way, the report said, they were shouting "Down with Nixon." This was the tinder for Monday's explosion in which a platoon of trigger-happy National Guardsmen shot and killed four students.

The effect on MSU, as on the rest of the country, was electric. For twenty-four hours, every college president in the U.S. held his breath, hoping somehow to escape the violence which could erupt momentarily. The president of MSU was no exception. Damage to the university buildings could be repaired, he said, even though the needed funds would necessarily reduce other programs. What worried Wharton was the safety of the student body in any general uprising. If trouble could be scotched in advance by a direct student appeal, his worries would end. On Tuesday afternoon, he went on MSU's closed-circuit television network to reiterate his confidence in the "37,000 students who had conducted themselves with common sense and restraint" in the face of "vicious and deliberate destruction by a tiny group." He wanted to assure the "37,000," however, that he did not construe their "good judgement as apathy or unconcern over the present world situations." He knew how President Nixon's April 30 announcement of the U.S. assault on Cambodia had frustrated and maddened many of them. It had offended him, too, perhaps more so because he had "been personally involved with Asians and Asia for many years." While he had labored to find a solution "to the grave problems of poverty" and had sought "economic development" to buttress peace, others had depended upon military force, which was seen as more important than "land reform." "Now, once again," he went on, "a President has unilaterally taken the step of expanding the war without prior consultation with our foreign friends or without the approval of the United States Congress. Based upon my experience in Asia, I am firmly convinced that the new expansion of the war is a serious error and miscalculation." This was his personal opinion alone. Others might well feel otherwise. But however they felt about the war, he was going to Washington soon to talk to Michigan's congressional delegation and would be delighted to take their petitions—for or against the expansion of the war—to place them before the representatives as an expression of their conscience.[21] It was a masterpiece of persuasion and would, in all likelihood, have collapsed the tension but for one development. A call was already sweeping U.S. campuses for a national "strike" to protest the invasion of Cambodia and the slaying of Kent State students. At MSU, approximately 2000 demonstrators laid plans to walk out the following day, demanding that the university be closed until all U.S. troops were withdrawn from Cambodia, ROTC abolished, black enrollments increased, and guns removed from campus police.

How to cope with this new turn troubled Wharton. If the students were frustrated, their president was equally tried. The university could not endorse a strike and had little to do with developments outside MSU such as Cambodia. It would do no harm, however, to point out to the entire student body the consquences of a closed university. "The effects would go far beyond what is viewed as a symbolic protest against the war," he explained. It would mean extending the school year beyond June 14 to make up for lost instruction, sending students home, possibly halting veterans benefits, and jeopardizing the University's 1970–1971 budget, which was under consideration by the state legislature. "Therefore," he remarked with complete candor, "it should be clearly understood that the effect of any course of action which forces closure of the University is to make the university community the target and the victim, not the policy makers in Washington." Nevertheless, Wharton decided on the carrot as well as the stick approach to blunt the threatening student movement. He would not sanction a strike, but would agree to a one-day suspension of regular classes "to encourage a number of 'teach-ins' on the war, racism, ROTC and other matters of interest." To a reporter of the Lansing *State Journal*, it had all the trappings of "a high school senior skip day ... with all classes enjoying an extra day off," but it was effective in cooling tempers.

Turning to the next demand—that ROTC be abolished—Wharton assigned the University's Academic Council responsibility for looking into ROTC's presence on campus. Composed of students and faculty, this influential body debated the question for three and a half hours before giving ROTC a decisive vote of confidence and promising to review its curriculum. On top of that, the *State News* polled the student body to sift out campus sentiment. It showed an overwhelming majority in favor of keeping ROTC on campus. Only 15 per cent of the 1140 students voting were in favor of excising ROTC.

Out of the complaint that blacks were being slighted, an agreement was reached to create an off-campus black cultural center. Beyond that, the university agreed to double its black enrollment 8 per cent by the fall of 1971, Wharton promised in his "Report from the President," May 11, 1970.

But these advances on the part of the administration only served to harden activist pressures. The demonstrators saw their influence waning despite a continuation of protests, the most notorious of which was a march on the state capitol in Lansing by 10,000 students following an American flag draped in black mourning cloth. The protesters had hoped to impress the legislators with their demands, but the effort boomeranged. Hearing what had happened, William R. Copeland, chairman of the House Appropriations Committee, fell into the generation gap with the words "Those people at the universities have got to do something about the disruptions. I am going to take a good look at the budget of Michigan State and other universities to see how they're going to pay for the damages and lost days of instruction." Crestfallen by the public apathy, the radicals decided to retaliate. On Friday, May 15, about two hundred anti-ROTC students entered Demonstration Hall, ROTC headquarters, to stage a sit-in, and refused to leave until the police threatened them with arrest. They finally came out, but turned abruptly around and began throwing rocks at the windows. Again, as two weeks before, it took tear gas to disperse the crowd. Then, three days later, more violence erupted when a number of students, calling themselves the Action Group to Combat Racism, wrangled with the administration. They demanded a closing of the University to memorialize the killing of two black students by police at Jackson State College, Jackson, Mississippi. It was a clear example of white students trading on black tragedy, for no MSU blacks took part in the protest. When the demand of the white students fell flat, some took to the streets for another round of rioting. The remainder stayed inside the Student Union building and refused to leave at the 11 P.M. closing hour. The police stood by until 1:30, then began arresting those inside, taking them to Ingham County Jail to be charged with loitering and trespassing. About 130 were arrested, 20 per cent of whom were not MSU students.

When Wharton heard what had happened, he was livid. In a pre-dawn release, he said, "It is an understatement to say the rioters have no legitimate cause which could in any way justify their actions. As was the case with the illegal sit-in in Demonstration Hall Friday night, provocation seemed the only aim." Some of the involved students had different views. They had not tried to aggravate the police; they were simply discussing racism and "didn't feel like leaving." A young honor student was "radicalized" by the police raid. "More and more kids," she told a reporter from the Grand Rapids *Press*, "want to go out thrashing [window

smashing] now, especially since that night. I even lean toward it. The administration has really been rotten. I used to
respect President Wharton before, because he had a tough
job to do, but not anymore. There was no excuse for sending those cops in that night. It was a political thing, that's
all, a repressive act to impress the Legislature."

Admittedly, Wharton was in a difficult spot. He was
damned if he did and damned if he didn't. Many of the
students felt his actions and his statements were unsuppor-
tive or non-responsive; at the same time people on the outside said he was inciting to riot. Small wonder that he lost
fifteen pounds during his first months at MSU and, while
vowing he had never been up against the wall, admitted
there were difficult and trying days. A special obstacle was
getting an accurate measure of the students. He had visited
fourteen residence halls since January and, looking back,
saw the residents as a "paradoxical" group. "I have found
the student body to be both more homogeneous and more
heterogeneous than I expected. The majority of students are
more homogeneous, but the remainder are much more heterogeneous than I expected," [22] leaving him, in a sense, between two chairs. One of the best cases of heterogeneity
was the so-called People's Park, a campus site which students appropriated for communal living. During the last
week of April they set up tents, some new, some old, some
canvas, some plastic, some even consisting of blankets tied
between trees. At the center of the camp was a rudely made
grill on which stood an iron kettle. Nearby a wooden table,
supporting a giant bottle of red-colored vitamins, completed
the kitchen facilities. In this bucolic setting, students whiled
away the hours, cooking, reading, playing cards, talking. It
was an answer to the alienation so many felt. "You can go to
MSU for four years and never meet anyone," declared one
girl quoted by the Flint *Journal*. "It's really wonderful to
get to know people again."

The sight of these youngsters made Michigan legislators

howl and was undoubtedly on Wharton's mind when he described to Robert Berg of the Detroit *News* his first six months in office. "I've had the works," he told him, "demonstrations, sit-ins, student riots—there's been everything you could conceive of. This is one of the most total jobs I've ever run across. You are on demand at all times for every conceivable kind of decision." Did it matter that he was black? Wharton nodded. "I've been more deliberate and more cautious than I normally would be. This is not because I don't want to make a mistake, but because I know there is a tendency to examine everything that I say and do with a microscope. And in fact, sometimes some of the reactions I get, especially the negative ones, are, I suspect, in part a reflection of this. There are a large number of people—though by no means a majority, I know—who would like nothing better than to see me not do so well. And, therefore, they are quick to find something they can point to and say, 'See, I knew it.'" What gave Wharton particular satisfaction at the end of this trial period, however, was an August editorial in the Michigan University *State News*, the paper that had excoriated him on January 21. The writer now found "the pressures phenomenal [but] Wharton had distilled a course that brought MSU through what could have been an academically, financially and politically crippling half-year." The *News* repeated its January statement that actions speak louder than words and that the "sounds of action had been gratifying."

As to the faculty, the mood vis-à-vis Wharton was similarly sanguine. "The first six months we just sort of waited to see," Professor Dale E. Hathaway, a member of the presidential selection committee, observed to Harry G. Salsinger, education editor for the Detroit *News*. "His handling of the situation in May and June, when things were hot and heavy on every college campus, convinced the faculty that he was very capable."

His association with black students has been equally gratifying. According to Tony Martin, a twenty-eight-year-old native of Trinidad who sits on the executive board of the Black United Front, Wharton has prevented any "serious confrontation" by deliberate counter action. "He has established a close working relationship with black students and involved them in campus affairs. I think our tendency toward him is favorable but we don't really know what he would do if there was a clash. I think we would both be in a bad position because I think he would act like a president."

With the majority of white students, he has built a close rapport. Only the activists who were unable to undermine his authority in the aftermath of Kent State are dour. They cynically refer to him as "Oreo" (black outside, white inside.) Yet their animosity has had little effect on his equilibrium. What the color of a man is inside or out, white or black, has little relevance to the present. "The only people who mention it now are in the media," he declared at the end of his first year in office.

And this distinction—or lack of it—one may add, is the key to Wharton's philosophy. A black, he has succeeded in a white man's world, is proud of it, and sees the system as a milieu in which other blacks with training and purpose can also succeed.

Shirley Chisholm

¶ If Harriet Tubman, stout-hearted, aggressive conductor of the pre-Civil War Underground Railroad, could be reincarnated, her spirit would undoubtedly find comfortable lodgings in Shirley St. Hill Chisholm, first Negro woman to be elected to the U.S. House of Representatives.

Every identity of the former finds fresh reflection in the latter—short stature, dark skin, sparkling eyes, raw courage, combativeness, and a fierce tenacity for overcoming obstacles. In preparing the two for their roles on the American stage, Nature seems to have surfeited both with an embarrassment of riches.

The only exception to their common heritage was a difference of environment. Harriet Tubman was a product of agrarian slavery; Shirley Chisholm is an example of urban upheaval. But this difference serves only to emphasize the fact that the human spirit, like the sprouting seed, inevitably breaks through its encasement, given creative strength.

Shirley Anita St. Hill was born in Brooklyn on November 30, 1924, the daughter of West Indian immigrants. Her father, Charlie, was an unskilled worker in a burlap-bag factory and her mother, Ruby, earned money as a cleaning woman, the proverbial pursuit of poor black women. As the oldest of three daughters, Shirley assumed the physical perquisites of family domination, and extended her rule peripherally as well. By age three she was cornering black children and boxing their ears. Kids three and four years older were punched and ordered to heed what she said.

But life in Brooklyn was enervating—hardship and income insufficient to make ends meet. The St. Hills, who originally came to the U.S. in search of economic manna, had by 1928 lost faith in their dream and reluctantly concluded that their children should return to Barbados to live with their maternal grandmother, a kindly provider in her mid-fifties. Grandmother Seales, however, despite a solid reputation for cooking pastry and coaxing the soil to produce staples, was a firm disciplinarian. A sharp blow, administered with a strap on the metacarpal expanse of one hand, was sufficient to preserve household discipline. On Sundays, the St. Hill siblings were decked in starched finery and marched two miles to the parish church for an introduction to the mysteries of the Christian faith. Yet, the most significant result of moving from Brooklyn to Barbados was neither home, nor food, nor shelter, but the opportunity of attending an elementary school in a British colony. Instead of exposure to drastically inferior ghetto schooling, the inevitable legacy of a Brooklyn black child in the early 1930's, Shirley was given an opportunity to master the basics of reading, writing, and arithmetic.

When, at age ten, a fiscal upturn in the St. Hill homestead permitted Shirley and her sisters to return to the U.S., the scholastic challenge turned out a breeze. The three were advanced a full year over their peer group, an advantage which lasted through high school. Not unnaturally, it filled Shirley with a new sense of her intellectual standing. She saw herself as something special.

And this "something special," which was entirely subjective until graduation from Girls High, took on objective overtones once she was enrolled in Brooklyn College—her choice of the four scholarships to come her way. For the first time, looking through the eyes of a sociology course, she saw the Negro race as the oppressed minority, surrounded by a white noose. As Shirley's personality acquired dash and effusiveness, stimulated by debating and mingling with other blacks, she came to the attention of Louis Warsoff, a political science professor. Warsoff was certain she had a political future and asked her to give it a try. "The idea was far from my mind," she looks back now, "because even today the word 'politics' in America has a connotation of corruption. In addition to that I was black and a young girl. It was impossible at that time for blacks to make progress in politics on the local scene and that is where you must start." [1]

Besides, anyone so young and expansive as Shirley could hardly be expected to commit herself to the drudgery and confinement of political office. She already suffered growing pains from her mother's admonitions against dancing and late hours. "We were a laughing stock, always the first to arrive at a party and always the first to leave. I remember one time dancing with a boy and trying to be ever so sophisticated until my sister Muriel came over, pointed at her watch, and said, 'Remember what time Mummy said we had to be home.' I wished the earth would open up and swallow me." Consequently, Shirley bridled over any suggestion that interfered with or impeded her actions, whether politics or maternal proscription, especially when, as in the case of the latter, it was due to misunderstanding. "I come alive on a dance floor. I'm very creative. I use my hands and my body. Even now I amaze people when I dance. I suppose it's part of my cultural heritage as a black woman. But my mother hated it. She thought I would go to work in a nightclub. She bought me a piano, I think simply to curb the surging activity she thought would lead to a theatrical life."

But if half the family influence was an umbrella to shield the St. Hill girls against urban temptations, the paternal half was a venturesome soul who swam on the tide of rising expectations. Though a wage-earner and the chief supporter of a wife and four daughters, he had accumulated by 1945 capital savings from which he bought a house for $10,000—three-storied, complete with iron railings to silhouette a front garden. Situated on Prospect Place in Brooklyn, at the edge of an area known as Bedford-Stuyvesant, its possession demonstrated what two decades in America had brought to the St. Hills. To Shirley, a product of two cultures—British colonial and American national—the feat carried as much psychological as it did financial meaning. "It was really remarkable," she said, "to bring up a family of four daughters on a laborer's pay, give them all an education and then buy them a house. My parents were obsessed with making sure we would not have to struggle as they had. This is something I have noticed about West Indian migrants compared with American Negroes. They are more ambitious and more prepared to make sacrifices for goals they consider important. They strive for home ownership and good schooling while American Negroes do not always have these priorities. I think the explanation lies in our history. We had slavery in the West Indies but it was not so brutal as in the deep South and it did not break up families in the same way. For 300 years in American slavery there was no family life after the day's work was over and we are still suffering the consequences." [2] What Shirley failed to mention was the unavoidable suspicion that she fell heir to Charlie St. Hill's daring and determination to achieve which took priority over her mother's caution and introversion. The world of household duties held no charms for Shirley. She desired a life of her own making.

A baccalaureate degree (*cum laude*) was only the stepping stone to higher learning. By day she became a teacher in a Harlem day nursery, by night a student at Columbia University, objective a master's degree in early-childhood education. Her schedule had few free hours. Besides, boys found her too brainy. "I dominated the conversation," she concedes. "One boy danced with me only on condition I never talked to him about my lectures."

There was a lone exception. One day in her twenty-fourth year, Shirley caught the eye of another West Indian, a Jamaican by the name of Conrad Chisholm. A private investigator residing in Brooklyn, Chisholm was intrigued by the sight of a woman who seemingly was never exhausted, never strayed from her schedule. Her reaction to his first advance was chilly. "I thought he was terribly fresh." Even the request to share a dinner with him failed to thaw her icy response. "I had all kinds of reasons why I shouldn't go, but he would never take no for an answer." [3] Later, she jokingly explained why: "Jamaican men always want the best," which explains their marriage a year afterward.[4]

While Conrad Chisholm continued his career ferreting out unscrupulous compensation claims against the railroads, Shirley went forward to teach tiny children. She became the director of a day nursery on the Lower East Side of Manhattan within shouting distance of the Brooklyn Bridge. The population included more than 150 Negro and Puerto Rican children, making it the "newest and biggest day nursery in New York City."

It was exciting work. For the first time, Mrs. Chisholm was able to inject her vast energies into a social need. There were the children who desired affection and the various command decisions to make. Her natural ebullience turned some on, others off. "She was a first class 'b.s.' artist," a coworker remembers. "She was often unfair, but she learned from her mistakes." [5]

But out of this experience came new awareness: a sense of social stewardship and a passion for authority. All about was evidence of the fate which awaited poor black families—ghettoized, crowded into substandard housing, victims of police brutality, forced to attend inadequate schools, exposed to crime and dope pushers. On the periphery of the

Bedford-Stuyvesant area of Brooklyn she saw the city's worst record. "I realized I had a good home, a well-paying job and a fine husband. All this had come because of my good education. I had escaped. But all around me was suffering and, even worse, ignorance. I had to do something."

In addition, Mrs. Chisholm could now witness the connection between bad government and the frightening position of American blacks. All the ills of municipal neglect were evident to anyone administering a day nursery. If the city copped out on public housing, the poor would live in wretched hovels; if the city permitted the "third degree," the chief victims would be black families; if the city dumped its worst teachers in the slums, still another generation would be lost; and if the city allowed the unmolested flow of narcotics, black children would be hardest hit.

About this time—1953, to be exact—a historic event was taking place in Brooklyn that catalyzed the changing Shirley Chisolm. The powerful Democratic Party had stupidly nominated a white "carpetbagger" for justice in the Bedford-Stuyvesant area despite its overwhelmingly black complexion. Blacks decided to rebel. They organized a new club, known as the Bedford-Stuyvesant Political League, to combat the white-controlled machine. Leading the challenge was Wesley Holder, a West Indian, English-trained, from British Guiana, possessed of keen political instincts. Hodder's man was as Brooklyn as Prospect Park, and following a knock-down, drag-out fight, the League's candidate won by 123 votes. In the ensuing pandemonium that engulfed the black community, Hodder's voice was heard predicting new honors for black Brooklyn. They would, in time, he said, put their representatives in the seats of the mighty. It might sound hyperbolic, but Hodder foresaw a black congressman one day. Unbelieving cheers greeted his words.

No one had been more impressed by Hodder's performance than Mrs. Chisholm. When she saw what the League was trying to accomplish, she joined in with enthusiasm. Within a year she was the League's vice-president, an ardent Hodder supporter. Trying to prod blacks into action, however, was a job of immense difficulty. Up to that time, their votes were little more than a fob on the Democratic chain; understanding this impotence, blacks had shown little concern for politics. In fact, they associated the word with white men and accordingly looked on black politicians as "house niggers" in the Man's preserve. It was the duty of Hodder and Mrs. Chisholm to change attitudes. "We had to tell them and show them where they could be helped," declared Hodder. "It was hard work with long hours, often unrewarding." [6] Yet, for Mrs. Chisholm, it was a means to an end. The long weekends she spent with neighbors, getting jobs for the unemployed and securing welfare aid for the needy, was the absolute *sine qua non* for political ascension. For a decade following the Supreme Court's decision to desegregate the schools, she remained in the ranks. She neither asked for nor sought political office. It was enough to back the black organization and its chief component, the Unity Democratic Club of the 55th State Assembly District. Back in 1960, a genial, politically astute black named Thomas R. Jones had provided the brains for establishing Unity, a role he parlayed into a seat in the New York State Assembly two years later. Jones was on the rise, burdened with the debts of campaigning, and when an opportunity to grab a civil court judgeship appeared at the end of his two-year term in Albany, he bowed out.

This was all the opening Shirley Chisholm needed. She announced her decision to campaign for the nomination. Members of the executive committee were shocked. "It was the first time a black woman had sought elective office in Brooklyn." Mrs. Chisholm recalls, "but I knew I could do it. I felt strong enough. There were people in that clubhouse who were saying, 'Why not give Chisholm a chance? She's got it. She can lead.' So I told them, 'If you need to have a discussion, have a discussion. But it makes no difference to me. I intend to fight.' " [7]

It eventually turned out that all the shock was not due to Mrs. Chisholm's sex. The ultimatum had come at a time when Mayor Wagner was feuding with the forces of Assemblyman Stanley Steingut, Democratic leader in Brooklyn. Unity was in Steingut's camp and did not want the boat rocked in such uncertain times. For a time, there was talk of drafting Jones, but it got nowhere and Mrs. Chisholm was eventually designated Unity's candidate. That fall she scored a resounding victory over her Republican adversary, defeating him by a landslide margin of almost ten to one.

The victory brought her scholastic career to an end. She gave up her job as Chief Educational Consultant for all of New York City's day nurseries in order to attend the sessions in Albany where Assembly figures with years in the imposing, green-trimmed Assembly Chamber were hardly prepared for her style. Petite (5 feet 4), attractively groomed, she jolted them with militant rhetoric. Her maiden speech brought them up in their chairs. "Hey, she's pretty," they began. But then Shirley Chisholm gave them a fighting speech and when she had finished, all they could say was, "Sister, where did you learn all that stuff?" [8]

It turned out pretty much as it had at Columbia. Members avoided her from fear of being outshone. Afraid of humiliation, they went their ways, leaving Mrs. Chisholm free to do as she pleased. In Albany, it is usual for cameraderie to develop among the legislators of all stripes. On the floor of the legislature, they erupt in diabolical accusations—one for the other—but off the floor, when the day's activity is finished, they gather in bars, restaurants, hotels to trade amenities and small talk, to engage in fun and frolic. This, however, was not for Mrs. Chisholm. She confided to Susan Brownmiller of *The New York Times:* "I don't blame the fellows for not asking me out to dinner. Men don't like independent women. Not many knew I was a regular gal. I think they were afraid to take the chance. I ate most of the time in my room. I had the TV and I read and I did my legislative homework. I went to bed early."

Still, such Spartan devotion, like virtue, had its own reward. Mrs. Chisholm became an arch-exponent of legislation to aid the underprivileged. She asked and received additional funds for the support of day nurseries, her first success. Then she turned her attention to the problem of unemployment insurance for domestic workers. "Every black woman in New York City, including my own mother," she explained to colleagues, "has done cleaning work at some time. But whenever they were out of work they got nothing. Thousands of women will feel the benefit of this bill," and they have.

But her greatest success—the legislation on which her name is indelibly stenciled—is a program called SEEK, an acronym for Search for Education, Elevation and Knowledge. According to Mrs. Chisholm, the bill gives funds to young Negroes and Puerto Rican students with potential. It enables them to go to college. A lot of ghetto schools merely provide dead-end vocational diplomas. Consequently, the graduates cannot compete with white children for scholarships.

They are the victims of a system of discrimination and segregation. "I know," she says, "because I visited twenty-six schools in black and white areas of Brooklyn—never telling them I was an Assemblywoman—so I could make valid comparisons. Four things stood out. One, the large number of substitute teachers in the black areas. Two, the lack of a good curriculum in the black schools that would give black boys and girls the chance to compete with whites. Three, the attitude of many of the teachers indicating they thought black children were inferior. And four, the inability of black parents, in many instances, to have a full voice in the Parent-Teacher Association."

The beauty of the SEEK program is that Negro and

Puerto Rican youngsters who show promise are given a chance to attend college. Despite shortcomings of a deprived secondary education, if they pass a SEEK-administered test, they enter college, take remedial instruction, and catch up to their classmates during the first year.

Following SEEK's incorporation in New York State, Mrs. Chisholm held a series of public hearings to test its efficacy. "I remember a boy of fifteen," she recalls, "who had been taken out of a dead-end school because he wanted to be a surgeon. I looked at his fine hands and I kept thinking that one day those hands would save both black and white lives. I thought back to my own youth. I was able to make it in spite of being black. But some of my peers never made it because of the system. It makes me sick and angry to think of the hundreds of thousands of brains which have been lost to America." [9]

The annual deep freeze that engulfs New York's capital city was hardly under way in 1969 when the State Legislature, acting upon a federal court order to comply with the one-man–one-vote dictum of the U.S. Supreme Court, carved out a new 12th Congressional District in Brooklyn, which for the first time contained heavily black Bedford-Stuyvesant, surrounded by peripheral white areas. Previously, Bedford-Stuyvesant had been so gerrymandered by white politicians that it looked like pieces of a gigantic pie. There were four or five congressmen in the area, all of them white. When the territory was cut afresh, the ethnic line-up was 70 per cent black, 30 per cent white. In addition, Mrs. Chisholm discovered registered women voters outnumbered men by between 10,000 and 13,000.

From a pragmatic angle, the situation was designed for Mrs. Chisholm's benefit. The only question was whether the people of Bedford-Stuyvesant wanted her to run. "I am the people's politician," she told Susan Brownmiller. "If the day should ever come when the people can't save me, I'll know I'm finished. That's when I'll go back to being a professional educator." In the process of reaching a decision, to be or not to be, she went to the front door of her Brooklyn apartment one cold February day, in answer to a knock, and found an elderly Negro woman standing at the doorstep. She had come to present Mrs. Chisholm with $9.69 in coins, garnered from coffee klatches and tea parties, the gift of a group of housewives, black constituents, who wanted her to run for Congress.

This was the cue she had sought. Tears flowing, she took the money, wrapped it up carefully, and put it away as a reminder of the public's trust in her. With such backing, she felt an obligation now to join the race. Her one apprehension was the opposition of male politicians who thought of politics as a man's world, something to be played according to the rules. "You see," she candidly admitted later to David English of the London *Daily Express*, "I cannot be manipulated. I have a fiery, independent, fighting nature. I'm not a machine or a hack politician. I'm part of the new breed of politicians. I cannot be bought and I cannot be bossed. As a result professional politicians respect my ability but they don't like me. I'm a maverick and they don't know what I'm going to do next." [10]

Opposition to her candidacy was not long in surfacing after she tossed her hat into the ring. Various Negroes made noises to indicate their interest in running, but held back because of pressures from above. It was a time when the national political picture was clouded by controversy. Lyndon Johnson had collapsed over opposition to the Vietnam struggle. His address of March 31, declaring himself out of the presidential race, had opened wide the doors of the Democratic Party to three hopefuls—Vice-President Hubert Humphrey and U.S. Senators Robert Kennedy and Eugene McCarthy. In the ensuing scramble, Congressional hopefuls in the 12th District—with the exception of Mrs. Chisholm—waited anxiously to see where to jump. One of the first to raise his head was Judge Tom Jones of Unity Club fame. A storefront on Fulton Street, emblazoned with JONES FOR CONGRESS, told the story. Jones visited his old club to test the sentiment, but the reception was strained. "You know a judge is supposed to be above politics," the leader who replaced Jones said, "and Jones hadn't been to the club much in the last few years."

Moreover, Jones was tied into the Kennedy orbit and the Senator was unwilling to release him. During the preceding year Kennedy had taken a leading part in the establishment of the Bedford-Stuyvesant Restoration Corporation, a plan that blended neighborhood initiative with private and government investment to refurbish the black ghetto. Jones was Kennedy's choice to head the local governing body and when he asked Kennedy for support, confident the Senator would aid him, he learned that he would be "more valuable" as head of the corporation than sitting in Congress. Crestfallen, his backing gone, he decided to withdraw, taking instead a nomination for the state's Supreme Court.

Just why Kennedy did not use his legendary prestige with blacks to aid Mrs. Chisholm, once he decided not to support Judge Jones, is something of a mystery. Both were liberal Democrats, pledged to reform. Yet he refused aid. "I was the top vote-getter," Mrs. Chisholm says, recalling the campaign, "but Kennedy never sought me out. I think there were some people who kept him from me." [11]

The "people" were evidently the brass in the Brooklyn Democratic organization, commanded by Assemblyman Steingut, who regarded Mrs. Chisholm's independence dimly. Kennedy was a close ally of Steingut, their friendship dating back to the presidential election of 1964, when Kennedy became the candidate for U.S. Senator. At the time, Mayor Robert F. Wagner of New York City was the Democratic kingpin in the state, but his failure to raise up a candidate for the Senate gave Steingut, the Mayor's ancient enemy, a chance to join with other state chieftains, in proposing Kennedy. If Steingut was cool to Mrs. Chisholm, that settled it for Kennedy.

On paper, however, the organization took an open stance. Any favoritism was to be handled surreptitiously. "This was an unusual turn of events," Mrs. Chisholm says, looking back, "because they had always supported a particular candidate for Congress and the reason, I think, was that the community—black, white and Puerto Rican—very much wanted me for their candidate."

The candidate who benefited most from this peculiar turn of events was State Senator William C. Thompson, a lawyer, elected to the legislature the same year as Mrs. Chisholm. In the eyes of the Kennedy-Steingut faction he was the one to support. Eight of the ten district leaders—all white— pledged their aid and, as part of a *quid pro quo*, Thompson promised to turn over delegate strength to Kennedy at the national convention. In appreciation, Kennedy would canvass Bedford-Stuyvesant in his behalf. With undisguised acrimony, Mrs. Chisholm says, "Willie felt the white boys were going to get out the vote for him." [12]

A third starter was Mrs. Dolly Robinson, a former employee of the New York State Department of Labor and former co-leader of the 56th Assembly District, Assemblyman Bertram Baker's bailiwick. A twenty-year Albany veteran, Baker was, like Mrs. Chisholm, a West Indian native. Born on the island of Nevis, he had obtained an education with British overtones at the Cambridge University Preparatory School on St. Kitts. Now seventy, he was nearing the end of a distinguished career, with accolades for his part in promoting open housing. He was uncertain what to do. Thompson had previously refused to support his choice for a judicial post and aggravated the disenchantment by challenging Baker for leadership of the 56th. In addition, Mrs. Chisholm, with a burst of staccato mirth, had humiliated him on the floor of the Assembly, crushing his pride and leaving him frustrated. He could always turn to his old friend Judge Jones, but the Judge was a Kennedy man and Baker refused to tear up his allegiance, as an organization Democrat, to Johnson and Humphrey. So after some hesitation, he decided to put forward Mrs. Robinson in the hope of picking up Johnson-Humphrey strength and thereby wielding the balance of power.

This, then, was the format as the three-way race finally got under way:

Candidate	Sponsor
Mrs. Chisholm	None
William Thompson	Kennedy
Mrs. Dolly Robinson	Humphrey

Mrs. Chisholm studied the forces against her. Instinctively she knew that Mrs. Robinson could not be nominated because (1) the Johnson-Humphrey forces were under attack in the black community for waging war in Vietnam and (2) her following among women was much greater than Mrs. Robinson's. With Thompson, the picture was entirely different. All her weaknesses turned out to be his strong points. He had Kennedy, she had no star-studded figure in her corner. He was the male symbol, she was the butt of anti-feminine sentiment.

To counter these disadvantages, Mrs. Chisholm plotted secretly. Let Kennedy support Thompson. She would appeal to his opponent, Eugene McCarthy, the ultimate voice in the anti-war arsenal. Working through the Coalition for a Democratic Alternative, she finally reached the Minnesotan, to chat with him a half hour. But the plan to get McCarthy's help was abruptly canceled because on the day Kennedy was scheduled to campaign in Bedford-Stuyvesant, his body was lying in state in New York's St. Patrick's Cathedral. Without Kennedy, there was no need to enlist McCarthy.

While Kennedy's assassination was an unfortunate and

unforeseen blow to Thompson's chances, even worse was
the opposition of Wesley Holder, Mrs. Chisholm's initial
mentor. He joined the Chisholm bandwagon and immediately drew a bead on Thompson's weakness in the black
community, his reliance on whites. "I had to be careful not
to get a white backlash," Holder said of the campaign, "but
in my last brochure to the voters I implied that Willy
Thompson was being backed by the whites. I made it clear
that the Negro leaders had not chosen him. It worked." [13]
Yet, politically agile as Holder was, he would be among the
first to point out that Shirley Chisholm's personality carried
the day. Her ability to inject other women with enthusiasm
was phenomenal. "She can pick up the phone," says Conrad
Chisholm, quoted by Susan Brownmiller, "and call two
hundred women and they'll be here in an hour." During the
primary campaign, they took up the cry "Unbought and un-
bossed," following their leader throughout the district, dis-
tributing campaign material in shopping bags, two thousand
pieces at each stop. "I have a theory about campaigning,"
Mrs. Chisholm declares. "You have to let them *feel* you."
The fact that she can speak Spanish fluently—after years
of working with Puerto Rican children in the city's day
nurseries—means that she communicates easily with the
major racial groups.

When the final arbiter—the people—handed up their
decision on June 18, the number voting was surprisingly
low. In the adjoining 13th District, for example, almost four
times as many people went to the polls. Although Mrs.
Chisholm lost six of ten Assembly Districts to Thompson,
she won her own 55th convincingly. That cushion of 1265
votes, contributed largely by the yeoman work of the Unity
Club, provided the winning margin of 788 votes out of 11,-
825 cast for the three candidates. The cause of the poor turnout, Mrs. Chisholm asserts, was public apathy. "Many
black politicians have not been delivering services to the
black people of their constituencies because they are hung

up in a system which requires first allegiance to a special interest group or clique and black people are thus quite apa-
thetic about all politicians in general."

There was no time to waste, however, in post mortems.
Three months before, James Farmer, former national director of the Congress of Racial Equality (CORE), had announced his candidacy on the Liberal Party ticket. Farmer
had some knowledge of the 12th District, having served six
months with the Bedford-Stuyvesant Development and Services Corporation working toward the establishment of "a
ghetto-based community college." But the fact that he lived
in lower Manhattan brought an immediate rejoinder from
Senator Thompson. "It's too bad he doesn't live in Brooklyn.
I think the people in our community want someone who has
lived here." Stung by this assault, Farmer announced that
"geographical boundaries" never were limitations to the
"problems of black and Puerto Rican communities." He
pointed out to a reporter for *The New York Times* by way
of illustration that," he had not lived in Mississippi in 1960
when he led the Freedom Riders in a campaign to integrate
bus lines and bus stops and spent forty days in jail there."

But the seed of alienation was planted. Despite an illus-
trious past, Farmer came through as a carpetbagger. Along
the way he had picked up the Republican nomination, and
this prompted a procession of GOP dignitaries to visit the
12th District to pound the election drums in his behalf. Voters grew resentful. It was a "terrible intrusion," as Mrs.
Chisholm saw it. "It was saying to them, 'You don't have
anybody worthwhile for this $30,000 [now $42,500] fruit-
cake.' It was a slap in the community's face. Everybody, Republican, Democrat, black and white, male and female, resented the intrusion." [14]

Farmer fought hard to change the image. He took an
apartment on Herkimer Street in Bedford-Stuyvesant to
maintain a mailing address, then went out of his way to
eliminate anti-Farmer sentiment among the district's black

militants. For a time it looked as though the Brooklyn CORE group, a radical outfit guided by Sonny Carson, would run a candidate against him, but the threat was finally withdrawn after Carson and Farmer smoked the peace pipe.

What the Liberal-Republican candidate tried to do was build the image of a successful national figure. "The racists and bigots are going to be in a strong position in Congress next year," he told audiences, "and we will need strong experienced people who can command national attention to stand up to them. I don't intend to be a freshman congressman. I graduated a long time ago." [15] This was just what Mrs. Chisholm's advisor, Wesley Holder, liked to hear. "I told Shirley that Farmer would appeal to the one or two per cent at the top of the pyramid, the intellectuals who had read about him. She was not to waste her time with them but to concentrate on the broad base of the pyramid which had all the average voters who knew her as a local figure." [16]

No doubt, Farmer was attempting to conduct a more sophisticated campaign. Not wishing to be caught up in the district's antagonism to the Nixon-Agnew ticket, he devised ways of impressing his name on the voter. His campaign material carried arrows pointing to his place on Columns A and D, with the slogan "Vote Farmer First." Likewise, he emphasized his gender by handing out printed material that expressed the need for a "strong male image" and a "man's voice in Washington," hoping thereby to fan the anti-matriarchal flames which Mrs. Chisholm symbolized. She recalls being greeted with "Here comes the black matriarch!" But she quickly points out that Farmer had a double-edged weapon in his hand, for the women of Bedford-Stuyvesant knew he was married to a white woman.

What it eventually came down to was a contest between a national figure without local roots and a relatively unknown with strong local ties. The public media, understandably or not, concentrated on Farmer. He was the figure the people knew; he was the candidate that most political pundits considered a shoo-in. NBC's contribution to the Farmer-Chisholm bruhaha was to devote almost its entire half-hour TV production to Farmer, which prompted Mrs. Chisholm to dub him the "national figure."

But being a "national figure" failed to cut the mustard. On November 5, the voters expressed their preference for a local candidate by a margin of 2½ to 1. The result was no surprise to Mrs. Chisholm, who had lost seventeen pounds campaigning. She was the candidate of the Democratic Party, which claims 80 per cent of the district's 91,000 eligible voters. "Farmer ran about as well as any Republican could," she commented. But Chisholm partisans were not so benign. "Why didn't he go up and run against Powell in Harlem?" one shouted during the victory celebration.

Mrs. Chisholm promptly vowed that she would speak out in Congress. "I am supposed to be seen and not heard," she ventured, "but I have no intention of being quiet." [17] One of her first objectives would be "to revamp the antipoverty program. It should be retraining people for jobs, giving them the skills to live in our automated society. At present it is nothing more than a Band-aid. It isn't getting to the root of the problem for blacks. The program is badly run. High salaries are paid to officials who are taking kickbacks and putting their families on the payroll. It's almost become a pork barrel and in the meantime idle minds are plotting to burn down our cities." [18]

A *New York Times* article datelined Washington, January 17, 1969, was enough to shatter Mrs. Chisholm's resolve. Under the headline HOUSE FARM PANEL TO GET URBAN VIEW was the report that Shirley Chisholm would be assigned to the House Agricultural Committee. The dispatch went on to explain that "requests by freshmen in Congress are not always heeded." Mrs. Chisholm had sought a place on the Education and Labor Committee, but the Democrats on the Ways and Means Committee, sitting as the Committee on

Committees, had other plans. "You gotta start somewhere," Republican Jacob H. Gilbert, Democrat of the Bronx, a member of the committee, said, revealing that Mrs. Chisholm would be a member of the agriculture subcommittee on Forestry and Rural Villages.

"Apparently all they know here in Washington about Brooklyn," Mrs. Chisholm told the press, as reported in *The New York Times* January 30, 1969, "is that a tree grew there. I can think of no other reason for assigning me to the House Agriculture Committee." Constituents added to her chagrin by bantering "Shirley, we don't grow hogs in this district. How did you get on that committee?"

Fighting Shirley Chisholm decided to object. She went to Speaker John McCormack and reported what had happened. He listened, shook his head. "Be a good soldier," was his paternal advice. "No," she replied to herself, "that's why the country is the way it 'is." Certain liberal Democratic House members attempted to remonstrate, saying the Agriculture Committee afforded a forum for consumer interests, but their words fell on unhearing ears. "It is not a question of getting off the Agriculture Committee *per se*," she answered. "It is a question of getting off a particular subcommittee."

When the House Democratic caucus met on the twenty-ninth, she was ready and eager for the showdown. Approaching Wilbur Mills of Arkansas, chairman of the powerful Ways and Means Committee, she sought removal from the Agriculture Committee. Taken aback over this break with tradition, Mills asked for reconsideration. "Will the gentlewoman from Brooklyn withdraw her amendment?" he intoned. Mrs. Chisholm remained unmoved in the face of his challenge and, after some debate, was gratified to have her name scratched from membership on the Agriculture Committee.

Following the closed caucus, Mrs. Chisholm released a full head of steam castigating the operation of the committee system. "It seems to me," she told the press, "that it is time for the House of Representatives to pay attention to other considerations than its petrified, sanctified system of seniority, which is the only basis for making most of its decisions." The nine black members of the House, she went on, "the largest number since Reconstruction," should be given priority in meeting the nation's "critical problems of racism, deprivation and urban decay." [19] The real clinker is that the committees do not reflect grass-roots opinion. A majority of the chairmen are seventy years of age or over. "They sit cloistered on the hill in Washington, D.C., and have their interminable hearings and believe this is indicative of national attitudes. People come up on the hill to testify on certain legislation and so often these people are carefully selected and don't know what's really going on in the hills and valleys of the land."

For three weeks thereafter Mrs. Chisholm remained in the dark as members of the Democratic caucus argued what to do. Finally, on February 18, she learned of her appointment to the Veterans Committee, a sop to be sure, but still an upward step in representing her district. The Veterans Administration operates a hospital in Brooklyn and she announced she would "make people more aware of their eligibility for the hospital and other veterans' benefits."

During the campaign of the previous fall, Mrs. Chisholm had called for the construction of over a million subsidized housing units a year. The lack of adequate housing in Bedford-Stuyvesant was reaching crisis levels, she pointed out. Joining Republican Jonathan Bingham, a Bronx Democrat, she now co-sponsored an amendment to the National Housing Act that established a fund for the construction of low-rental housing. But Washington, unlike Albany, paid scant attention to a freshman congresswoman. "It's a very secluded and exclusive kind of organization," she explained. "The first two years you are told that you can't get legislation passed." Of course, she adds with an understanding twinkle, "I don't exactly behave myself."

The seriousness of the housing situation in her district, with buildings abandoned and huge areas cleared for the Model Cities Program, had led her to the conclusion that rent controls must be rolled back. "We're really going to have to do something or New York will be abandoned completely." In her view, recovery could not be achieved by conventional capital; what is required is a huge investment of public funds. "The problem is beyond the control of the cities and the states," she warned.

And, besides, the problem of housing extends beyond Bedford-Stuyvesant. The white noose of suburbia acts to lock in ghetto residents. They are, generally speaking, powerless to leave either because they cannot afford rental and construction costs or because discriminatory housing patterns bar them. "Many blacks," Mrs. Chisholm contends, "would like to work out on Long Island, but they can't, so we are building the seeds for another kind of destruction if the government doesn't recognize that the availability of jobs goes hand in hand with the availability of housing." In answer to the question "What is Congress doing to solve this problem?" Mrs. Chisholm replies, "Congress is too busy with the Vietnam war. I am not attempting to be facetious when I say, 'Look at the appropriation bills coming out of the U.S. Congress and you know right away that domestic corners are really at the bottom of the list.' This is what is so terribly frustrating."

Mrs. Chisholm's more immediate concern, in view of the congressional mood, is the deliverance of jobs. Bedford-Stuyvesant has one of the highest unemployment rates in the nation. "I talk with so many black men who are unemployed," she explains. "They want a 'piece of the pie,' as they phrase it. 'Look, Chisholm,' they say, 'I want some training, I want some education so that I can earn at least $100 a week, take care of my family, maybe open a little bank account, or have a little luxury or something.'" These are basic desires, not dependent upon the color of the capital-

ism, white or black. "The masses of black people," Mrs.
Chisholm declares, "cannot see themselves as capitalists.
Let's be pragmatic—the masses today want training to acquire jobs that are going begging because they lack the req-
uisite skills and education." If such training is available,
blacks "will move up the economic ladder, buy homes, save
money to educate their children." Nothing makes the Congresswoman more angry than the knowledge that blacks are
being exploited menially because of the color of their skin.
Upon learning that black hospital workers in Charleston,
South Carolina, were receiving as little as $1.30 an hour—
lower than whites performing the same job—she complained to *The New York Times* (April 16, 1969) in a communication which said, "How long must the inhumanely
paid Charleston hospital workers be forced to strike and suffer jailings before they are treated as first-class citizens?"

On March 26, 1969, Mrs. Chisholm gave her maiden
speech in Congress—a polemic against the Vietnam war.
She had tarried a time over opposition to the war, but now
she was vigorous in condemnation. She would oppose every
defense money bill, her colleagues were informed, "until the
time comes when our values and priorities have been turned
right side up again." It was time for "every mother, wife and
widow in this land who ever asked herself why the generals
can play with billions while families crumble under the
weight of sickness, hunger and unemployment" to inveigh
against the conflict. Like the arms of an octopus, her wrath
crept out to enfold members of the House. She knew "many
gentlemen with sons eligible to serve in Vietnam who are in
reserve units. I know one who has six sons, all in the reserves. He can afford to get up and talk about escalating the
war. But I'm compiling a list, and as soon as the public sees
what is going on, they may start asking a few questions." [20]

Mrs. Chisholm's counter thrust was to call for a volunteer
army to replace the Selective Service System. "The present
draft system is indentured servitude, a sixteenth-century
anachronism," she informed the House. "We wonder why the

youth of this nation are rebelling. Could it be because we treat them as mindless, subservient cannon fodder?" Her faith in volunteer service rested on three premises: (1) the willingness of young men to flock to the colors in time of crisis. Doubting Thomases, undoubtedly, see America, particularly American youth, as moral and physical cowards, but "the average critic," she charged caustically, "is well over the draft age of twenty-six and most could not pass the induction physical even if they could meet the mental requirements. In short, most of them, because of their age, are too old to fight; they only wage the wars, while those who do the fighting and the dying cannot even vote, cannot even decide whether or not to fight"; (2) the inadmissibility of calling a volunteer army a luxury when the government has contrived to make second-class citizens economically out of Selective Service draftees; (3) the farfetched argument that political power would despoil volunteer service. "The argument is based on the assumption that all volunteers would be of a similar bent," Mrs. Chisholm heatedly suggests. "Hogwash. A volunteer army would not significantly alter the political power of the Armed Forces. In the final analysis, there are only two basic differences between a voluntary army and the present draft army—costs and personal liberties. I am willing to pay the higher costs for a volunteer army if that army will do two things: First, if it will provide an effective citizen check on our foreign policy and bring it back to the inner limits of sanity and good sense, and second, if it will guarantee each citizen, a soldier or not, that the personal and political liberties of a democracy cannot be abridged at the personal whims of any one individual." [21]

Not unnaturally, because so many of Mrs. Chisholm's interests tend to gravitate toward youth and the turmoils of young people, she constantly dwells on their contributions to the U.S. She says they are breaking the bonds that have held previous American generations in thrall. Ghettos, according to the Congresswoman, are not confined to "rat-

and roach-infested, garbage-laden slums." They exist wherever human beings try to cut themselves off from those who dwell in different subcultures of our society. "In my speaking engagements around the country," she likes to point out, "I am often approached by white people who tell me that they have played golf at such-and-such a country club for so many years and that they were so naïve that it took the Kerner Commission Report to make them realize that there were no Negro members in their club. Many of them are liars. They not only realized it; they actively opposed black people and other minority groups joining their little exclusive ghetto. Others of them are liars also, but liars in a different vein; they realized it and just didn't have the guts to confront those most responsible for it. Of course, a few of them might have been telling the truth.

"But whether they were lying, whether they were moral cowards or whether they were truly naïve they are all members of the sub-cultural ghetto that their country club represents. Closed in—walled off from the rest of the world— choosing to remain there quietly rather than incur the social and economic sanctions that are often the penalty."

But not today's youth. Because they refuse to accept this alienation, Mrs. Chisholm is optimistic over their future. She is confident they will succeed where previous generations have failed to rise above bigotry. "For most of them, it is just not enough to make money. . . . Most of them have a commitment, or at least, an interest in social equality. . . . They are reaching out . . . touching . . . other . . . different people . . . other different cultures," she avers. This way the isolation of the cultural ghetto is being ended. But it is not a minute too soon, for her generation has "attempted to denude, to foul and contaminate their legacy beyond recall." [22]

One reason for Mrs. Chisholm's utter disdain of vitriolic criticism is a prophetic sense of her own importance. She knows instinctively that her role is less than permanent. Thus she had no qualms about renouncing a relatively secure Assembly seat to enter the quest for Congress. In Congress, she informed her colleagues who might be wondering about their futures, "many of us will be out of the picture within the next ten years or so." Perhaps the best illustration of this scorn for propriety occurred in 1969 during the New York City mayoralty campaign. The previous year she had been named Democratic national committeewoman to succeed Republican Edna F. Kelly of Brooklyn. The unanimous choice of the party's delegates to the national convention in Chicago, Mrs. Chisholm sat out the proceedings in her hotel room, convalescing from a recent abdominal operation, and has the distinction of being the first Negro woman elected to the Committee. Presumably, the professionals thought (in the words of Thomas Collier Platt, a former New York Senator), she "would stand while hitched." They were wrong, as they were shortly to see.

It is a rule in Old Gotham that mayoralty campaigns arouse more interest than a majority of state and national elections, and 1969 was no exception. The Democrats led off with an array of candidates that included such notables as Republican Hugh L. Carey of Brooklyn, Republican James H. Scheuer of the Bronx, former Mayor Robert F. Wagner, Controller Mario A. Procaccino, and Borough President Herman Badillo of the Bronx. Interest ran high because Mayor Lindsay was, by universal concession, in trouble. The Republican Party, which endorsed him in 1965, found his views too liberal, especially the concern he demonstrated for deprived blacks. The stakes rose higher when State Senator John J. Marchi, of Staten Island, a popular Republican with impeccable family credentials and the cynosure of conservatives, decided to challenge him.

In the confusion of candidates and issues, voters had trouble sorting out their preferences in primary voting. On the Democratic side, liberals split their votes between Wagner and Badillo to give Procaccino, a conservative, the brass ring—and moreover the mood extended into the Republican

ranks, dumping Lindsay. Fortunately for the Mayor, the
Liberal Party had already endorsed him for re-election, thus
assuring him of a place on the November ballot, admittedly
some solace for being rebuked by his own party.

But the liberals, who included Shirley Chisholm, refused
to remain buried. "The situation," she said a month afterward, "is so critical and so important that none of us should
let partisan politics stand in our way. All the liberal and Reform people have to support Lindsay." What worried her
was the admonition that New York was becoming "virtually
paralyzed by fear and hatred," and that Marchi and Procaccino were exploiting these "corrosive emotions." Her endorsement brought immediate reactions: from Lindsay, the
paean that Mrs. Chisholm was a person who "always spoke
from conscience" and had "never been shackled by out-
moded political institutions," but from John J. Burns, chairman of the Democratic State Committee, the advice to get
out. "If I found I could not support Mr. Procaccino," he
said, "I would resign my party position." The Procaccino
camp fumed over her defection. Taking the chairman's cue,
one spokesman said she should be "read out of the party." [23]
But Mrs. Chisholm refused. To various messages of disap-
proval threatening to remove her, she replied, "I am not
afraid to be brought up on charges, but we're not going to
do it privately, we're going to do it publicly," and the Democratic leadership had no stomach for that. According to
Mrs. Chisholm, this was just one more example of the
"handwriting on the wall," a phrase she likes to use in referring to the changing role of professional politicians. No
longer do their words carry Olympian authority. "Many see
the handwriting," she strongly avows, "and are afraid to
face what the handwriting is telling them. When they get
up to speak before groups, they become irrational because
of the fear they are losing out." They suffer from political
chauvinism. "If you are a professional politician, the party is
the thing. The party, regardless of the candidate, is the
thing. I don't happen to believe in that." But the voters are

becoming surfeited. "Quite clearly, the American people, particularly the younger people, the younger citizens, don't have any compunctions about voting for or against a person because he is a member of a certain political party. People today are looking at the candidate and the issues, and if the candidate or the issue belongs to another party, they don't hesitate to cross over and vote in a general election for that candidate. The handwriting on the wall shows that political bosses can no longer deliver their districts. That day is over!"

When the votes were counted that November, Mrs. Chisholm's thesis was amply proved. Democratic districts went overwhelmingly for Mayor Lindsay in his march to victory. "And yet," the Democratic Congresswoman points out, "if you had been following their voting patterns over a number of years, you could be sure the Democratic bosses would have delivered them, which shows that the younger voters don't have the hangups about political labels that their grandfathers and great-grandfathers and great-great-grandfathers did. The latter didn't ask whether the candidate was a Democrat or Republican. They pulled the lever all the way down out of sheer habit."

Returning to Washington at the end of the Lindsay-Procaccino-Marchi campaign, Mrs. Chisholm was immediately involved in a variety of projects. In December she appeared before the subcommittee on Health of the Senate Labor and Public Welfare Committee to promote legalized abortion or, the term she prefers to use, "pregnancy termination." She had long advocated family planning, but more had to be done to limit births. "Certainly, no one should be forced to have an abortion," she declared. "The decision to have a child should be a personal private decision. Unfortunately, as the law stands now, there is no choice. Under the present circumstances we are imposing the Catholic view of abortion on the entire population."

The result: "Between 250,000 and 1,250,000 illegal abortions are performed annually in the United States. Botched abortions are the single largest cause of maternal deaths. Il-legitimacy is a growing problem. By 1967, approximately 4.5 million children under the age of eighteen in the United States were illegitimate. If a white girl gives up her child for adoption there is a pretty good chance that the child will be adopted. This is not the same for black and other minority group children. They spend their lives in orphanages and foster homes. This is one of the prime reasons so many black girls keep their babies. The number of children in orphanages or in foster care totals 316,000. Only 25 per cent of the black children are in public institutions—18 per cent are in voluntary institutions or homes. This contrasts sharply with the 71 per cent of white children in public institutions and 80 per cent in voluntary care."

Knowing she faced an audience that wished to stay aloof from problems etched with emotion, Mrs. Chisholm directed her next remarks to their pocketbooks. "Some of you gentlemen," she said, "may think this is all too hearts and flowers. Well, I've got an even more practical reason why you should be in favor of abortion repeal. It costs you money. The number of illegitimate children on Aid For Dependent Children has been steadily increasing. Until now [as of 1967] 1,100,000 or 28 per cent of all AFDC children are illegitimate."

"The most frequent reason married women seek abortions," she went on, "is that they feel that they have too many children already. A recent in-depth survey of 5,600 persons by Dr. Charles F. Westoff of Princeton's Office of Population Research has revealed that of all economic groups, the poor were most anxious about this issue. Among the poor (i.e., earning under $4000) 42 per cent of all legitimate births are unwanted. The principal reason seems to be financial or financially related, e.g. crowded housing. Indeed, there is a high correlation between the number of children in a family and the ability to break the poverty cycle. The risk of poverty increases rapidly from 9 per cent for one-child families to 42 per cent for families with six or more children. Nearly half of the children growing up in poverty in 1966 were members of families with five or more children under eighteen. More than one quarter of all families with four or more children live in poverty. The risk of poverty is two and a half times that for families with three children or less." [24]

A second interest, also associated with the plight of poor blacks, is the repeal of Section 11 of the Internal Securities Act of 1950 which permits the federal government to establish and maintain detention camps for suspected subversives. During hearings before the House Committee on Internal Security, Mrs. Chisholm said "its mere presence on the books" was an insult to Americans whose color was not white. "It was not the Italians and Germans who were rounded up during World War II when more than 100,000 Japanese-Americans were interned," she reminded the committee, but those "who were easily identifiable because of their skin. Today, it is not the Ku Klux Klan or the syndicate whose doors are being kicked in, it is the Black Panthers. Skin, skin, skin color, gentlemen, that is the criterion. It makes us special targets." [25]

What undoubtedly contributes most to Mrs. Chisholm's vaulting reputation (her incoming mail is already among the top five in Congress) is her sensitivity to youth. No matter how pressed she is with the need to see dignitaries, she can always find time for young people. This means talking to visiting school delegations in Washington and an endless journey in Bedford-Stuyvesant to all the district schools. Though childless, she loves children, loves to be with them, to talk, to hear their problems. She knows firsthand the terrible crunch of narcotics on youth and their militancy in wanting the vote. When the House Select Committee on Crime held hearings in the fall of 1969, she called for legislation that would "cut off the source of supply." Speaking as one with authority, she said: "We can do it if we really desire to do so, but the truth of the matter is that the drug traffic is a network of circumstances involving known criminals as well as respectable-looking individuals who are making money out of this insidious business that has now eaten at the core of our most precious product—our children.

"The real problem is not drugs or crimes by individuals per se. It is rather the social organization that makes both of these things necessary. It is common knowledge to the people of my district that policemen take bribes to protect the numbers racket, drug pushers and prostitutes. It is common knowledge that some politicians take instructions and money from local racketeers." [26]

In the infested jungle of the ghetto, such words are heard but seldom taken seriously. After Mrs. Chisholm's allegation, the New York City police department said it "was investigating" the charges and would have "no immediate comment," which said worlds without saying anything. What one forgets living outside the ghetto, but is never forgotten inside, is the vengeance that organized crime visits upon its informers.

One wonders, however, how long society will submit to having a gun held at its head. The City of New York, together with the State of New York, spends millions annually to care for the city's narcotic addicts, who make up 60 per cent of the U.S. total. Hospitals are built to house the victims, methadone clinics are set up to aid heroin users, but the vital ingredient, and the police power to cope with the pushers, is lacking because payoffs are plentiful and lush. Currently, the tail enjoys wagging the dog, and until New Yorkers wake up little that Mrs. Chisholm or anyone else says is going to rid the city of this scourge.

Happily far more sanguine than the work to halt addiction is the effort Congresswoman Chisholm has put forth to get eighteen-year-olds the vote. They are the "most unrepresented minority group" in America, she says. According to the U.S. Bureau of the Census, at the time of the 1968 presidential election, there were 21,679,000 Americans between the ages of sixteen and twenty-one—about 10 per cent of the nation's population. "The size of that figure alone," declares Mrs. Chisholm, "would seem to warrant their occasional refusal to participate in the war in Vietnam and other salient activities and aspects of our society on the basis that they have no direct representation."

Despite the fact that opinion polls showed that 64 per cent of the American voting public favored lowering the voting age to eighteen, Congress did little to indicate a changed posture. Then, in the spring of 1970, the tide suddenly turned. Whether the members of the House became apprehensive over youth's challenge—after all, most of 1968's crop between sixteen and twenty-one will soon be marching to the ballot box—is a moot question. In any event, June 18, 1970, Mrs. Chisholm voted with a 272-to-132 majority to lower the voting age to eighteen, climaxing a hard-earned campaign.

Summarizing her many political activities, one is impressed by the fact that Mrs. Chisholm's radicalism functions so effectively within a conservative framework. Despite her defiance of political authority, she has no yearning to work outside the system, no desire to junk the American system for some untried political nostrum. She is determined simply to make the U.S. live up to its constitutional commitments, which is to say patriotism in the market place. She takes encouragement from a belief that the "whole attitude and the whole approach to politics is changing. It is my humble opinion that you cannot change unless you know just what it is that you are attacking and you can't attack anything on the outside looking in; you can only ascertain the weaknesses and the strengths of people and institutions by being in the system. I feel that change must come from within the system."

Of course, the system is white-oriented and Mrs. Chisholm is black. "One ever feels his twoness—an American, a Negro," wrote William E. DuBois in *Souls of Black Folk* about such ambivalence, "two souls two thoughts, two unreconciled strivings; two warring ideals in one dark body, whose dogged strength alone keeps it from being torn asunder." And Mrs. Chisholm appears able to survive well in two cultures. While clinging to the established political system on the one hand, she talks militancy to blacks on the other. At the July 1969 annual convention of the National Urban League, held in Washington, she called up memories of Frederick Douglass, the historic black militant, to say, "Power concedes nothing. We must liberate ourselves. It was true then and it is true now—'power concedes nothing.'" She went on to say that "nearly 60 per cent of all black people, Black Americans, today still live in what some people have called and are calling 'colonies,'" proof, if proof were needed, that "power concedes nothing." She explained that her definition of power was not the old-fashioned idea of power generated by wealth and influence, but the "kind of power that comes from the people." Political robber-barons must go "against the wall" with them. "We are tired and tiring more each day," she added, "of the illegal, immoral and anti-human war in Vietnam; we are tired of brush-fire skirmishes and field exercises that pretend to be a war on poverty; [of] leaders who okay without thought $25 billion for an expedition that can't even bring back green cheese to feed our hungry citizens."

This was "soul music" to black ears. But where some militants tended to talk about the bullet, Mrs. Chisholm was referring to the ballot as the weapon to reduce hunger, build housing, improve education. "I believe that the goals of this Social Revolution must be the preservation of human resources—human potential—and human life. That leaves only the ballot." Surprisingly, her attachment to the system did not reduce her standing with important militants in Bedford-Stuyvesant. Questioned about her relationship with Sonny Carson, Albert Vann and Rhody McCoy (three of that ghetto's best known militants), she answered, "I have a good relationship with all of them—I'm very proud to say

UP FROM WITHIN

Shirley Chisholm

*The dynamic, nationally famous member
of the House of Representatives.
She was the first black woman ever
to hold that office.*

UPI

Horace Julian Bond

The thirty-one-year-old member of the Georgia Legislature. Bond was originally denied his seat in that body and took his case to the Supreme Court. After winning his case he was catapulted into national prominence and in some circles is currently mentioned as a potential presidential candidate.

UPI

Kenneth Allen Gibson

Mayor of Newark. Gibson, who rose to
power from the ghetto of the city's Central
Ward, was the first black mayor of a metropolitan
city. Gibson, thirty-nine and full of self-confidence,
never bucked the system, but chose instead to
work from within and make it work.

John Mackey

Twenty-nine-year-old tight end of the
Baltimore Colts. In 1970 he was elected president
of the National Football League's
Players' Association, the bargaining
agent for the 1200 players of the American
and National Football Conferences.

Andrew F. Brimmer

Trained in economics at Harvard, Brimmer has worked with the Federal Reserve Bank in New York and was appointed Assistant Secretary of Commerce for Economic Affairs in 1965. He is now a member of the Federal Reserve Board, the first black ever to hold such a position.

John Conyers, Jr.

Forty-one-year-old member of Congress from Detroit and quickly becoming the acknowledged leader of black congressmen on Capitol Hill. Conyers struggles tirelessly to remove the deeply etched stains of white racism in the United States.

Clifton R. Wharton

President of Michigan State University.
Wharton was the first black to be named
head of a major American university.
He sees the white man's world as a
"milieu in which other blacks with
training and purpose can also succeed."

UPI

Alvin F. Poussaint
Associate dean and associate professor of psychiatry at Harvard Medical School. Poussaint has lobbied strenuously to gain more power for the black members of the American Psychiatric Association.

BLACKSTONE-SHELBOURNE

that despite the fact that some of the militants, the extremists or the ardent nationalists, don't agree with my philosophy or my approach to problems, I have a good working relationship with these three. I can communicate with them because one thing they all say: 'Shirley is sincere in whatever she believes.' It doesn't mean that I agree with everything they say or that they agree with me, but because of the sincerity and integrity I have demonstrated thus far in my political life, I have an open relationship with them."

Like most black politicians, Mrs. Chisholm carries a mental dubiousness about "white liberals." She told Susan Brownmiller, *New York Times Magazine* writer, that they were the "favorite parlor conversation" for Negroes. "They were fine," she adds by way of refinement, "when they were relieving their pangs of guilt with their contributions and their participation in the panels and the forum groups, but now that it has come down to a matter of putting into practice what they've discussed in their forums and panels, they've got a lot of hang-ups." Pressed for an in-depth definition of *hang-up*, Mrs. Chisholm replied, "I think the main hang-up with white liberals is that they become identified with the cause of social and economic justice for blacks, but when it really comes to fitting the action to the word, quite often they draw back. You find they're not ready to give that last strong commitment. Their convictions are not strong enough to take a stand which will cause repercussions with their neighbors. Take, for example, block busting or selling homes to blacks. White liberals will not come out in the open and say, 'We are going to lead the fight and sell the homes,' because they fear what their white neighbors or their friends or families might do. It's a lack of a certain kind of guts that is needed to follow through, particularly when they are trying to bring about changes in a society that has had a particular attitude toward a certain segment of the people."

One of the fascinating talents Mrs. Chisholm conveys is

her ability to sort the chaff from the wheat, to differentiate the mirage from the substance in the black movement. She is not impressed, for instance, with symbols of power. "Black leaders in particular," she avers, "must do more than grow Afros—wear dashikis—buy African artifacts—extoll the virtues of 'soul' food." Not that these are "wrong," in her mind, but "too often irrelevant." What is relevant is the sight of "black students asking for more black courses, black instructors, black people asking for community control of education. This is saying to White America, 'You have kept me back for so long, you have determined my destiny, you've been telling me how to live, what to do, how to work. I now want to assert myself and my ego to make some determination about my life and my destiny, in other words, here I come whether you like it or not—this is my way of telling you that I am here.' In order for them to assert their egos which have been deflated for so long, they have to prove certain things to themselves. It's part of the struggle for identification, showing the world and those forces that have kept them back so long, that they can do something about their destinies—can make a contribution. They offer to do this within the system, but if the system refuses them, they may become separatists."

Indeed, this is one of Mrs. Chisholm's greatest worries. "I have been predicting for quite some time that unless our government begins to turn around, we're going to see blood in the streets. I mean this because I have traveled all over this country. I've been in thirty-six states in the past fifteen months. I have visited college campuses and talked to all kind of people. I've been in Appalachia, the black delta of Mississippi, and I tell you black people and white people are frustrated. They're upset and they're just about ready to do anything they have to do and that frightens me."

A chink in this wall of gloom is the victory of Kenneth A. Gibson, black civil engineer, who won the Democrat nomination for mayor of Newark in the spring of 1970. Instru-

mental in the outcome was the endorsement of John P. Caufield, former Newark Fire Director, Mr. Gibson's principal
white supporter, who placed fourth in the initial voting and
then swung to Gibson. This for Mrs. Chisholm was a beacon
lighting future hopes. It indicated that black people "can
really" get behind a particular candidate, and given the
right circumstances, "even white people will come to a Kenneth Gibson because of the need for change." Gibson's opponent, then Mayor Hugh J. Addonizio, was being tried on
federal charges of extortion and income tax evasion.

But such victories, as they relate to black candidates, can
only result—*à la* Mrs. Chisholm—when blacks exert pressure. A perfect case was Mrs. Chisholm's appearance at the
Democratic State Convention at Grossinger's in the heart of
the Catskill Mountains in April 1970. She went there to lead
the fight for the nomination of State Senator Basil A. Paterson, a Harlemite, for lieutenant governor. Arthur J. Gold-
berg, former United States Supreme Court Justice and U.S.
delegate to the United Nations during the Johnson regime,
was the favorite candidate for governor, and the chief issue
was therefore getting white delegates to accept a Jew and a
black at the head of the ticket. The ethnic makeup was further complicated by Arthur Levitt, a New York Jew, running for re-election as comptroller, and Adam Walinsky, a
third Jew, striving for the attorney general position. Mrs.
Chisholm kept hearing "three Jews and a black man. That
just won't go over upstate.' I told them, 'O.K., if that's your
problem, take one of the Jews off.' " [27]

Once the emboldened Congress woman reached the mi-
crophone, she shouted, "You're nothing but robots and au-
tomatons," fearing the delegates would nominate William J.
vanden Heuvel, a perennial hopeful and friend of the late
Senator Robert Kennedy, as well as Senator Paterson, in the
hope that a primary battle would give vanden Heuvel the
edge. Under state law, both candidates could appear on the
ballot if each obtained the support of at least 25 per cent of

the delegates. The scheme was political chicanery at its worst, and an aroused Chisholm roared, "You give the vote the way the bosses tell you to—you don't want to change this party." She attacked the "wheeling and dealing ... footsy and games," as she called it, and concluded the twenty-minute harangue by saying, "Will those with courage and guts—and it takes guts in a rigged convention—leave this floor and meet with us?" A woman from the Nassau County delegation yelled "Get off that stage!" Not to be outdone, jaw jutting, Mrs. Chisholm screamed back: "You come and get me off." When about a third of the 345 delegates—black and white—followed her in order to caucus, the vanden Heuvel candidacy died abruptly and Paterson was acclaimed the winner.

In Mrs. Chisholm's quieter, more relaxed moments, however, when the fires are banked, what comes through is a woman of sensitive uncertainties. She has doubts about where her career is leading. She is not unaware of the perils of public office. "I'm fighting for my people," she likes to say, "and in fighting for my people, as somebody said, 'I keep telling it like it is' and this jars certain forces in our society. I never dreamed that a little woman like me—a little black woman like me—would become such a threat to anybody because I myself don't have that much power—but evidently, my voice on the American scene is very disturbing to certain elements." [28]

Her strongest advocate and perfect companion is Conrad, her husband, who understands the toils and tribulations of political life, and the reasons for Shirley getting the family's chief billing. Whatever the future holds—and Shirley talks about retiring to two homes, one in Brooklyn, the other in the West Indies—much of her success can be traced to the quiet, attentive affection of this perceptive man, who quite agrees with Ethel Kennedy that "there's only one woman who belongs in politics today and that is Shirley Chisholm." [29]

Horace Julian Bond ═══════════

❡ It was the year 1944. In the state of Georgia, Jim Crow was very much alive, although here and there an isolated incident heralded the approach of black militancy after the long domination of white fear. In this instance, oddly enough, the key was a white arch-segregationist, Governor Herman Talmadge. It had been the custom for some years at Fort Valley State College, a Negro institution in central Georgia, to hold a ham dinner for supporters in the contiguous territory. Talmadge liked such affairs and was not one to pass up a ham-and-egg supper with the opportunity to shake hands and exchange political palaver. He would even, if the mood was right, sit and talk with local blacks. And so it happened that photographers caught him eating with Negroes, an unpardonable sin in white Georgia.

Of course, the pictures never saw the light of day because they were impounded deep in the files of Valley State president, Dr. Horace Mann Bond. But the following January, when the Georgia legislature met in Atlanta, Dr. Bond sent the pictures to Talmadge with a note, "Gov. Talmadge, here are the pictures. Do you want me to send them to the *Journal* and *Constitution?*" "No, Dr. Bond," Talmadge hurriedly wrote, "you'll get your appropriation this year." [1]

Some years prior to this incident, Dr. Bond had earned a doctorate in education at the University of Chicago and went on to sharpen his academic skills at Fisk University in Nashville. Before going to Valley State, teacher Bond married a Fisk student, who—being a native of Atlanta—was unprepared for the highly segregated life of rural Georgia. When she discovered that her first child would be born in the most primitive hospital facilities, she returned to Nashville and there on January 14, 1940, gave birth to Horace Julian Bond.

Something in that initial act—the effort to escape Valley State—came to be symbolic of the distance that separated the child from the rigors of Southern segregation. From birth to manhood, he was continually isolated within the walls of academe. "I never really lived the life of a Southern Negro kid," Bond would say later.[2] At five, he was transported north to Lincoln University in Pennsylvania when Dr. Bond assumed the presidency. Young Julian recalls that his parents provided "a stable home, a fine education and an atmosphere in which there was a great deal of respect for learning. There were always books in the home. Reading wasn't something that you had to do, but was something that you just did as a matter of course." The carrot without the stick turned Julian into a reader of incredible speed. He learned to read at age four and at seventeen was able to devour *Gone with the Wind* in one night.

Julian Bond's elementary teaching at Lincoln began on campus. "We used the gym and the tennis courts. My playmates were the other faculty kids. We all went to the laboratory school on campus that was used for teacher training. It was a very pleasant, very insulated life," he reported to Douglas Kiker of *Playboy* magazine. Bond was nine before he finally ventured from isolation and then it was only as the result of court action. Faculty members at Lincoln were incensed over segregation in the public schools and sought relief in the state's Supreme Court, using their children as plaintiffs. Once the ban was broken by a successful testing,

Julian entered public school, where he remained for three years.

When he was twelve his parents decided he would benefit from broader horizons and dispatched him to George School, a Quaker prep school in Bucks County, Pennsylvania. Being the smallest member of his class and the sole black in the student body were initial handicaps, but in five years at George, Bond became goalie on the soccer team, backstroke on the swimming team, and graduated with first-class grades. His one traumatic experience was the request of the headmaster not to wear his athletic jacket with school insigne in Newtown whenever he took his white girl friend there on a date. "That was just like somebody stopping you and slapping you across the face," the ultimate of indignities for Bond.[3]

When he entered Morehouse College in the fall of 1957, he was easily taken for an Ivy League product. Boyish, thin, tall, with classic features, he looked the part of an establishment scion. The academic environment added to the mood. He concentrated on literary output, wrote poetry, and was delighted to see his verses included in six anthologies in four countries. Martin Luther King, Jr., fresh from his triumphs in the Montgomery bus boycott, taught philosophy. According to Bond, the martyred civil rights worker would open his book to the lesson, glance at the passage, read the first line, close his book, and recite from memory. "You could follow him by the text. I didn't learn too much philosophy because the class always degenerated into discussions of the civil rights movement, which had nothing to do with Plato or anyone else." But for all that the attitude at Morehouse remained relatively quiet. "Except for a few verbal militants, there was no militancy on campus," Bond states. "We discussed indignities, but never in terms of 'let's do something about it.' We seldom went downtown, except maybe to go to the Fox theater and sit in the balcony, because the local movie house was so filthy. But on the whole, there were so many attractions on campus, we simply didn't have to face segregation; houseparties at big homes with swimming pools, and all the campus culture, all that," he recalled to Douglas Kiker.

This brand of euphoria suddenly became passé in February 1960, after student sit-ins were staged in Greensboro restaurants by students of North Carolina A & T College. Campus activists in Atlanta, stirred by these reports, were moved to join the lancing of racial boils. But Bond, by his own statement, was not among them. It was a little far-fetched, come to think of it, for one so sheltered. Demonstrators were having their heads cracked and bloodied, not exactly the role for a man of Bond's sensitivity. Besides, there was still the sanctuary of family renown, if the need arose, from having a distinguished father who was now dean of Education and Social Research at Atlanta University, and a remarkable mother turned librarian after earning a second M.A. in library science.

With such mental cushions to fall back on, Bond was hardly prepared for what took place one morning in early February at the Yates and Milton drugstore, a campus hangout adjacent to the Atlanta campus. As Bond tells it, "A student approached me whom I didn't know very well, a fellow named Lonny King, a football hero who was active in campus politics. He showed me a newspaper headline which read GREENSBORO STUDENTS SIT-IN FOR THE THIRD DAY."

" 'What do you think of that?' he said to me."

"I've seen it," Bond replied crisply. "I read the paper too."

"It's pretty good," King went on. "Don't you think something like that ought to happen here?"

"Well, it probably will. Someone will do it."

"Why don't we do it?" King entreated Bond.

Bond was surprised, first because he was not particularly close to King and secondly because King assumed that Bond would be interested in sponsoring a sit-in demonstration in Atlanta. "Why me?" mused Bond.

But King snatched him from the reverie. "You take one

side of the drugstore and I'll take the other, and we'll run up and down the seats. Let's call a meeting in front of Sale Hall for tomorrow morning." When the crowd gathered in response to their call, the die was cast in a form Julian Bond never anticipated. Overnight he was rooted out of the quiet past and thrust into a movement of revolutionary proportions. Making plans to change society was unlike anything he had ever attempted. In no time, he found the work absorbing all his energies. If an effective scheme were devised, it must include total analysis of the problem: a count of restaurants and lunchrooms with their locations, a list of all public buildings in Atlanta with segregated facilities, the name of every civil rights lawyer or white liberal, NAACP officials, and the various school forces willing to enter the fray. They decided to call themselves the Atlanta Committee on Appeal for Human Rights. They would aim their first sit-in demonstrations at the public restaurants in City Hall, the two bus stations, the two train stations, the federal building, and the state capitol.

"I was in charge of the group that hit the City Hall cafeteria," Bond told *Playboy*'s reporter. "Nobody knew what to expect, whether the police would beat us, or shoot us, or what. I told everybody in my group we'd be out of jail in half an hour, and I really believed it. It was the first and only time I've ever been arrested. We stayed in jail for ten hours before bail was arranged. I got out, went back to school and picked up Alice [Clopton], who was in rehearsal for a production of *Finian's Rainbow;* she was a dancer. I drove her home, then went home myself and got up the next morning and read about myself in the paper. We all felt very proud of ourselves."

The voice of protest could now be heard throughout the land, and among the first to sense the intensity of student involvement was Martin Luther King. For a time, prior to the Greensboro sit-in, his star seemed to be setting. Some people were saying, as Loudon Wainwright of *Life* magazine told it, "King is a great cat, but what's he done lately?" His name had slipped from public view. Now King saw a chance to revive his foundering Southern Christian Leadership Conference by cooperating with the young dissenters. In April 1960, the SCLC invited militant students from Southern Negro colleges to Shaw University in Raleigh, North Carolina, to plan civil rights strategy; out of this convocation emerged the Student Nonviolent Coordinating Committee, with James Forman as the first executive director. Julian Bond, Morehouse activist, was one of the chief instigators.

Back in Atlanta, an overworked Bond had all he could manage to keep his scholastic seams from splitting. In the catalogue he was still a junior with one year to go, but in fact he was finding it difficult to continue. He had enlisted in the racial battle and there was no turning back. The demands on his time were limitless. He was also in love with Miss Clopton, the shy, attractive daughter of a restaurant chef and a Home Ec major at nearby Spelman College. The question was how to remain in school, contemplate marriage, and continue as a field officer in COHAR, campus acronym for the Committee on Appeal for Human Rights.

Bond solved the dilemma by protecting all flanks. He continued at Morehouse, married Alice, and to support her joined the staff of the newly formed Atlanta weekly Negro newspaper, the Atlanta *Inquirer,* as reporter and feature writer. At the same time, he developed new techniques for integrating Atlanta's lunch counters. Tactically, Bond introduced the waterproof placard and two-way radio communication which enabled headquarters to check the picket lines. Strategically, he perfected the technique of the "hit-and-run sit-in." According to Bond, "We'd sit there until they either looked like they were going to arrest us and then we'd leave—or we'd sit there until they'd refuse to arrest us and simply close down the place."

After attacking the public lunch counters, COHAR

turned its fire on the big department stores. Rich's was the prime target. It is the largest store in the Southeast—what Nieman-Marcus is to Dallas or Macy's and Gimbel's to New York. "If you want anything at all," says Bond, "you can get it at Rich's." He was quite certain that since Rich's was *the* department store, all the others would have to integrate if Rich's did. So Bond's group met Mr. Rich secretly in the office of the Chief of Police in Atlanta and stated their case. "I can't afford to do it," he told the students. "My competitors would crucify me." Then he added something which really irritated Bond. He said, "I'm Jewish; I know what discrimination is and I sympathize with you, but I can't do it." Tempers flared, accusations flowed. Finally, Rich exclaimed, "I don't care if another Negro ever comes in my store—I don't need your business and I don't want it." Bond was incredulous.

Rich's, for all its faults on segregation, was the one store in Atlanta where the clerks were courteous to blacks—they would call you Mister or Mrs. It was the one store in Atlanta where you could return anything—if your wife bought a dress and wore it to a dance, she could take it back in the morning and get her money back. But if this was to be Mr. Rich's attitude, they would stop Negroes from coming into his store.

"First, we started a campaign to have people turn in their Rich's credit cards, but this was an utter failure. Then we tried another tack. We set up a picket line around all of downtown Atlanta with particular concentration on Rich's. After a time, we could see the result of our work in the declining figures of the department store index for the southeastern region, published by the Federal Reserve Bank. Each time they fell, we would cheer. We also serialized a pamphlet, written for the Nashville Council on Human Relations about how sit-ins had succeeded there. The weekly run of 20,000 to 30,000 copies was passed out Sunday mornings at church. It all helped."

After about eighteen months of this, the stores gave in, the Atlanta lunch counters were integrated and Bond and company moved on to other things.

The "other things" were slowly gestating. SNCC, gathering momentum, had absorbed COHAR, with its $6000 bankroll and 4000 membership list. Forman needed a publicity spokesman. Instinctively he turned to Bond, who was by then managing editor of the *Inquirer*. Even though Bond only helped in his spare time, this new effort was the straw that finally broke his connection to Morehouse. Barely months from a diploma, he stopped going to school, withdrew, and signed on full-time with SNCC at $40 a month. "There was a time," his mother recalled later, "when we tried very hard to send him back to school," and his father once loaned him money, on the stipulation that he return to Morehouse, but Julian promptly filed the contract in a convenient limbo.[4]

As Communications Director of SNCC, Bond faced two major problems that sprouted from tiny seeds. One was SNCC's continuing quarrel with the SCLC of Martin Luther King. What Bond found upsetting was the fact that SCLC had acted as midwife at the birth of SNCC. But the child was not prepared to accept the role of being seen and not heard; he was now more aggressive than his godparent. As Bond likes to point out, recalling SNCC's early days, "SNCC was the pioneer, the thrust. We went to Mississippi before anybody did. We went to Selma a year and a half before Dr. King came there, and formed the base that grew to be the Selma movement. So there was the inevitable clash. We went in, did the spadework; SCLC came in and got the gravy. All civil rights groups, SNCC included, raised money on the basis of their accomplishments and when SCLC stole our accomplishments, we couldn't raise any money. Bad feelings developed between the two organizations, not between King and us, but between the mechanics who ran the two organizations."

SNCC workers, Bond among them, referred to King as "de Lawd," yet their respect for him ran deep. There came the day after King had broken the racial barrier at the old Albert Hotel in Selma (a landmark built with slave labor, since torn down) that Bond dropped by to visit the older man. As he recalls it, "I walked into King's room and he was smoking a cigarette. I was literally scandalized. I couldn't have been more surprised if I had seen him taking dope, you know, or lying on the floor drunk—just to see him lift a cigarette to his mouth. I said to myself, 'My God, Dr. King, what are you doing?' I wanted to leap up and grab it from his lips, even though I smoked at the time. I don't know why I had that reaction."

"Could it be," I asked Bond, "that you were close to his philosophy, what he was trying to do?"

"Oh, yes—very much so," he replied.

"You don't agree quite so much now?"

"No, not now, I don't, but that's all hindsight."

The second difficulty SNCC encountered arose, strangely enough, from its magnetism for Northern white students. Struck by the injustice of the South's Jim Crow laws, the courage and endurance black youths displayed in opposing these discriminatory practices, they streamed south in droves. Intelligent, idealistic, filled with a burning fervor to overcome racial prejudice, they literally overwhelmed the black cadre who were already on the job. Bond puts it this way: "I mean, you'd see a Negro girl just learning how to type who grew up in Greenwood, Mississippi, went to high school there, is just learning how to type on the office typewriter and some chick from Vassar says, 'Let me do that. I can do it faster.' And she does it, and so this girl says, 'Well, hell, I'll never learn how to type if this chick is going to come down here huntin' and peckin' and by the end of the summer, she'll whip back up to Vassar and I'll *still* be here, huntin' and peckin'.'" There was also the white syndrome (white on black) that irritated black SNCC workers. The re-

quest to register at the polls brought different reactions
from elderly blacks, depending upon the color of the solici-
tor's skin. "You get a young white kid," Bond observed, "to
come up and say, 'Mister Smith, we want you to go register,' and he'd say, 'Oh, yessuh, captain, yes, suh, be right
down there,' something they would not do for the blacks. It
became people doing the right thing for the wrong reason
all over again." Moreover, there was the lurking fear of
white retaliation against any black who worked with white
"outsiders." All this reacted adversely on relationships that
were entered into originally with the best of intentions.

Throughout these perilous days of the early sixties, Bond
was closely tied to SNCC headquarters in Atlanta. Little
wonder that he told John Neary of *Life* that "I felt like a
whore, or a pimp—feeding those tapes to radio stations,
handouts to reporters, tearing around the South" on fast-
moving expeditions.[5] "SNCC had twenty projects in Mississippi and I'd hit them all in the course of a week and then
go into Arkansas, Louisiana, Tennessee and Georgia." Although he never was assaulted or tossed in jail, he did survive some harrowing episodes, as on the day he drove with
Bob Moses and two other SNCC field secretaries to visit a
longtime leader of the NAACP in Mississippi, E. H. Steptoe.
At that time, NAACP was so unpopular that Steptoe would
buy fifty one-year memberships from national headquarters
and sell them to blacks, who would immediately destroy
them so as not to be incriminated if stopped by the police.
As Bond recalls the incident, "We drove late into the night
and finally pulled up in his front yard. Moses told us to stay
in the car, but we had been driving from Jackson for six
hours and I wanted to stretch. So I got out and came up on
the front porch, walking right behind Bob. He knocked on
the door and you could hear Steptoe say, 'Who is it?' And
he said, 'It's Bob Moses,' and Steptoe said, 'Who's with you?'
And Moses, thinking we were back in the car, said, 'No one

is with us.' And Steptoe opened the door and immediately thrust a shotgun out which stopped about two inches from my face." Fortunately for Bond, he didn't pull the trigger and Moses quickly explained. What had happened was that Steptoe thought Moses was being commandeered by someone who had a gun in his back and was trying to gain entrance to Steptoe's house. Steptoe was ready to shoot it out.

On another occasion, he was in Gasden, Alabama, with his wife, Alice, during a particularly trying period of lunch-counter demonstrations. Marlon Brando and Paul Newman, the Hollywood actors, had flown in to convert local businessmen to the virtues of integration. SNCC personnel wanted to see what would happen, but they were late and the two stars had gone. A disappointed Bond placated his wife by suggesting they go to a restaurant for a late snack. About eleven o'clock, he had had enough. He knew he had to drive back to Atlanta the following morning. Taking Alice and Mrs. James Forman, who was a member of the party, he drove off in Forman's car. In minutes, Bond recalls, "we were in a black neighborhood locked between a police car and a car with four white men in white shirts, no neckties, all with automatic rifles. After pulling us over to the side of the road, they came up to me and asked, 'What's your name?' And I told him. 'Let's see the registration of your car.' I turned to Forman's wife, and she gave it to him. The man turned out to be an officer in the Alabama Bureau of Investigation, the state's equivalent of the FBI. He discovered Mrs. Forman's name on the registration of the car, and said, 'Where's Jim?'

"She feigned ignorance and said, 'I don't know where he is.' And he said, 'Let's see—he was in Newark, New Jersey, last night, he was some place in Connecticut the night before, and somewhere else three days ago.'

"So we were very much taken aback and engaged him in a long conversation about integration and segregation, with neither side conceding a point; finally, they simply drove away and left us there, all the while holding their automatic rifles at the ready.

"The next day our plans unexpectedly changed and we decided to spend the night in Gasden instead of returning to Atlanta. Quite by accident, I ran into a man who accosted me, 'Didn't I see you at the corner of such and such street last night?' he asked. 'You know we had fifty men in the bushes around you. If they had tried to take you away, we would have killed every single one of them.'"

Still another time, Bond had gone to Greenwood, Mississippi, SNCC headquarters in the Delta, "really a bad, bad little town," to use his words. He arrived just after a fire had gutted the office, forcing SNCC's removal to a one-room facility. Bond spotted a sofa and stretched out. In the middle of the night he remembers opening his eyes. "Here is this fellow, black guy, guarding me, literally with a Thompson submachine gun, the only one I've ever seen in my life, the old kind with the stock and handle in front. I said to him, low-key, 'Pardon me, what are you doing?'

" 'I'm protecting you,' he answered. This was an era when people in SNCC didn't believe in guns, carrying weapons, in self-defense for that matter, but I was not about to argue philosophically.

" 'Thank you very much. Where did you get that weapon?' I asked.

" 'Oh, I just got it from someplace.' And I went back to sleep. When I awoke in the morning, he had vanished."

Students of the black movement have often concluded that it vaulted the great watershed in the summer of 1965 with the burning of Watts. Up to that point, the civil rights program was crowned with one success after another, culminating in the passage of the Voting Rights Act of 1965, still considered the Magna Charta for Southern blacks. After Watts, as the battle turned to the Northern metropolitan centers, civil rights took on an empty ring in the black ghettos because the masses were unable to get better jobs, better education, or better housing as a result of congressional action. Dr. King, the overpowering personality, even heard himself booed when he toured Watts, only weeks after his greatest achievement—the Selma March.

But, for SNCC, the watershed was earlier. It was raised during the Democratic national convention in the summer of 1964. Until then, whatever their differences, black and white had cooperated in the South and black activists worked alongside white liberals. But that year Mississippi was torn between the regular Democratic Party and the Freedom Democratic Party for control of the delegates to the national convention. FDP said the regulars were illegally elected because blacks were excluded from the primary election. In Atlantic City, the point was pressed home on an embarrassed party that had stood for racial equality. Principle gave way under pressure from the White House with Lyndon Johnson snapping the whip; white delegates one by one gave in. At the end, in a feeble offer to assuage the disillusionment, FDP was offered a compromise: they could have two of the delegate seats reserved for Mississippi. To young black activists who had worked night and day, often at the peril of their lives, this was too much. When they saw erstwhile friends succumb to political pressure, they walked out, said to hell with the whites, and turned into black militants.

While Bond never went as far as Stokely Carmichael or Rap Brown, future heads of SNCC, in advocating war on the whites, he began to wonder where SNCC was taking him. Trouble, perhaps prison, awaited those militants who went on to violence. He had to think of his wife, their two children, and the third one who was on the way. His mind drifted back to the days at Lincoln University and the value of parental stability. "It was not a matter of becoming disenchanted with civil rights," he recalled, "but of giving the children some of the advantages I had as a child." He pondered whether leaving the movement to take a better-paying job in public relations would be the best solution.

But while he was weighing the option of working in or outside the system, the Georgia Legislature reapportioned the state, in compliance with the Supreme Court's one man–one vote decision. Bond found himself suddenly tantalized by the possibility of running for office. "I thought, hell, why not? It would bring SNCC into town. And, besides, it would really be an experience." [6] And, of course, it would be laboring inside the system.

SNCC officials were not so positive. Some liked the idea, some didn't. A minority argued that Bond would have to compromise, that politics was the art of compromise. They were as skeptical of the system as Carmichael and Brown had been. Furthermore, how could anyone as radical as a SNCC worker be elected? What they overlooked was the insider; in Alabama, where Carmichael and Brown challenged the system, they were the outsiders—Carmichael from New York City and Brown from Baton Rouge. As Bond put it, "Atlanta was my home, my neighbors were my real neighbors." Thus a political career, in the standard meaning, was a reality to the one, only a mirage to the others.

Bond got his way. Black Atlantans walking down Hunter Avenue in the spring of 1965 were surprised to see that wigmakers and seamstresses in Pearl's House of Bazaar had been moved to the back room to make way for the Julian Bond Campaign Headquarters. On the tables facing the windows, piles of pamphlets and campaign posters awaited distribution to the 30,000 people in the 136th House District of whom 90 per cent were black. SNCC workers buzzed up and down the streets leaving them at the poverty-stricken homes. Bond's campaign promises were low-key. He confined himself to local issues like unemployment and housing. He would introduce a minimum-wage bill for domestic workers, he vowed. It didn't seem to matter that he was only twenty-five. On June 16, voters flocked to the polls and gave him a resounding 82 per cent of the ballots.

Being a representative-elect to the Georgia legislature was a novel experience. Bond well remembered an incident four years before, when he and Benjamin D. Brown, executive secretary of the Atlanta branch of NAACP, had unsuccessfully tried to integrate the House gallery in the capitol. They had barely taken their seats before the Speaker spotted them in the segregated white section. "Mr. Doorkeeper, get those niggers out of the white section of the gallery," [7] he had bellowed. Now Bond and Brown were going back, this time as elected members, Brown also having won in another district.

The mood had changed—or so it seemed. Blacks had taken their seats in the Georgia Legislature and no one for a moment dreamed that Bond might have difficulty. What happened during the first week of January 1966 came as a thunderclap. It followed the murder of Sammy Younge, a veteran SNCC worker, who was gunned down from behind for daring to enter a white toilet in Tuskegee, Alabama. Prior to the assassination, SNCC was planning to issue a statement on the Vietnam war, castigating U.S. involvement, but the text was for some unexplained reason held up until Younge's death brought the issue to a head. Then similarity between murder abroad and murder at home prompted an emotional polemic. "We believe the United States government," the statement read, "has been deceptive in its claim of concern for the freedom of the Vietnamese people, just as the government has been deceptive in claiming concern for the freedom of colored people in such other countries as the Dominican Republic, the Congo, South Africa and in the United States itself." The murder of a Southern civil rights worker "is no different from the murder of peasants in Vietnam. We take note of the fact that 60 per cent of the draftees from this country are Negroes called on to stifle the liberation of Vietnam, to preserve a 'democracy' which does not exist for them at home. We maintain that our country's cry of 'preserve freedom in the world' is a hypocritical mask behind which it squashes liberation movements. We are in sympathy with, and support the men in this country who are unwilling to respond to a military draft which would compel them to contribute their lives to United States aggression in Vietnam in the name of the 'freedom' we find so false in this country."

Did Bond stand behind the statement? A radio reporter, sensing his vulnerability, moved in to find out. The query was unfair because Bond had had nothing to do with the writing. But his innate loyalty to the organization firmly closed all exit doors. "I concur fully," he answered, and added, "I would not burn my own draft card, but I admire the courage of those who do." With this, the roof fell in.

Lead-off man in Georgia's officialdom was Lieutenant Governor Peter Zack Geer, who said, "There is no way that Bond can take the oath of office as a member of the House to honestly uphold the Constitution of the United States and the State of Georgia in view of his endorsement of SNCC's subversive policy statement." His solution: bar Bond from being seated.

Representative Jones Lane of Statesboro, the man who had invited Governor George C. Wallace of Alabama to speak to the Georgia legislature during the previous year, offered to spearhead the fight against Bond. Others joined in, but the stoutest opposition surprisingly came from the Atlanta press. The liberal Atlanta *Constitution,* piloted by the renowned Ralph McGill, crawled all over SNCC, saying its position on Vietnam was akin to racism and anarchy. Editorially, it maintained the SNCC statement went "far beyond dissent and doubt about policy." After printing scare headlines to alarm the public, the *Constitution* had second thoughts and, three days following the initial blast, printed the full statement. The paper wrote that Bond had actually said "I wouldn't burn my [draft] card, but I understand why people burn theirs, and I admire their courage *because I think they do it with full knowledge of what the penalty is*." McGill's part in the onslaught shook Bond. Up to this point, McGill had been *the* Southern liberal, but as Bond saw it now, "times had passed him by. His liberalism had brought him to a certain point and the thrust of the movement passed that point. Afterwards, he began to be less of a liberal."

But Bond had no time for philosophical reflections; the tide of dissent, like a huge wave, was carrying him along. Friendly forces tried hard to divert the pressure. The seven Negro legislators who had won office in the special June election begged him to countermand the SNCC statement. "It was every other Negro in the delegation against Julian," his campaign manager Ivanhoe Donaldson said, reporting the futile effort. The next morning, January 10, 1966, the twenty-five-year-old legislator walked into the capitol to find five petitions in the hands of the House Clerk, all demanding he be refused his seat for committing "treason" and giving "aid and comfort to the enemies of the United States and the enemies of Georgia." Typically, Representative Arthur J. Funk of Savannah fumed, "I don't care if he's innocent of making these remarks. All those people tend to think that way, and every day he's on this floor is a disgrace." [8] When 204 other legislators stood to take the oath of office, the Clerk remanded Bond to his seat. He stalked out to await the verdict of the special committee hastily called to consider his case. The threat of what might happen seemed infinitely more serious to bearded black supporters roaming the corridors in their fatigue jackets and blue jeans than it did to Bond. He strolled into a room off the corridor, curled up, and went to sleep on a Formica-topped table. In between he told newsmen, "The fact of my election to public office does not lessen my duty or my desire to express my opinions, even when they differ from

those held by others." Only once did he rankle—when a reporter inquired whether he was a Communist. "I tell you
now that I never intend to answer that question again," he
cried. "I will take the oath [to support the United States
and Georgia constitutions] but I am putting you on notice
now that I am not going to answer that question again." [9]

By afternoon, the twenty-six member House committee
was prepared to interrogate Bond. The atmosphere was
reminiscent of a medieval confrontation between lord and
serf. "Do you admire the courage of persons who burn their
draft cards?" special prosecutor Denmark Groover, a former
legislator, began, hoping to nettle Bond. Calmly he answered before a hushed house: "I admire people who take
an action, and I admire people who feel strongly enough
about their convictions to take an action like that knowing
the consequences they will face." On the other hand, he assured members of the committee, he had not burned his
draft card and "had never suggested or counseled or advocated that anyone burn his draft card." Somehow Groover
had obtained a tape recording of Bond's original interview
on the SNCC statement and proceeded to play it over the
House's loudspeaker system: "I don't believe in that war [in
Vietnam]. I'm against all war. I'm against that war in particular and I don't think people ought to participate in it.
Because I'm against war, I'm against the draft. . . ." [10]

That was precisely what the House committee needed to
hear. Their hearts were in their lapels in the shape of tiny
tin American flags, worn for the occasion. They barely listened when Howard Moore, Bond's personal attorney and
brother-in-law, took issue with Grover. It was not a matter
of patriotism. His client was a supporter of the U.S. and
Georgia constitutions. All that was involved was his right to
dissent. Charles Morgan, Jr., Southern director for the American Civil Liberties Union, carried the argument further by
pointing out this was a case of the kettle calling the pot
black. Had not the Georgia legislature itself resorted to mas-

sive resistance in defiance of the decision of the U.S. Supreme Court banning segregation in the public schools? Was it possible to say Bond had betrayed his country when the legislature was equally guilty? The committee sat impassively, refusing to be moved by appeals from the Reverend Howard Creecy, Bond's defeated opponent in the Democratic primary, or Malcolm Dean, his defeated Republican adversary. Since Bond had refused to capitulate to white Georgia supremacy, and instead had flouted their antagonism, they would be adamant too. It took only minutes for the Committee to reach its decision. By a vote of 23-3, the recommendation was to refuse Bond a seat. He had been judged by a kangaroo court, not a court of law, by men anxious to lynch reason. Watching the spectacle and peering down from the gallery at her husband, alone behind the podium and scorched by the gaze of unfriendly eyes, Alice Bond, Julian's wife, had difficulty not to scream. But nothing would stop the House majority—or Bond—now, although "it was the worst thing he'd ever been through." No sooner had the full House voted 184-12 to exclude him on a charge of "disorderly conduct" than he promptly announced he would be a candidate in the next election to fill the vacancy.

Reaction to the expulsion was swift. *The New York Times* (January 12, 1966) called Bond "a misguided young man" for "encouraging draft-card burners and others who seek to avoid service in Vietnam," but said this should not serve "as a bar to his right to public office." Showing greater sensitivity, the *Christian Century* on January 26 reminded its readers that "much tea was spilled and much blood to secure the Americans the right to be represented by the man they elected." With measured asperity, the editorial went on to ask the Georgia legislators, "Why then do they refuse to seat in their house a man who now practices dissent which their forefathers took to the point of secession? Have Georgia legislators suddenly become federalists? Hardly. They don't like this Negro; they don't like SNCC; they don't like suggestions that the State Department and the Pentagon may not be omniscient. So they smite Bond, who combines all of their dislikes in one person." Others were simply furious over what had happened. In Washington, a group of twenty-three U.S. Representatives wired Georgia's Governor Carl E. Sanders, expressing opposition to the legislature's action. "We strongly protest the denial to Julian Bond of his seat in the Georgia House on the basis of the unpopularity of his political views on one of the great issues confronting our nation," they said.[11] In Atlanta, Martin Luther King joined the fight in support of Bond after flying home from Los Angeles. A resident of Bond's 136th District, King charged the House members with racism for voting to oust Bond and promised demonstrations to fight the decision. In answer to the appeal, a noisy crowd numbering hundreds of community leaders and civil rights workers gathered in Mount Moriah Baptist Church to praise the name of Julian Bond. "Julian Bond is a man," shouted Mrs. Dorothy Bolden, a leader from financially pinched Vine City. "We don't have many men in Georgia," and Bond is a Negro leader, not a "leading Negro, selected by the city fathers downtown." [12]

But while editorials and telegrams and words were used to influence public opinion, the only sure recourse for Bond was to take an appeal to the courts. This was the sole action the Georgia legislature would seriously consider. Consequently, as soon as the hearing was concluded, Bond's attorneys went to work. Three days following the House action, they filed suit in Atlanta's Federal District Court, charging the House with violation of the right of free speech, guaranteed by the First Amendment. "If there was ever a more blatant violation of the First Amendment, we have not located it," said the lawyers. "Had a member of the Ku Klux Klan or the John Birch Society or the White Citizens Council spoken against Federal policy, he would have been cheered." The complaint also declared that Mr. Bond's rights under the Fifth and Sixth amendments had been denied, since he was not indicted by a grand jury or tried by an impartial jury. Finally, because Bond was black, the suit charged violation of the equal protection clauses of the Thirteenth, Fourteenth, and Fifteenth amendments. Dr. King signed on as one of the plaintiffs.

Although there was some question as to the jurisdiction of the court in matters affecting the legislature because of the constitutional separation of powers, the District Court agreed to hear the dispute and named a three-judge panel that included Chief Judge Elbert P. Tuttle of the United States Court of Appeals in the Fifth Circuit, Appeals Judge Griffin B. Bell, and District Judge Lewis R. Morgan. The justices brushed aside the alleged violations of the Fifth and Sixth amendments and found no evidence to support the contention that Bond suffered because he was a Negro.

But they did carefully explore the charge of unfair limitation on the right of free speech. "A central question [said Justice Tuttle] is whether Mr. Bond's denunciation of the nation's involvement in Vietnam is 'a protected area of free speech' under the First Amendment to the Constitution." When the trio finally reported their findings on February 10, they upheld in a split decision the right of the Georgia legislature to exclude Bond. The majority view, supported by Bell and Morgan, was that Bond could not approve the SNCC war statement and still take the oath to support the U.S. and Georgia constitutions. "Mr. Bond's right to speak and to dissent as a private citizen," they said, "is subject to the limitation that he sought to assume membership in the House." This contention was spiritedly denied by Tuttle, who wrote in a dissenting opinion that the legislature had exceeded its constitutional powers. The Georgia charter specifically lists the reasons for disbarment as being under twenty-one years old, a non-resident, having a criminal record. To go beyond that, to bar him under "undefined, un-

known and even constitutionally questionable standards,"
declared Tuttle, "shocks not only the judicial, but also the
lay sense of justice." And this, he added, did not go to the
heart of the free speech issue and the "grave" question of
whether Bond's rights had been violated under the First
Amendment.

Reaction in the Bond camp was to promise an "immediate" appeal to the U.S. Supreme Court. But this time Bond
decided to replace the American Civil Liberties Union as
chief counsel. In its place he selected Leonard B. Boudin, of
New York City, a person well known for representing
clients whose radical views had brought the federal government running. Boudin and his partner Victor Rabinowitz
had appeared in behalf of more people before the McCarthy Investigations Committee than anyone else—reason
enough, Bond thought, to select them for this assignment.
Within four weeks briefs were in Washington contending
that Bond had been barred "solely because of his public
statements on issues of national concern. This is the first
case before the Court in which a legislative body has refused to seat an elected representative because of his public
expression of opinion." [13] This was the crux of the issue, not
whether the special legislative committee which heard his
case was an adequate substitute for a court of law (for, after
all, legislatures are empowered to regulate their own functions) and not the fact he was barred for being black (for
other Georgians sitting in the House were Negro). The district judges had understood this, had thrown out the charge
of discrimination when attorneys for the ACLU had been
unable to produce satisfactory evidence. On the real
question—the question of free speech—the majority had
skittered, resting its case on the fact that Bond could not be
a political dichotomy, that if he tried, his oath to support
the federal and state constitutions was worthless. It was
now for the highest court to decide.

The first clue to the court's attitude came in early November when Arthur K. Bolton, Georgia's attorney general, presented the state's position. Bond, he said, was "eager and anxious to encourage people not to participate in [military service] for any reason that they chose," and, therefore, could not conscientiously take the oath to support the federal constitution. Up went the eyebrows of Supreme Court Justice William J. Brennan. "Is that all you rely on?" he snapped. This "comes perilously close to saying that a person is unqualified to sit if he opposed the war in Vietnam," Justice Abe Fortas added.

On December 5, the Court unanimously ruled that the Georgia legislature had erred in denying Bond a seat. Chief Justice Earl Warren wrote the historic opinion which for the first time in American history restricted the authority of a state legislature to judge the qualifications of its membership. The First Amendment, he said, "requires that legislators be given the widest latitude to express their views on issues of policy. Legislators have an obligation to take positions on controversial political questions so that their constituents can be fully informed by them and be better able to assess their qualifications for office." Referring to the specific question of the oath requirement, the Chief Justice wrote that it did "not authorize a majority of state legislators to test the sincerity with which another duly elected legislator can swear to uphold the constitution. Certainly there can be no question but that the First Amendment protects expression in opposition to national foreign policy in Vietnam."

As *Newsweek* magazine pointed out to its readers, the "unhappy political life of Julian Bond had begun to look like an exercise in how to try without really succeeding," but now with the Supreme Court turning things around, Bond's future had a brighter hue. The Bonds, to be sure, had always leaned heavily on the High Court to solve their problems. As a member of the Board of Trustees of Berea College, Julian's grandfather had unsuccessfully sought in 1908 to put an end to segregated education in Kentucky. In 1954, Bond's father had helped prepare the brief for *Brown vs. the Board of Education of Topeka,* which struck down the "separate but equal" provision of *Plessy vs. Ferguson* that permitted the South to operate a *de jure* segregated public school system. And now young Julian had seen the same Court deliver him from a personal dilemma. After the initial refusal of the Georgia House to seat him, he had run a second time in the special election of February 23. No one sought to challenge him and he had received 682 votes of 695 cast. The House had previously considered what the outcome would be and before adjournment had authorized its Rules Committee to pass on Bond's qualifications before permitting him to take the oath of office.

The axe fell three months to the day after election, when the committee unanimously rejected him a second time. Thereupon Bond announced that he would run for the House a third time in the September primary and, if successful, in the November election. Although Bond was fast becoming a national personality, by now a change in the political climate was emerging. Through the public media he was also becoming the victim of adverse public opinion in his own district. An older, more conservative group of blacks disliked what Bond had to say on Vietnam and the juxtaposition of civil rights and the war, as advocated by SNCC. They especially disliked SNCC's increasing resort to violence. In January, after Martin Luther King had led a demonstration of a thousand people to the steps of the capitol to protest Bond's exclusion from the House, the peaceful gathering later deteriorated into a riot between SNCC workers and the state police. The provocation was resented, although King and Bond had both already left. In the aftermath, Dr. Samuel W. Williams, president of the Atlanta chapter of the NAACP, spoke what was in the minds of many of Bond's elder constituency. "The civil rights issue in this country is not identical with the Vietnam issue," he said. "I think it is important for us to keep the two separated." [14]

Further resentment of SNCC arose from its conversion to the concept of "black power," promoted by Stokely Carmichael, SNCC's new head. Only weeks after taking office, Carmichael had joined the Mississippi march of James Meredith, first Negro to collect a diploma at Ole Miss, and then had raised a national furor by shouting "black power" in every hamlet along the route from Memphis to Jackson, Mississippi. To Bond's embarrassment, Carmichael chose Atlanta to fan the racial flames and appeared there just seven days before the primary. Within hours he was jailed, charged with two misdemeanors: inciting to riot and disorderly conduct.

For anyone as closely allied to SNCC as Julian Bond, this latest episode posed a serious election threat. It was well known that antagonism between the organization and its public relations director had been rising for some time. It was the SNCC stand on the Vietnam war that had triggered his first exclusion and now, because he was running on the Democratic ticket and not on a third-party "black power" platform, they had begged off riding his bandwagon. Bond could envision his strength ebbing if he continued to support SNCC while they held out. There was only one thing to do. He handed in his resignation—as it turned out, none too soon. In the election he defeated Malcolm Dean, dean of students at Atlanta University, his previous opponent, but by only fifty votes where a year before the margin had been 1819. The rest was comparatively easy. In November, he carried the 136th District by more than two to one; in December, the Court upheld his right to be seated. There were some grumblings from members of the House, but they meant little. "Certainly, I will abide by the final decision of the Court," said Republican Jones Lane, the man who marshaled the opposition originally. A second antagonist rounded up support for the "silent treatment," but that didn't upset Bond. All he wanted was the $2000 in back pay the state of Georgia owed him and the right to take his seat with the other members.

The actual swearing-in ceremony scarcely caused a ripple. The House was so embroiled in deciding the gubernatorial contest between Lester G. Maddox, of Pickwick chicken-restaurant fame, and Republican Howard H. Callaway, a wealthy conservative, that it had time for little else. Callaway had won a paper-thin victory over Maddox, and under Georgia's constitution the House had to make the final decision. Since Maddox was a Democrat, as were most of the House members, his victory was not unexpected. The only unpleasantness arose when Republican James H. Floyd walked out rather than witness Bond take the oath.

For the first few weeks Bond remained silent. He was surprised to be appointed to three of the House's choice committees—Insurance, Education, and State Institutions and Properties. The latter two were financial plums in that out of session they paid a per diem of $25 on top of the legislator's base salary. Despite this, there was the ever-present threat of animosity his name might engender. With some trepidation he put in a resolution, along with seven other Negroes, asking recognition for National Negro History Week. He wanted to discover if his name would kill the joint effort. When the vote in favor of the resolution was unanimous, he knew he had passed the initial test. "I sort of expected him to try to stir things up by introducing Vietnam and civil rights legislation," a white supremacist declared, "but he's off to a good start. He's listening, but he isn't saying much."

Bond was surprised to find out what lengths certain white members would go to not to speak to him directly. His seat was next to Ben Brown, his longtime NAACP friend, who "got along well with everyone." Whites would approach him and say, "Ben, how is Julian?" with Bond only one foot away. Brown would look at Bond and look back at them,

"Well, he's fine, I guess." And then, they'd look at Brown and sort of wink and say, "Well, you tell him to keep out of trouble," as though Bond literally weren't there.

Among the whites who did talk with Bond were some who wanted to know more about the SNCC situation. Surreptitiously they would ask Bond, "What was it you said back then that made me vote to throw you out of the Legislature? I never did understand it. Do you have a copy of the statement?" So Bond would dig up a statement and wait for the reaction. "Well, oh," he'd reply, "is that all it was? I'm awfully sorry." At this, Bond would gasp in amazement. "My Lord," he breathed to himself, "I spent a couple of thousand dollars, missed one whole year from the Legislature, and this guy didn't even know what it was I was talking about."

In common with other state legislatures, the Georgia House was noted for its conservatism and flowery language. It took some time for Bond to get used to both. As a former SNCC operator with liberal tendencies, he was ill prepared for a body in which, said ACLU attorney Morgan, "Hitler would be a middle-of-the-roader." [15] The House oratory defining these views was awesome. Of his initial recollections, Bond remembers how the "members were able to bring tears to their eyes in an instant and conjure up visions of their elderly grandmothers being forced into the street if some horrible piece of legislation was passed." Such rustic corn, delivered with all seriousness, is one reason why Julian Bond, a speaker of national celebrity, has never delivered a speech on the floor of the Georgia House. He would not try to emulate their standards. Besides, he offers as explanation "I've never really felt that I had anything that earth-shattering to say. If it were an issue I am sincerely interested in, I'm not sure whether or not I would hurt it or help it. My position is such that if I got up and spoke in favor of something, I don't really know, but I think a great many people would vote against it, just as a matter of course." Humorously he adds: "Now, I've thought about the strategy of speaking against things that I really am for, but I don't think they would fall for that. They're not stupid by any means."

This curious pragmatism of Bond's has enabled him to take an objective view of presumably his worst enemy in the capitol—Lester Maddox. Maddox stands for everything Bond abhors—white supremacy, separation of the races, segregated schools. Yet Bond sees in him something else, the creature of Southern poverty. "He knows what it means to be poor, and he has a lot of sympathy for poor people. He doesn't care if the poor people are black or white, but if he thinks he can do something for poor people, he'll try to do it." One day Bond went to Maddox's office to ask why there were no Negroes on any draft boards in the state of Georgia except in Atlanta, and the Governor without a second's hesitation replied, "Y'all fight in the Army, don't you? You ought to be on the draft boards." "He did it just like that," Bond recalls, "he didn't have to study it or anything. He saw that some things are right and some things are wrong." [16]

In the legislature, Bond serves both as state representative and district alderman under a system that is indigenous to Atlanta. At the state level, his strength is severely limited by the arithmetic of having nine black representatives among 204. Yet, Bond is happy to say that he is one of six blacks on the eighteen-member Education Committee, not enough to block the segregationist majority on school issues, but far more than the black strength warrants. In a hot dispute, black unanimity could be decisive. Bond is also one of seven blacks on the twenty-four-member Fulton County Committee (Atlanta and some suburbs) that must approve local legislation by a two-thirds vote. Since Atlanta is 43 per cent black and white legislators depend upon black votes to remain in office, the strength of the black bloc is substantial. If two whites should desert the majority on an issue of black import and the black bloc holds firm, the minority is in a position to blue-pencil any white proposal, something whites have not previously faced.

But Bond's day-to-day usefulness as a Georgia representative has additional meaning. In a true sense, he is the real district alderman. "The thing to remember," he says, "is that in Atlanta the aldermen come from city wards, but are elected citywide, so although an alderman lives next door, he doesn't represent the people in the neighborhood alone, he represents the people in a city of one million, while I come from a district with only 30,000 people in it. Consequently, people in my district feel much closer to me than to their aldermen and I am called upon to perform such aldermanic duties as obtaining a street light, a sidewalk, monitoring garbage pickups and checking on police protection." In this connection, he reported to Reese Cleghorn of the Atlanta *Journal,* "Almost every call I get is related to city and county affairs. I never get any of my constituents asking me about the sales tax, or teachers' salaries. What really bothers me is that a lot of people my age say, 'Well, aren't you just placating people by paving their streets and picking up their garbage and putting in new street signals?' and so on. And I always say no, because I think it's insulting that some people would think that somebody in my district is placated and made satisfied by his condition in a basically segregated society simply because a street is paved. I think what it does is maybe the opposite. It gives him more time to think about his over-all problem if he doesn't have to wipe the mud off his feet when he comes home. . . . Politics is getting ordinary things. That's the way you help people. That's what government does."

Bond likes to mix with people in his district, listen to their problems, answer questions. "The one advantage," he says, of having a House with 204 members is that the districts are small. I can walk across mine in an afternoon and see a couple of hundred people as well." To cement his district relationship, Bond sends out a monthly newsletter to about five hundred constituents. In some he jokes, as when he wrote: "I asked Governor Maddox to kill this bill and he did. It was one of the few nice things he has done since he became Governor." In others he is serious. "We will never have an end to poverty until we have an end to war," he commented in referring to a proposed $70-billion national-defense budget.[17]

Bond's salary as a Georgia legislator ($5200 a year) is augmented by the fees he receives as a speaker. For approximately five months a year he travels, appearing two and three times a day at colleges and universities and various other forums where the payments range from $750 to $1000. They are booked tours ("from which," he says, "my agent takes an enormous amount—much to my chagrin"). It is hard, grinding work, but it has its laughs too. "The first thing I hear when a person greets me is 'How was your trip?' Now, unless the plane crashed, I think the trip was a success. The second question is 'Do I have a bag?' If I get off the plane in Boise, Idaho, I wonder if he believes I would come all the way to Boise without a bag. Now I'll tell you something else which does happen on occasion. I like to wear three-piece suits and I've been wearing them since I was in high school and although I have blue jeans, slacks, sport shirts and everything else, I like three-piece suits. I always have and I always will—I think it is the most perfect outfit ever made for man. I was making a speech at one of the city colleges in New York City one day, dressed in one of my three-piece suits, when a student with a neatly trimmed beard, rather long hair, blue jeans and sneakers, raised his hand, 'Why do you wear such funny clothes?'"

Few Americans see and talk to as many students as Julian Bond. "The first thing I've begun to realize—and I realize it more and more as I travel across the country," he says, "is the frightening similarity between students. Someone who didn't know would believe that students in South Dakota,

Illinois, California, and Mississippi were different people. But they're really not—even if they have a rural background, have lived in the city, may have lived in an all-white neighborhood or community, never met any black people, never seen real poverty—they all look at TV, they all see Huntley-Brinkley, Walter Cronkite, they all read *Time, Newsweek* or their newspapers, which carry UPI or AP reports. So there is a frightening similarity among them and a lot of the regional differences that used to exist in this country don't exist among these young people. Another thing I've noticed about these youngsters is their need for the proverbial knight in shining armor. They ask, 'Who can beat Richard Nixon?' And I think it is not asked as the standard complaint of people in the out party wanting to get in as much as it is an attempt to embody all of the hopes and dreams and aspirations into one man. 'Where is Robert Kennedy, where is Eugene McCarthy? Who is going to take their place?' And this is very dangerous because all of us have feet of clay, all of us are here today and gone tomorrow, yet I sense this yearning as an attempt to discover a rescuer who can sweep down and snatch up the hopes and dreams of all these young people and carry them off into some kind of Camelot."

Just as this fixed similarity exists among students, so there is a similarity to the issues he encounters. One of the most difficult to answer is the unending query about the Negro's future. Should he support integration or separation? Bond's reply is ambivalent. He is for integration of the public schools in the South and blames the Nixon administration for the current snail's pace. Neither the Justice Department nor the President has provided leadership, in the Bond view. Because of this, "it is no wonder that black children have reacted against integration, have come to despise it." But let there be no mistake about Southern attitudes. Despite talk that blacks want separate schools, "black people in the South want and are going to fight for integrated, quality education." Yet, politically and economically, Bond sees no hangup in black separatism. "I like to believe the black-white separation which already exists and the growing impulse for political and economic separatism that you see in black communities all over the country mean simply the beginning of a new kind of power and strength in the black community. For instance, if black people in Detroit engage in political separatism, the result is two black congressmen. If they engage in economic separatism, it means the beginning of economic stability, greater control of goods and services, the flow of capital in and out of their own community, which is vitally important in every big concentration of black people all over the United States. That kind of separatism, that kind of segregation is very healthy and enhances the possibility of eventual integration. At present, we deal with white Americans on an unequal basis for obviously we are outnumbered nine to one, we have little or no money or economic or political power so we must take advantage of our large concentrations in the cities and parts of the rural South and by making the best of that, increase our ability to join in with the rest of society." What this has done for Detroit since the riot of 1967 is to add a black bank, three car dealerships owned by blacks, and several new and large black-owned businesses, to lend substance to the Bond theme on finances.

Another favorite topic which Bond encounters on the college campus is interest in the Black Panthers. "What is to happen to them? Will their organization disintegrate?" Bond sees them currently on a suicidal course. The constant battle with the police, the jailing and exile of leadership has to take its toll. "No organization can generate and continue to thrust articulate and intelligent leadership to the top," he says. Consequently Bond suspects they will moderate their position. "You know," he goes on, "they already have moderated part of their earlier position. They began as a unit that simply policed the police. They switched from that to a

political entity which puts forth a political and economic
program for the black community. They have stopped
carrying weapons openly. A great many have stopped wearing the Panther uniform, the black jacket and black beret.
And I think they are likely to undergo that kind of moderation. I'm not attempting to suggest that they modify their
position, their political program, but I think they are likely
to become more acceptable to more black people and if they
are not exterminated, or extinguished, I think they are
going to be a permanent and viable force on the American
scene for some years to come."

But for Eldridge Cleaver, the Panthers' loudest spokesman, Bond has other words. "I have a feeling that he's losing his popularity. When Malcolm X was killed, his [Mal-
colm X's] popularity mushroomed. When Cleaver disap-
peared, his popularity diminished. It mushroomed for a
while, and now it's diminished because people are saying
that, if you're the leader of a revolution, you cannot absent
yourself from it." [18] The slightest suggestion that Bond, too,
may have left the Movement by engaging in politics stirs
old fires. He resents any implication that he has embarked
on a softer path by becoming a state legislator. "I have a
faint, faint, faint hope," he emphasizes, "that this is one of
the ways to solve your problems, but I'm really not making
much of a dent in the Legislature. If I weren't there, I don't
think it would be any better or worse; the things I do for
my constituents in my role as alderman-ombudsman someone else could do as well if not better. What does irritate me
at times is that people think that all my life I've been inclined to do what I do now. I've marched in the streets, I've
broken laws, and I've been to jail, and did all the things
which Stokely Carmichael and Rap Brown did and, in fact,
did them before they did and was with SNCC from its very
founding, so I don't like people to put me in a mould and
pose me as opposed to them, for there are a great many similarities between us." As a matter of fact, Bond claims to

identify more closely with Rap Brown than with any other individual because Brown is the one really honest person he knows "utterly without fear."

But, unlike Carmichael and Brown, Bond has had strong reservations on the use of violence to achieve ends. "If you could demonstrate to me," he has said, "that we would have a better state of affairs than exists now, and that it could succeed, then I'd be all in favor of it. But I doubt if it would work, especially right now." [19] The police, in Bond's view, hold the trump cards. They "have too many armaments, like helicopters and tanks that shoot through whole rows of buildings. The techniques learned in Vietnam are being brought back to this country, ready for use against the local insurgents." [20] What Bond suggests is a "program that calls for pressure both inside and outside the system. There are times when black people in governmental positions, state legislatures, city councils, and the U.S. Congress are rendered eunuchs" because of opposition. "So you need the pressure on the outside to make institutional society move in the proper direction." Then he adds somewhat darkly, "Now, I tend to be against violence. I am not a pacifist, as I once was or considered myself to be, but I am beginning to believe more and more that some violence may be a necessary ingredient in bringing progress to us."

A third question that constantly confronts Bond during his campus peregrinations is to find his antidote for ending white racism. As in so many areas of racial concern, his answer covers a wide field that includes public as well as private areas of society. On the one hand, he says the "government is the force to control it. If government doesn't sanction it, its manifestations will be less severe. Some predicted that when lunch counters were integrated, blood would flow in the streets. But the government said the counters would integrate. As resentful as white people were, and as much as white people dislike black people, blood didn't flow. There was no official government sanction for it." [21] On the other hand, speaking of the private sector, Bond declares, "People have to look for racism in places where they might not believe it exists. When a home or a school is built, you should look at the employment pattern among the builders, the workers, who is hired, who isn't, who is kept from getting a job, who gets one. In a hundred daily actions, you have the opportunity to see racist actions or racist acts or racist behavior and do something to strike it out. Ultimately, the individual acts of hundreds of thousands of people make the grand difference and unless hundreds of thousands of people are willing to make the individual acts, there will be no grand difference."

Interestingly, Bond takes a dim view of the part miscegenation or the white churches will play in the eventual solution of white racism. "It seems likely," he told veteran Georgia politician Roy V. Harris, "—over a period of hundreds and hundreds of thousands of years—that there may be a one-race society . . . I don't think there should be a prohibition against it . . . [but] you can solve the race problem without that kind of fusion. You can solve it by having an equitable division of power in this country. As power begins to be divided more equitably, then you're going to see a lessening of what you call the racial problem." [22] Although the white church is the presumed moral guardian of American society, Bond sees it as "pretty much a Sunday-morning institution.

"Churchmen *do* perform deeds of great bravery, but they do them over the objections of their denominations. I just cannot see the American church as a national institution taking very great strides. It seems to me to be nearly bankrupt, as far as social matters are concerned. It just doesn't have the get-up-and-go to do it, and I include the Catholic and Protestant churches, the Jewish synagogue—all of them."

When will racism end? "At least a hundred years," Bond answered early in 1970. "It's going to take some deaths and

births. Take my senator, Senator Russell, there's no remov-
ing him, there's no changing him, he's just got to go to the
great Senate in the sky and when he does, I think the situation will improve a mite. And then we might not ever eliminate racist feelings. I think it's sad, but maybe true, that as
long as there are observable differences between men, there
will be some sort of prejudice and men of darker or lighter
skins will distrust men whose skins are a different color from
theirs. The important thing is the elimination of their ability
to do anything about their distrust or their prejudice."

Up to now, the failure to eliminate white distrust and
prejudice has worked havoc on black America, Bond points
out. "It has made us the last to be hired and the first to be
fired; it has recently, as any reading of Vietnam casualty
lists will show, made us first in war if not first in the hearts
of our countrymen. It has given black children an opportunity to attend school for twelve years while receiving five
years of education. It has placed us on relief to be scored as
lazy and shiftless while 6000 white American farmers are
paid $25,000 each year not to work, and while oil million-
aires receive an automatic $27\frac{1}{2}$ per cent tax writeoff every
year. In short, we are in bad shape." [23]

To counter this, Bond demands the immediate reordering
of the nation's priorities. The Vietnam war has to be ended
at once so as to concentrate on domestic issues. "The war is
pressing," he explains; "people are dying visibly from it and
while people certainly die from domestic concerns, their
deaths are not visible, and therefore the concern is not
there. So ending the war is the first thing. Second, the political system must be reconstituted, by exchanging some of
the older leadership, the reactionaries from the South, the
conservatives from other parts of the country in both parties, and replacing them with not necessarily younger but
certainly younger-thinking people, more progressively
thinking people, a reconstitution, indeed, of all the people in
government." A big order that, but Bond actually believes it

could be a "rather simple task. If young people put the kind of energy into selected congressional campaigns in 1972 as they put in the McCarthy and Kennedy campaigns in 1968, I think it could be done rather easily."

This idea of "reconstituting the political system" has intrigued Bond for years. After election to the Georgia House but prior to taking his seat, he had joined with others to establish the National Conference for New Politics, a group of civil rights and anti-war militants. The "new politics," said the group's manifesto, should "reverse the tendency of our politics toward the monolithic conformism of 'the great consensus' and can revive the free-swinging politics of traditional American democracy." Its first convention a year later in Chicago was all the manifesto promised and more. While some white delegates looked on in awe, a black caucus (representing 10 per cent of the convention) asked and got 50 per cent of the delegates' voting strength, which assured control of the convention and acceptance of militant black demands. Free-swinging it undoubtedly was, but not in the sense of "traditional American democracy." As writer Walter Goodman noted in a piece for *The New York Times Magazine*, "Julian Bond had the good luck or good sense to leave Chicago before the first plenary session was called to order." [24] But this abortive effort to change the thrust and structure of American politics merely whetted Bond's appetite for further ventures. On his tours to college campuses, he speaks of "trying to bring an almost discredited New Left policy, participatory democracy, to the poor, so that Southern black people scattered all over the Southeast region can have a chance to have some say in their lives, in their economic and political future." He is far from certain what political vehicle should be used along the way. "The politically sophisticated black people of this region," he notes, "are beginning to wonder whether this remaking process will be done under the wings of the Democratic Party, as many had once believed. It may be the party of Hubert Humphrey, to whom they gave ninety-plus percent of their votes in 1968, but isn't it also the party of Eastland and Stennis and Wallace in Alabama, and Maddox? Isn't it the party which gives credibility and responsibility to the Russells and Talmadges, and must it always be the only one we've got?"

For the moment, however, such questions remain rhetorical. Bond works, loosely harnessed to be sure, but still he works inside the Democratic Party framework, as he did during the Chicago convention of 1968, when he abruptly rose to national stature. There was—and is—something anomalous in the fact that of all the cities in the United States, Chicago would be the one to make Bond famous. He once said of the Windy City, "Chicago strikes me as the most hostile city of any I've ever been in. I always get the feeling, as I'm walking down the street, that anybody, white or black, at any moment, is going to hit me for no reason whatsoever." [25] Nevertheless he went there in mid-August to dispute the seating of the "regular" Georgia delegation, handpicked by Governor Maddox. He saw it as a one-day experience—reaching Chicago in the morning, going before the Credentials Committee of the Democratic National Committee, spending a couple of hours in testimony, and taking the plane back home. Mistakenly, he thought the Credentials Committee served the purpose of a jury—to hear the evidence and deliberate in private. "What we didn't know," he said, "is that this jury is not locked up. We found we could lobby by remaining at the convention." And that's what he and his friends did. Thereafter it was a tale of personal privation, mixed with convention scarcities. He tried the quarters in the local YMCA, but couldn't face them: room tiny, no running water, showers outside. So he commandeered a sofa in the delegation's communal room in the Hilton. Without fresh clothes, he had to sit nude each day in the Hilton laundry while his wardrobe was cleaned. "One day," he recounts, "it took almost four hours, and all this time I was sitting there wrapped in a sheet."

But the effort paid off. He and his friends had the support of Eugene McCarthy's organization and when the committee handed down its decision on August 23, it was to divide forty-one of forty-three seats between the two competing delegations. Chairman Richard J. Hughes, governor of New Jersey, declared there was no "perfect solution"; the factions would have to select the delegates they wanted on the new slate. Still, Bond was elated when four days later the convention opened and he found himself in the center of a floor fight over the seating of the Georgia delegation. The Maddox group objected to getting only half the seats. Quick to take advantage of the impasse, McCarthy men moved to bar them entirely and replace the "regulars" with Bond's delegation. Across the floor of the convention hall, they raised the chant "Ju-lian Bond!" "Ju-lian Bond!" in a growing crescendo. Eventually the motion lost, but in working out an accommodation the insurgents won nearly half the state's delegate votes, as the Credentials Committee had advocated.

When the time to select candidates arrived, Bond was a logical choice to second Senator McCarthy's nomination. Not only was he young, black, handsome; he also represented the force in the convention that had just killed the unit rule by which machine politicians, like Maddox, controlled whole delegations regardless of minority opposition. McCarthy had seen it used by the Credentials Committee to destroy his campaign of months. Now he sought Bond's help.

Bond agreed to speak, went backstage, behind the podium, to be "made up" for the television cameras. There he found a little room, plushly furnished with sofas, a TV set and bar, and two bathrooms converted into makeup rooms. Jokingly he remarked to an operator at a large telephone switchboard, "Has the big fellow from Texas called lately?" "Not in the last fifteen minutes," she answered, leading him to conclude the President was on the phone every fifteen minutes, saying "Do this, do that, do the other." Governor

Harold E. Hughes of Iowa eventually put McCarthy's name in nomination, followed by liberal spokesman John Kenneth Galbraith of Harvard, and then Bond. Although McCarthy had considerable strength, the forces against him were so tightly knit that Humphrey received almost three times as many ballots—1761 to 601.

Yet the McCarthy supporters were not yet finished. They might be run over by unit rules and big-city pressures, but they still wanted a chance to discuss the Vietnam war and the police violence in Chicago before the convention adjourned. To do this, they needed to nominate someone for Vice-President and employ the time of the nominating and seconding speeches to discuss the issues. The gesture lacked validity because it was conceived at the end of the convention when tempers were high and when Humphrey's choice of Senator Edmund S. Muskie of Maine as running mate was certain to be approved by the delegates.

But the liberals were desperate for a token of recognition after McCarthy's defeat. They asked Governor Philip H. Hoff, of Vermont, to buck Muskie. Hoff had resented the "atrocities" of the previous evening, but bowed out, saying Muskie was his friend. Then, on a spur-of-the-moment impulse, Richard Goodwin, writer and intimate of the slain John F. Kennedy, came over to Bond. Bond looked up to see "Groucho Marx without a mustache," holding a cigar in one hand. "How would you like to be nominated for Vice-President?" Goodwin asked. "I'm too young, Dick," Bond answered. "That's okay, you know why it's being done." So Bond agreed.

Ted Warshafsky, a forty-one-year-old Milwaukee lawyer, vice-chairman of the Wisconsin delegation, put the Georgian's name in nomination from the floor, saying "We have stood with the people throughout this convention and we will stand with them now." With a reference to the violence that had erupted the evening before in Grant Park, Warshafsky called for the "American dream" that would be as meaningful for the "affluent" as for "the young people who march in the parks," and said Bond would speak for the "wave of the future." It was a disappointing performance, spoken in a voice so low that most delegates never heard. When he tried to secure time for a second speech by Allard Lowenstein, of New York, the professionals arose to stop him. Convention chairman Carl Albert of Oklahoma emphatically said "no."

Meanwhile, Bond was having his own difficulties. While delegates were preparing to ballot for Vice-President, John Chancellor of the National Broadcasting Company approached the Georgia legislator for an interview. "Not now, John, I'm busy," Bond said, trying to avoid him. "Please, just five minutes won't hurt," Chancellor countered. "Really, no. I'm too young to be Vice-President," was Bond's reply. "Please, I insist," Chancellor persisted. So Bond, feeling the options closed, said "Go ahead." The first question that Chancellor popped was "Don't you know you're too young to be Vice-President?" and left the impression with millions of people either that Bond didn't know the constitutional requirement for Vice-President or, knowing, he didn't care. It was okay for Bond to be nominated at twenty-eight, but not for anybody else. Bond was shaken but remained remarkably cool. The count began and the tally reached 48½ before Georgia was called. Then, in a "graceful" speech, Bond withdrew, declaring he had not yet reached the prescribed age of thirty-five. Blandly, someone asked him if he was prepared to seek another high office. "I've already been cut out of the vice-presidency," he smiled. "If I can't have that, I don't want anything." He was also game for the second question. "How had he come so far, so quickly?" "Clean living," he quipped.

His one searing experience during the convention was returning to the Hilton Hotel on the night of the student rioting to find bloody fingerprints all down the wallpaper in the corridor. "It looked as though someone had been beaten against the wall and had put his hand to the wound and then touched the wall—a horrible sight. Seeing that, I wandered into other rooms and found they had set up aid stations. It looked like a field hospital. I didn't see policemen hitting anybody, but I saw the results. Later, the police accused youngsters of throwing stuff out of the window down into the street, but this was impossible. The Hilton is the world's largest hotel with floors built on recessed ramps. We were on the third ramp back. In order for somebody to throw something into the street, he would have had to throw it up ten stories in the air, over the top of the hotel, and down into Michigan Avenue in front. It was just an impossible feat, so there was no excuse whatever for the police to come up there except to get the McCarthy kids."

It is difficult to speculate on the future of Julian Bond in light of his record at Chicago. John Lewis, his comrade-in-arms during SNCC days, says Bond displayed "real potential" to create a new political force out of the remnants of the civil rights movement, now that Martin Luther King and Senator Kennedy are lost. And the Reverend Channing Phillips, a Negro minister and Democratic National Committeeman for the District of Columbia, who was nominated for the presidency at Chicago, says, "It's realistic to think in terms of a black man for the vice-presidency as early as 1972. And I suspect that whoever runs will be clearing the way for Julian Bond in 1976—which is not a bad idea. He'd be of age by then." [26]

Whether or not these predictions materialize necessarily depends upon the uncertainty of politics and, above all, upon the man himself. Bond is basically a political theoretician with compassionate instincts, not an activist eaten by visceral tendencies. He possesses great personal charm, and "still doesn't know how magnetic he is," his Housemate Ben Brown says. It is not unusual for him to be mobbed by girls in the course of his appearances on college campuses. Yet a certain shyness persists. He dislikes large crowds and when

he is home, he shuns gatherings in favor of informal meetings with old friends from SNCC days. He and his wife and
their five children live in a modest brick residence close to
the Atlanta Negro college complex. His preferences are not
on a politician's standard fare. He drives an unpretentious
car and is chary about giving out his telephone number.
Alice Bond helps him maintain anonymity by refusing to
answer the phone during the day. She is said to dislike politics, claims she "*thought* she was marrying a writer," and is
jaundiced by the sight of the double-barreled shotgun Julian
keeps next to his bed to ward off any intruders bent on assassination, according to Douglas Kiker of *Playboy*. Of their
life in Atlanta, Bond observes quietly: "I like it. I think it's
just a friendlier, happier place for my family than if they
lived in some big Northern city. They'd be better off personally here; not necessarily educationally and not even
economically, but just personally I think they'd be better off
here." [27] It could be, of course, that Bond is biding his time,
saving his energies. At any rate, he appears to be a man
who enjoys what he does and is not eager—yet—to embark
on new seas.

When he talks of his future at all, it is generally in terms
of campaigning for Congress. There is a strong likelihood
that the 1970 census will enable Atlanta to have two congressional districts, one white, one black. If this happens,
Bond could be the natural choice in the black district, but
there is nothing certain about politics, especially with other
Negro aspirants eager to go to Washington.

Moreover, there is a lingering suspicion that Bond doesn't
feel tied to one constituency. Just as the states of the Old
Confederacy were his objective during the SNCC days, so
he now appeals to all blacks in that area, not just those of
the 136th House district. He is too modest to serve as their
spokesman; rather he wants to stimulate them to action, political action, which he says "ought to mean the art of deciding who gets how much of what from whom."

Bond speaks of vast changes in the works, now that the Southern black is coming alive. "It is not a new politics in the Eugene McCarthy sense," he emphasizes, "with bright, clean young people knocking on doors and soliciting votes. It is a new political process that began in Watts in 1964, and traveled from there to Newark and Detroit. It is a new process that began in Berkeley and moved to Columbia and Cornell. And while it is new and strange to many, it is as old as America itself. It is a part of the process that believes that when life becomes intolerable and government unresponsive and unrepresentative, then men have not just got the right, but the duty to rise up against it and strike it down." [28]

Not unlike the spirit which prompted the Boston Tea Party. Julian Bond is in this all the way.

John Mackey ===================================

❡ Baptist minister Walter R. Mackey was a creative man
with the persistence and determination to get what he
wanted. With his wife, a daughter, and two sons he had left
Aiken, South Carolina, hoping to find a better world in the
North. But Brooklyn in the early forties was already an embryonic ghetto, not exactly the spot to warm a pastor's
heart, and after their fourth child, John, was born on September 24, 1941, he moved to the Bronx in search of another life style.

That too was disquieting to the elder Mackey until finally
he found a site in nearby Roosevelt, Long Island, on which
to build a home. It was a patriarchal decision, as all decisions in the Mackey family were, and nothing could stop
him until he had raised a new edifice with his own hands.

A second chapter in the Mackey odyssey was Walter's
ambition to construct a church. Lacking money but not initiative, he corraled his sons (now five), his friends, in fact
the entire community, to put up the structure. We built it
"hand and foot, all the way up," John can recall. "I used to
go over every Saturday and help him." Throughout his
childhood, there was never a doubt that his father's hand
held the tiller, whether the issue was the church or his relationship to the neighbors.

One day John came home, proudly displaying a pennant on his bicycle, expecting to be acclaimed the family's cynosure. "I loved that pennant. My father asked me where I got it. I told him. He said to give it back. My friend had a new, shiny bike with a pennant on it. There I was, dragging along on my rusty old bike with no pennant." [1] Crestfallen and wondering how a father could act so curmudgeonly, John returned the present, not realizing for some years that pater Mackey had been his own Pinkerton and, piecing together the evidence, had discovered that the son's envy was stolen merchandise. The effect of the denial, though originally bitter, taught him a lesson. "There were things people expected you to do or not do, just because you were a minister's son," he now says. This kept him from hanging out on street corners with a crowd of youngsters prone to drink and dope. It also meant a midnight curfew, a particularly onerous restriction when parties were in the offing. Thinking back to those days, he remarked "there was always one going on somewhere and I hated to go home." Finally he had to accept the additional responsibilities of being a pastor's son. Mt. Sinai Baptist Church had to be swept and locked after choir practice and there were the little ones to escort home each week. Fortunately, these religious restraints, while making young Mackey impervious to urban lawlessness, did not stifle his ebullient personality.

This was due in part to neighborhood influences such as Bubba, a youth who lived next door and liked to wear a football uniform to impress his peers. "All of us wanted a uniform like Bubba's," Mackey recalls, "because he played football and made it sound so exciting." As a result, "when I went to Hempstead High School, I wanted to play football my freshman year." At Hempstead, however, no one could play football without a parent agreeing to accept responsibility for any injury incurred on the gridiron. Walter Mackey refused to give permission on the grounds the sport was "too dangerous" and his belief the school should under-write the medical costs of restoring injured players.

A year later, the situation had changed through a tempo-rary shift in the Mackey family's chain of command. John's father had gone to the hospital to have a cancerous growth on the larynx removed; in the interregnum all decisions were in the hands of his wife, who was more sympathetic. John pleaded with her to let him play and was so persistent that finally she gave in. "If you really want to play, you have my permission," she said. Excitedly he ran off to tell coach Bob Schuessler the good news. The coach took one look. "Mackey," he said, "you're too small to play—go back and fatten yourself up a little and we'll look at you next year." Recalling their conference, Mackey (who is now 6 feet 2 inches tall and weighs 220 pounds) thinks he weighed "about a hundred pounds."

Happily, during the next year he shot up to 165 pounds, then to 180, and finally in his senior year to 190 while his reputation on the gridiron, now that he had commenced playing, was correspondingly meteoric. The coach had orig-inally asked him what position he wanted to play, and Mackey (harking back to Bubba's record as a Freeport end) said, "I want to play end." Within two years he was known throughout Nassau County and capped his high school ca-reer by winning the coveted *Newsday* Tom Thorp Memo-rial Award, given annually to the county's outstanding foot-ball player. "Johnny's certainly the finest end I've ever coached and maybe the best we've ever had on the island," Schuessler said to a *Newsday* reporter after learning about the selection. "He can do everything and do it well. He's a rough, tough player on the field and he's going to get big-ger. Yet, he's the nicest kid you could find." The latter im-pression was the one that stuck to the hats of his classmates. "I was very happy," an admiring distaff member wrote in Mackey's *Colonial,* the school yearbook, "when you acquired your fame but worried too—I thought it would change you, make you conceited. But it didn't—you're still the great guy you'll always be." The complimentary reaction was actually a tribute to Mackey's affinity for the system. He wanted to learn, to get as much out of the instruction as possible. Impressionable, he talked of the "big influence" that mathematics teacher Robert Kennan had on him. One day, years afterward, he asked Kennan why he had singled him out to go to college when so many others dropped out at the twelfth grade. "You were different, John. You used to listen to what I said."

With such encouragement, Mackey began to think in white terms of Notre Dame, Michigan State, and Syracuse instead of black-oriented institutions like Howard and Morgan State College. He found the mood enhanced by offers from leading universities in all parts of the country which wanted him to play football. Also, there was Hempstead's basketball coach, John Mills, who talked of Mackey as "the greatest of them all." Midway through his senior year, Mills asked his protégé what he wanted to do about college. Finally, forced to sort out the various possibilities, Mackey replied, "I want to go to Syracuse." [2] In a few weeks—courtesy of John Mills—Mackey had an invitation from Ben Schwartzwalder, the football coach, to visit the campus. The Hempstead senior immediately was impressed by the freedom of the school. "They just didn't keep me in the gym; I was on my own. I did anything I wanted, talked to professors, went to classes, and was more or less loose. They never put pressure on me, you know." Also, he discovered that he could matriculate on an academic grant-in-aid. "As long as I maintained my average, even though I didn't play football, I could stay in school." This won over Walter Mackey, who originally thought Syracuse would be too expensive for his son. When the doors opened in September 1959, John Mackey was among the entering freshmen.

By then Schwartzwalder was a revered name on Piety

Hill. Since his arrival a decade before, his football teams had scored impressive records. They had won the Lambert trophy, emblematic of Eastern supremacy, twice—in 1952 and 1956—and had participated in three bowls: Orange, 1952 and 1958, and Cotton, 1956. His 1959 team was about to win national honors. Schwartzwalder was a rather remarkable figure. Short, stocky, commanding, he once played center at West Virginia under famed Greasey Neale, pitting 152 pounds of courage against competitors far heavier. During World War II, he served with the 82nd Airborne, jumping three times in combat, picking up a Silver Star for bravery under fire and at war's end was a major. He was long on discipline, short on patience when mediocrity was the issue. His teams bore the trademark of grinding perfection. One look at Mackey convinced him that here was an ideal prospect, the kind that one day might evoke high praise. Years later, authenticating his prediction, he declared, "Mackey was a most motivated player. He would remain on the field as long as anyone would throw to him. He had a great talent, but he would never have gotten where he did without hard work. He supplied his own incentive," adding "the great ones do; when they get on that field, they're ready to go."

But in the autumn of 1959, Schwartzwalder could afford to savor Mackey's prowess vicariously. With a team of national champions in the making, he didn't need the freshman giant who could run the hundred in less than ten seconds. The dazzling speed, however, convinced the freshmen coaches to reassign him from end to right halfback. For a time he was sidelined by a bone injury, later traced to calcification, but he got back into uniform in time to lead the Orange cubs to a shutout victory over their traditional rivals from Colgate.

As the 1960 season opened, the Schwartzwalder behemoth was under tremendous pressure to maintain its victory skein. In regular season play it had not lost one of its last sixteen games. Successively, the Orange overwhelmed Boston University, Kansas, Holy Cross, Penn State, and West Virginia, coming up to Pittsburgh with another undefeated season in the balance. The strain of winning finally overwhelmed the players. On October 29, before a stunned crowd of 41,872, the Orange succumbed 10–0, with famed Ernie Davis, Syracuse's All-American halfback, held to a minuscule twenty yards during the first half. The Orange's best effort sputtered out on the Pittsburgh 37-yard line. When it was over, the gloom on campus was so heavy the local *Herald-American* bowed to the despondency by rimming its account of the debacle in mourning lead.

The only consolation for Mackey was that he and Davis were now the closest of friends. The two blacks had rapped well since John's first appearance on campus and Schwarzwalder had asked Davis to show him around. "You should have met Ernie," Mackey once told George Vecsey of *Sport* magazine, describing their relationship. "He was one of the nicest people you could ever know. I mean nice, real nice. The kind of guy who would help an old lady across the street, that kind of nice." Time ripened their relationship. "I was the only black on the freshman football squad," Mackey remembers, "and since he and I were about the same age, it was natural to hang around with each other." They roomed together during John's sophomore and junior years, and just as two cronies might conjure plans to help each other, Davis imparted his pigskin knowledge to Mackey. "A lot of people say I'm hard to bring down. Ernie showed me how to do this. Many ball carriers have a tendency to absorb most of the punishment when being tackled. I was taught [by Davis] to try to dish it out. If you can hit your man first, use your forearm to keep him away from your legs, you have a chance of going on." [3]

The lives of the two young men were for those days relatively free of racial discrimination. The campus unrest which began with the 1960 student sit-ins had not yet disturbed the tranquility of Northern schools. Moreover, Mackey had lived in an integrated neighborhood and attended an integrated school before coming to Syracuse. His only open encounter with white racism was during a boyhood trip to South Carolina with his father. He remembered stopping on Route 40 in Maryland to get food. The restaurant proprietor had looked at his father—a very light-skinned Negro—and then at John. "Come on in," he said to the elder Mackey, "but leave your darkie outside." In college, the word carried less overtness, but a thread of subtle ostracism was there. He could recall a football official saying "Don't be like Avatus Stone," which meant nothing to Mackey because he didn't know who Stone was. (Stone had allegedly "raised hell" by going out with white girls and the white alumni took umbrage.) But such caveats were wasted on the big sophomore because the campus milieu was about what Mackey had always experienced and he didn't care who Stone was anyway.

In the fall of 1961, the presence of Ernie Davis plus an in-depth supply of superlative backs persuaded Schwartzwalder to try Mackey at end. Besides, "we just didn't have any ends," he said in explanation. "John can play anywhere. His only problem is that he's so high-strung and excitable." To Joseph Szombathy, end coach and ex-Orange star, the word was simply "over-eager. He's too aggressive on defense, that's his trouble. He charges in there too fast sometimes and gets fooled. But he's doing fine on offense. He can block and, though we haven't thrown to him very often, he's caught every one we threw." To such criticism Mackey merely replied "I got a lot to learn" [4] as he hustled to correct the flaws.

In the Orange's seventh game against its historic foe, Pittsburgh, the effort finally paid off. He took an eleven-yard scoring pass to put the Orange ahead. The final 28–9 score sent the coach into high fettle: "The greatest team effort since I've been coaching at Syracuse," he exclaimed. On the Saturday after Pittsburgh, thousands of central New York fans gathered in Archibald Stadium to bid farewell to Ernie Davis and to give the "last hurrah" to a sixty-two-year rivalry between Syracuse and Colgate. Davis played magnificently, whipping a touchdown pass to Mackey for seventy-four yards as Syracuse routed the Red Raiders for the eleventh successive time, 51–8.

All fall, Schwartzwalder had been aiming for the following week's game with Notre Dame in South Bend. The two teams had not met since 1914, when the Fighting Irish outscored the Orange 20–0. Syracuse had to win this one to get a post-season bowl bid—or so the coach thought. From the opening kickoff the battle raged, and with two and a half periods gone the Orange trailed 14–0. The Orange was headed for defeat when suddenly the offense came to life. Dave Sarette, its scrappy quarterback, decided to gamble on a fourth-and-one situation with the ball resting on the Orange 43. Instead of punting, he hurled a pass to Mackey. As a Binghamton sports writer described what he saw, "The ball traveled about seven yards in the air and Mackey did the rest with a stiff arm that almost decapitated George Sefolk, the Irish defender." The fifty-seven-yard gallop ended in the end zone with the left side of Mackey's shoulder pads exposed beneath his torn jersey. Again Sarette chose to gamble, this time a two-point conversion pass which made the score Notre Dame 14, Syracuse 8. Moments later, an aroused Orange team got the ball on its 47 and drove for a second touchdown. With the extra point and ten minutes to go, Syracuse led 15–14. An Orange line that had performed superbly on defense completely bottled up the Irish. On the final play of the game, with defeat all but certain, coach Joe Kuharich sent in Joe Perkowski, the Irish place kicker, to make one last desperate attempt for a field goal from Notre Dame's 45. Off went the gun as Orange linemen swept in. When they saw the kick had missed the uprights, they went wild and turned to leave, not realizing the umpire had ruled a roughing penalty against Perkowski. Again, the two teams faced each other; this time, with the ball moved up fifteen yards, Perkowski booted the pigskin to score three points. The Irish had won 17–15. Schwartzwalder offered no excuses. "It was one of those things," he said, "that you believe didn't happen." Neither could the Eastern Collegiate Athletic Conference, which said the officials had committed an error in giving Notre Dame an extra play and that Syracuse was entitled to win 15–14. But the controversy died after Notre Dame refused to concede defeat. At season's end, the Orange record stood 7–3–0. Although Mackey failed to get All-American recognition, Schwartzwalder knew what the judges had not seen. "He's a helluva kid," he smiled knowingly. "If he isn't the best end in the country today, he's certainly going to be next season."

In 1962, Mackey's final year with the Orange, Schwartzwalder had even more good things to say about his star end: "He blocks, tackles, catches passes, runs . . . does everything well," he said, but graduation had completely stripped the backfield and the new ball handlers rarely threw the ball. In six games, John had snagged only six passes for sixty-five yards, not one a touchdown play. Schwartzwalder in desperation shifted Mackey to right halfback, playing behind the strong side of Syracuse's unbalanced line. In his first game against Navy, Mackey exploded with two touchdowns and sixty-three yards on six carries. On one, a thirty-six-yard dash into the end zone, he was seemingly stopped at the line of scrimmage by three Navy tacklers converging on him at once. He spun around, shook them off, and then scored with a tremendous burst of speed. On another thirteen-yard run he "stiff-armed one defender so hard that the Middie was rendered momentarily senseless." After absorbing a 34–6 defeat, a Navy scout told what happened: "Our boys never bounced off anybody all year like they bounced off him."

The final game of Mackey's collegiate career took place in

Los Angeles against UCLA. Neither team had had a winning season. Each needed a victory to prevent a losing year. After ten minutes of play, the Orange had moved into the lead with a touchdown drive, but the Bruins quickly responded, earned a conversion (which Syracuse had missed), and led 7–6. Thereafter, the game seesawed with Syracuse eating first downs but choking on the gains. The Orange piled up 320 yards, but costly fumbles, pass interceptions, and the Bruin line cut off each advance until 9:56 of the last period, when Mackey took a punt return on the UCLA 40, churned up the field, shook off three tacklers, and went over standing up. In the locker room, smiling under an avalanche of accolades and the honor of being named top performer in the 12–7 victory, Mackey could only observe modestly, "I'm glad we finally did something right."

Others, too, were reaching the same conclusion about Mackey. Five days before the Syracuse–UCLA kickoff, the Baltimore Colts had picked John Mackey as their second draft choice, and on Tuesday following the game, general manager Don Kellett and scout Buddy Young, former Illinois All-American who played for the Colts during 1953–1955, visited Syracuse to discuss contract terms with Mackey and his attorney, Allen Brickman. The Orange star was too elated over the victory in Los Angeles and too excited over being chosen for the East-West game in San Francisco two weeks later to initial any agreement. But the conversation did point up his growing prestige among players in the pro ranks. He could now visualize himself following in the steps of Jim Brown and Ernie Davis, the two Syracuse All-Americans, who joined the Cleveland Browns after graduation. For the moment, however, much depended upon his performance in the annual Shrine bruhaha between East and West. When the game ended, Mackey had demonstrated once again coolness under pressure by scoring two of the victor's touchdowns as the East overwhelmed the West 25–19. In the first quarter, the 61,107 spectators in San Francisco's Kezar Stadium jumped to their feet as he raced behind defenders Larry Balliett, of California, and Jim Johnson, of Missouri, to catch a pass on the West's 7 for a forty-one-yard scoring play. Later he sped downfield, passing Balliett and Johnson a second time, grabbed the bomb on the 30 from Notre Dame's Daryle Lamonica, and raced the rest of the way unmolested. The play covered sixty-nine yards.

Mackey returned to Syracuse more convinced than ever of his ability to play pro ball. He could hardly wait now to emulate Brown and Davis, but the continuing reports of Davis' serious illness were raising fears about his former roommate's future. Mackey had gone the previous July to watch Davis play in an all-star game. The minute he saw him on the field, he knew something was wrong, but he wasn't sure what it was. Davis seemed to have lost his blinding speed and talent for warding off tacklers. Mackey noted that he went down after being hit once, something he rarely did at Syracuse. He even wondered if Coach Woody Hayes of Ohio was trying to upstage Davis by giving Bob Ferguson, a Hayes product, the nod at fullback. This prognosis was shattered a month later when Mackey learned that Davis had been taken sick while practicing for the game with the National Football League (NFL) champions.

Rumors flew that he was ill with leukemia. Mackey had to know whether it was true. With two friends he drove to Cleveland and talked to Davis. When their conversation was finished, Mackey couldn't tell whether Davis was putting him on or not. He didn't act as though he had leukemia, he certainly didn't want any sympathy, but the way he thanked Mackey for coming was touching. The only outward appearance of what was rampant inside was a tendency for Davis' nose to bleed. Mackey didn't view this with alarm for the same thing, come to think of it, had occurred at Syracuse. Just because a man's nose bleeds doesn't mean he has leukemia, he told himself. Yet the fear could not be dismissed that easily. He recalled that Davis had won the Heisman Trophy as a senior, the first black to earn the honor, but it had entailed great sacrifice. Davis never got sufficient sleep. He would go to banquets and then study all night to prepare for next day's classes. Perhaps the fatigue had activated his troubles, but who was there to tell? In any event, unknown to Mackey, the sands of his former roommate's life were running out: at an accelerated speed. Davis returned to Syracuse on May 4 to attend the annual alumni-varsity football game. He didn't play, but helped the coach and joked with Mackey. "You know," he told his ex-roommate, "I'll still be a rookie this year and I'll be battling you for the rook-of-the-year honors."

"Yeah," Mackey replied, "I guess we'll find out which one is the better football player now, won't we?" The two men were physically identical—6 feet 2, weight 215. Davis' time for the forty-yard sprint was one-tenth of a second better than Mackey's, but otherwise they were the same. After the game, when the two gathered at a friend's house to discuss old times, the difference became crystal-clear. Mackey was robust, filled with health; Davis was thinner, noticeably drawn. The host, who had known Davis during his college days, saw the change. "He was the same guy, cheerful as ever, but I think he knew for a long time what the eventual outcome would be. He was too well educated, too smart a boy not to know, but he was so unselfish he just pretended to everybody that everything was all right. He knew better, but he knew if he came into a gathering with his head down and talked about his troubles, the conversation would stop and there would be a certain awkward atmosphere hanging over things. Ernie didn't want that. He wanted things to remain jovial. That's why I think he went along pretending." Eventually, the borrowed time had to be paid. Before the month was out, Ernie Davis lay dead.

The pall left by his passing was still in the air as Mackey traveled to Baltimore to ink his contract with the Colts on

May 27. There was talk at the signing of his having joined
the New York Jets because he would be playing in Long Island, his own backyard, but it hadn't happened. "Amid
an array of bright lights, microphones, taped interviews,
pointed questions," the conversation turned to lacrosse, the
Baltimore *Sun* reported. Had Mackey enjoyed playing lacrosse as much as Jim Brown, he was asked? Brown was
supposed to have said he would like to play lacrosse six days
a week and football on Sunday. "No, I don't love lacrosse
like he does," John replied. "I never played it in high school
and would rather play football seven days a week." After
the ceremony, Mackey hurried back to Syracuse to pick up
a sheepskin in American history. Only a few weeks remained before he was scheduled to join the Colts in July at
their training camp, Westminster, Maryland, thirty miles
from Baltimore. He knew the first weeks would be crucial.
Many college greats failed to survive the first cut. Of course,
he could always go to law school if he failed, but in the
meantime he was determined to give it his all. Very shortly,
veteran Colts were to discover what giving "his all" meant.
He "loved to hit" in order to show his prowess, a Colt official declared. "Running into Mackey," said another, "was
like slamming into a concrete wall." But when he was not
on the field, he spread charm. Within a week of his arrival,
Gino Marchetti, all-time NFL end, was telling him, "Rookie,
you're gonna make it big," and another veteran of the grid
wars, none other than Johnny Unitas, the Colt quarterback,
invited him to have a beer. "It was the first beer I ever
had," recalled Mackey to Baltimore *Sun* writer John
Schmidt. "I didn't like it, but I had another one. I couldn't
say no to somebody I had been hero-worshiping since I was
a kid."

Baltimore's new head coach, Don Shula, was also impressed. "Mackey looks good. He can really catch that ball
and go." The Colt camp was already debating whether
Mackey should play fullback or tight end. Since an arm as

prized as Unitas' needed strong receivers, Shula eventually decided to play him at end. Initially, Mackey found himself psyched by the Unitas image. "I used to get in the huddle," he said, "but I could never hear the plays." Sensing the trouble, offensive end coach Jim Mutscheller exclaimed, "Do you want to play?"

"Sure, I want to play," said Mackey.

"Well, why don't you get in the huddle?" he asked.

"I don't want to get in there with John," he replied. "I don't mind getting in there with Gary Cuozzo because he is a rookie, too, but I don't want to get in there with John. I just can't hear anything when I'm in there with John."

"You got to get in there and you got to stay in there until you start hearing things," Mutscheller said. Thereafter Mackey did, but it took time for the atmosphere to clear. Unitas, tipped off to Mackey's sensitivity, decided the huddle was the place to quiet Mackey's nerves. "Don't worry, rookie," he'd say with a wink, "everything is okay. I'm going to throw the ball to you this time." And if Mackey dropped the pass, he would not frown. Instead, he would toss him another to build his confidence. Gradually Mackey awakened to the fact he was another Colt, a member of the team. "But I still never talked to John Unitas," the ex-Orange star said. "Raymond Berry, the Colts renowned end, was the man who actually started me talking to John. Between plays, he'd ask, 'Can you get open?' and I'd say, 'Yeah, I can beat my man all day.'"

"Well, why don't you tell John?" he'd ask.

"You go tell him," Mackey replied. And Berry would then intervene. "Mackey can beat his man on this play," he'd remark to Unitas. Until, finally, Berry concluded it was time for Mackey to speak. "Look," he said, "you got to start talking in the huddle." And about halfway through the 1963 season Mackey sounded off, and after that Unitas made a point of asking his advice.

It was downfield, however, that Mackey suffered most.

Opponents took advantage of his inexperience to shout distracting comments. Against the Chicago Bears, he had outrun Richie Petitbon, the safety man, and was lofting his arms to catch the Unitas bomb when Petitbon yelled, "Welcome to the League, rookie," and Mackey, flattered by the unheralded affection, let the pigskin drop. The same thing happened at Los Angeles. Again Mackey was beyond the secondary, poised for the touchdown play. "If I scored, we went ahead," he recalls thinking. As his hands went up to grab the ball, one of the Ram players shouted "Look out." Automatically his head jerked for a glimpse of the danger and the ball slipped through his fingers. "Everybody in the Coliseum said the sun got in my eyes. Heck, I just got fooled by the oldest trick in the world." Out of such frustrations Mackey was learning the game as the professionals knew it. He began to use the same gambits himself. During the heat of battle, if he knew that saying certain things would upset an opponent, he'd say them, anything to get the edge. Conversely, he'd ignore everything said to him because if he worried about an individual, he couldn't do the job. At the end of his first season he had compiled an amazing record—thirty-five passes caught for 726 yards and seven touchdowns. He was the only first-year man to receive an invitation to play in the Pro Bowl, and those who had seen him play against the Minnesota Vikings in early December understood the reasons for the selection. He no longer was a liability on passes. In Unitas' words, he had "worked very hard to improve, listened to instructions and practiced." The result was fabulous. He grabbed a twenty-yard pass, squirmed out of the arms of Lee Calland, who had him pinned around the thighs, gave Ed Scharockman a straight-arm that toppled him like a tenpin, and sped forty yards to the goal line. On a second pass of seven yards, he broke through three Viking defenders for a twenty-yard scoring play. Awed by such feats, a Colt assistant bubbled, according to sportswriter John Schmidt, "There aren't many safetymen around who can handle that guy. Once he catches the ball, the great adventure begins. Those people on defense climb all over him. The lucky defenders fall off, the others may be trampled. They attack him as though he's a giant redwood. But he's also moving in high gear. And he can dig out, you know. He does 40 yards in 4.7 seconds."

Off the gridiron, Mackey was beginning to know his teammates. His natural gregariousness seemed to open the doors to the Colt great. He liked to visit Jim Parker, the Ohio State graduate who starred at offensive guard. "He was always laughing and jolly," Mackey recalls, "he kept the team loose all the time. There were occasions when I wondered how he could be so mean on Sunday when he was so nice during the week. The one thing I noticed about Jim was that he hated to lose. He would laugh and play and joke, but whenever he started losing, he became very serious. Jim told me what a great wrestler he had been at Ohio State and would let me get a hold on him I thought he couldn't possibly break. Then, the next thing I knew, he'd throw me against the wall. At first I actually thought he was trying to hurt me, but it was all in fun." Gino Marchetti was another Colt figure who impressed Mackey. Their lockers were next to each other—because Mackey's jersey number was 88 and Marchetti's 89. The latter, in contrast to Parker, was always nervous before games. "I guess he would walk ten miles, back and forth, back and forth. I used to get nervous just watching him." Mackey had the same difficulty trying to understand Steve Stonebreaker, who would roam through the locker room hitting the wall with his forearm. "Setting his pads," was Stonebreaker's explanation, "getting ready for the game." Everyone did his own thing, Mackey concluded. "Some were quiet, others loose, others never really said anything anytime." Pregame meals were in a category of their own. Some would eat huge helpings of steak and potatoes, which Mackey abhorred. "If I eat," he explained, "I'll always throw up. And if I don't eat, I'll always gag—but I always feel better when I gag and nothing comes up than if I eat and throw up. I play better on an empty stomach. I'm more aggressive and I guess I'm meaner when I'm hungry."

The year 1964 found Mackey on top of the crest. By now he had earned the unanimous encomiums of the Colt coaching staff. Mutscheller, for instance, was saying, reported the Baltimore *News American,* "The boy has everything, size, speed, and power. But what makes me go overboard most about him is his attitude. He's the kind of kid who means so well and tries so hard and is so coachable he could be among the best on sheer effort even without the marvelous physical equipment he has. Since he does have it, along with the perfect attitude, there's practically no limit to what he can do." One reason for this "perfect attitude" was Mackey's marriage at the end of his first year with the Colts to Sylvia Ann Cole, of Washington, D.C. He had met her during his undergraduate days at Syracuse. She was a Russian-French major who now wanted to continue her studies at nearby Johns Hopkins. Sylvia was ideal for John because she involved herself in the trials and tribulations of professional football without sacrificing her own aspirations or permitting football to dominate her altogether. Her worst ordeal, she discovered, was to watch the games at Memorial Stadium with other team wives. "I'll be sitting there," she says, explaining her reaction, "and a couple of guys behind me will get into an argument over John's merits. Then one of them will yell something like 'throw out butterfingers Mackey!' It's hard not to say a word."

Oddly enough, the fear of what injuries John might sustain on the gridiron doesn't worry Sylvia, for she is a confirmed stoic who believes what will be will be. "John doesn't think about injuries either," she adds. "We never discuss his playing in terms of danger or risk. Any ballplayer who worries about getting hurt isn't going to last very long. He's not giving all his attention to the game, his performance is going to suffer, and eventually he's going to get hurt. Since John doesn't worry, I automatically don't either, I guess. Even if he gets up slowly from a play, I still don't worry because I know he's not going to risk getting up unless he's all right." One reason John remains in superb condition is the fact that Sylvia has a job modeling for several Baltimore dress shops and has to watch her weight. Neither Mackey eats breakfast, although John is apt to drink a half cup of coffee with cream. "We believe that what you eat in the morning stretches your stomach for the rest of the day. I don't know if there's really anything to that, but it seems to work for us," Sylvia explains. Lunch normally consists of lean meat and a green salad; dinner, rare beef with vegetables, so mundane in its regularity that it qualifies for a gourmand's apostasy.

Since football was at best a six-month job, John had to unearth other ways of earning a steady salary. Following his first season with the Colts, he became sports director of WEBB, a local Baltimore radio station, while Sylvia continued her studies at Johns Hopkins. Mackey was determined not to live on his football earnings—a gridiron career might end momentarily and leave him stranded. Accordingly, he invested his football earnings in the stock market and supported Sylvia and their daughter with what he received from WEBB. After a time, he decided Sylvia should know what he was doing with his investments. "I took her down to the stock exchange near us and showed her around. First thing you knew, she was going to classes at the exchange and asking questions of everybody we knew. Before long, she knew more than I did. I gave her $500 to invest. She had it up to $5,000 in a year." Naturally, this added spice to the family dialogue. "When John comes home," Sylvia likes to point out, "I don't want to bore him with what went on around the house all day. . . . We talk about the market, interest rates, situations which affect us." Even the milieu has no connection with football. A visitor in the Mackey homestead finds copies of *Forbes, Fortune, Business Week,* and *The Wall Street Journal,* not sport reviews acclaiming the owner's pigskin mastery.

But back in the fall of 1964, when Mackey was beginning his second season with the Colts, talk of stocks, dividends, and profits was not a pressing issue. He only wanted to be the "great" football player that Mutscheller had predicted. Unfortunately, in the final exhibition game with the Pittsburgh Steelers, he suffered a bruise deep inside the thigh which curtailed his speed. The man who barely missed being selected rookie-of-the-year in 1963 had to work overtime to perform 60 per cent as well. Not until the last game of the regular season, against the Washington Redskins, did he display top form by scoring on a twenty-two-yard pass, his second of the year. Up to then, head coach Shula had dubbed him his "one-legged player" and, according to the Baltimore *Sun,* had been repeating to the press " 'he's not 100 per cent yet,' more times than Tommy Manville had heard the wedding march." For Mackey it was, he said, a gainful experience. "I don't feel you're a pro until you can play when you're hurt. It was new to me because I had never been really hurt before. So having an injury did a lot for me."

It began to show in 1965 when Mackey returned to the form he displayed as a rookie. He grabbed forty passes, gained 814 yards, and scored seven touchdowns. The Colts played excellent football, winning ten games and losing only to the Chicago Bears and the Green Bay Packers, but the latter proved their nemesis, defeating Baltimore twice in the regular season and knocking them out of the Western Conference title in a 13–10 overtime victory, the third time Don Shula had succumbed to Vince Lombardi in one year.

The year 1966 opened on a note of "here's where we came in." In the opening engagement, the Packers again took the measure of the Colts 24–3, but following that loss, Baltimore dropped only four of the succeeding thirteen.

Oddly enough, it was during two of these losses that
Mackey rose to the heights he had seemed destined to scale.
At Chicago, on October 10, he caught a ten-yard pass from
Unitas and ran toward Richie Petitbon, the Bears' strong
side safety who had made him look foolish his rookie year.
"I knew from experience that Richie would not try to tackle
me by himself," Mackey said afterward. "He'd stand his
ground and try to force me into making a move." This was
tailored to John's style. He slowed momentarily, bent over,
and then exploded upward with his right arm and right
knee. Petitbon went up in the air like a man riding his pe-
tard and fell backward stunned. On went Mackey to confront Dick Butkus, one of the League's fiercest linebackers.
John flashed his speed, feinted left, went right, and with an
arcing sidewinder swept Butkus behind. That was the last
obstacle. He outdistanced Roosevelt Taylor, the Bears'
safety, to score on a seventy-nine-yard touchdown gallop.

At Detroit on November 20, another Mackey spectacular
went into the record as he ran sixty-four yards for a touchdown, knocking down seven defenders on the way. Gary
Cuozzo, the Colts' alternate quarterback, threw him a five-
yard pass which appeared innocuous enough. Detroit's Dick
LeBeau mistakenly thought so as he dove to stop him and
careened backward. A pack of Lions closed in to finish its
prey, but it turned out not to be as bad inside the den as it
looked from the outside. "There were so many of them,"
Mackey recalled, "they were gettin' in their own way. And
nobody had a real good shot at me." He chanced to peer out
of the circle and saw Alex Karras, Detroit's renowned line-
backer, moving in for the *coup de grâce.* "That's when I
knew I could get out," Mackey suddenly realized. "Karras
looked like he was running hard, but I could tell from the
way his body was back that he was jogging. He figured the
other seven would get me, so there was no need to hurry."
LeBeau aided the mirage by returning to the fray a second
time. In one supreme effort, he climbed Mackey's back and

tried to wrestle him to the ground. Mackey twisted, turned, shed him like a tattered coat, and, bolting through the swarm, sped by Karras into the open. At first, remembering the fate of Roy Riebels, he feared he was going in the wrong direction from being turned around so many times. But then he spied teammate Lenny Moore on the ground and two more Lion uniforms looming up ahead. Jerry Hill, the ex-Wyoming star and reputedly the finest blocking full-back in the League, moved in to cut him down, while Mackey outraced the other Lion to the end zone. Back at the Colt bench, Tom Matte was shouting "Greatest individual effort I've ever witnessed," and eleven-year veteran center Dick Szymanski was yelling "I've never seen a run that even approached it." In December that year, Mackey was selected for the first time as tight end on the NFL All-Star team. His ability to run over, around, or through the opposing team was becoming legendary.

In other ways, too, he was becoming prominent. Teammates saw a dynamic personality who was not reluctant to voice his thoughts. Ben Schwartzwalder had noted the trait when Mackey was a Syracuse undergraduate. "A natural leader," he called him, noting his candor. Mackey had demonstrated this independence the previous July when he walked out of the Westminster training camp in a dispute over salary. "I thought I shouldn't be practicing without a contract," he said, according to the Baltimore *Sun*. "When I came to camp, I came to play. I didn't want to talk contract. I got a one-track mind. I can't concentrate on football and salary at the same time. I'll never come to camp again without a contract." Colt officials were angry and said he would be fined $100 for every day away, but Mackey scored his point. Two days later, following negotiations with Carroll Rosenbloom, club president, he signed a contract. It was not that Mackey had any illusions about Colt control. Written into his 1965 contract was an option clause giving the club the exclusive right to his service for 1966 whether he signed a contract or not, but the Colt management was on notice henceforth not to take him for granted. Above all, Mackey wanted a peer relationship with the club as well as the players. When he joined the Colts he noticed that blacks and whites were separated on the road. Blacks roomed with blacks and whites with whites, but never the two races together. If there was an extra black or an extra white, he usually had a separate room. This struck Mackey as a racial anachronism. "If you're going to win together," he thought, "then you should live and eat together." He discussed the polarization with Bob Vogel, the giant offensive tackle from Ohio State, who had been the Colts' first-round draft choice in 1963. A religious man, member of the Fellowship of Christian Athletes, Vogel understood the problem perfectly. A natural rapport had blossomed between the two after Vogel was chosen player representative for the Colt team and Mackey his alternate. One day the two decided to approach head coach Shula and ask why he couldn't "forget about the color thing." Shula agreed with the request and after that, blacks and whites began rooming together.

If ever a season during Mackey's career in Baltimore appeared doomed to failure, it was the 1968 one. The great John Unitas was a shadow of his former form, sidelined with tendonitis in his right elbow. Sizing up the situation, Mackey had to admit, a bit ruefully, "We used to put all our faith in him. If we were down ten points with two minutes to go, we figured he'd do it." Without him the Colts had to develop a new attack around another quarterback. Shula providently had obtained Earl Morrall, a former Michigan State great, from the New York Giants, and the acquisition proved eminently timely. Morrall and Unitas had had coextensive careers of a dozen years in professional football and, although Morrall's statistics were only half as imposing as Unitas', he was on the threshold of amassing his greatest year. In sixteen games during the regular season, his record was 182 completions in 317 attempts (57.4 per cent) for 2909 yards and 26 touchdowns, enough to win the NFL passing championship and the League's Most Valuable Player. Morrall's only defeat was at the hands of the Browns in mid-October. "This is the greatest football team ever," Mackey proudly told the press. "I'll tell you why: we have a great defense, a good offense and a spectacularly special team plus a terrific place kicker and a fine punter. The great teams have had one or more of those things, but rarely all five together. Then there is the 'togetherness' on our club. We're in great shape." If Mackey was slightly prejudiced, there was nothing discriminatory about Joe Kapp, quarterback of the Minnesota Vikings, who said the Colts "were the finest football team he'd ever seen." After the Colts had dumped the Cleveland Browns 34–0 in the season finale, winning the NFL title, "a quick poll taken in the press box failed to find a single expert who believed the Jets would have a chance to beat the Colts" for the World Championship in Miami on January 12, 1967.

Unfortunately for the Colts, the team read the clippings and agreed with the experts. How could a team from the American Football League defeat the old pros of the National League? Subconsciously, they were thinking the only thing the NFL had to do was appear on the field and the AFL would succumb. And why not? Hadn't the NFL won the World Championship against the best of the AFL in 1967 and 1968 by lopsided scores? The Jets, led by coach Weeb Ewbank, were delighted to encourage the feeling of overconfidence. Ewbank knew the Colts well. The 5 foot-7 inch 197-pounder had coached them nine years, winning the World Championship in 1958 and 1959 against the New York Giants. In the spring of 1963 he had informed everyone in the Baltimore organization that he wanted John Mackey of Syracuse. "He will make us champions again," said Ewbank, but before he could sign the Orange Star, Rosenbloom had fired him and hired Shula to direct the team. A change of venue had not destroyed his admiration for "that great giant," as he called Mackey. In fact, he announced from the Jets' training headquarters in Fort Lauderdale that Mackey would get double coverage. "Nobody's going to cover him one on one. You have got to get help from elsewhere. He's just that good." The only player on the Jet team who was not showering the Colts with praise was Joe Namath, the quarterback, who said, "We're going to win. I guarantee it." But, as *Time* magazine pointed out, "Whatever slim hope the Jets had of winning centered on Namath's arm—and the only thing he seemed to be exercising was his mouth."

Yet the psychology worked. Within minutes of the opening whistle, the 75,377 spectators in the Orange Bowl, plus a television audience estimated at 60 million, could see the Colts were no 7–1 choice, favored to win by eighteen to twenty points, as the odds makers had maintained. Instead, the Jets scored a touchdown against the vaunted Colt defense and kicked three field goals. Not until midway in the third quarter, when the game was beyond retrieving, did Shula send in the ailing Unitas to replace Morrall and the Colts scored their only touchdown. For completing seventeen out of twenty-eight passes for 206 yards, Namath was labeled by Dave Anderson of *The New York Times* "pro football's best quarterback" in the 16–7 upset. Mackey caught three passes for thirty-five yards, but the Jets swarmed around him like bees. "We sort of panicked," he said, explaining the metastasis, "and when you panic, you can't do what you usually do." Bill Curry, center, ex-Georgia Tech star and close friend of Mackey's, was more pointed. "If I live to be ninety-seven," he moaned, "there won't be a week I don't think about it. For two weeks after that, I was like a basket case. I never left the basket even to get a newspaper. It was the single most traumatic experience of my life except for losing a member of my family." Time, that healer of depression, was somewhat kinder to Mackey. He had always had a lot of respect for Joe Namath so there was no need to swallow the ashes that lay in Curry's mouth. "Joe learned the hard way in the AFL," Mackey declared, looking back at the Jets' victory. "There was a time when I didn't think Namath could read defenses, but AFL teams follow a different style from the NFL. Their rules are not standard, and because of it, the AFL has generated more imagination. In the future, they could be the tougher League." But on the afternoon of January 12, no boxing of the philosophical compass could compensate for the dreadful assault on Colt pride.

Indeed, one seriously wonders whether Shula ever recovered. His 1969 season was the second worst in his seven years with Baltimore, and early in 1970 he departed for Miami to take over the Dolphins. His going on February 18 was a boon to Mackey, who never accepted Shula's attempt to transform him into a fullback. Baltimore fans, aware of Mackey's tremendous power, had been crying for years to play him in the backfield and when Terry Cole and Jerry Hill, the Colt running backs, were incapacitated in training camp during the summer of 1969, Shula ordered the move. "I talked with John about the switch," he said, "and he was very unselfish about making the move. He told me, 'Coach, I'm willing to give it all I've got.'" But it lasted only a week. "We experimented two days," said Shula. "He looked very good the first day. On the second, he got hurt. So John will go back to tight end."

Unfortunately, it was a knee injury which failed to heal. Even a slight bump thereafter was enough to cause swelling. "I can't run like I would like to run," John told Cameron C. Snyder of the Baltimore *Sun*. "Before I hurt the knee, I would catch the ball and say to myself 'I'm going to trample that defender in the ground.' Now I'm more conscious of the knee and try to avoid getting it hit." The statistics told their own story: thirty-four passes caught for 443 yards and two touchdowns—the lowest yardage since 1964. While openly Mackey would say nothing that could be mis-

construed, privately he resented the cause of his predicament. He had spent seven years learning to play tight end
and he didn't want to learn another position, especially after
being named to all-league honors three years in a row.
Moreover, it was only days after Mackey's knee injury that
the Associated Press announced his selection as the greatest
tight end in half a century of NFL play, professional football's supreme honor. For such superior qualifications, only
the barest few could qualify. "The true test of the tight
end," the award read, "is his ability to maintain an emotional balance. Because of the demands of the position, the
personality of the player can easily be influenced, if not dis-
torted. Spread-eagled between the poles of finesse and sav-
agery, Mackey has met the challenge better than anyone in
the game, remaining a sensitive, positive and productive
human being while dispatching his assignment with professional elan. In an unyielding environment, Mackey displays
the grace of a man larger than his job." Small wonder in the
light of such praise that Mackey decried the effort to turn
him into a fullback.

The only "something else" he cared to accept dropped his
way in January 1970 when he was elected president of the
National Football League Players Association, bargaining
agent for the 1200 players of the American and National
Football Conferences. According to Mackey, the post fell to
him quite by accident because he was the "least of all evils."
The story went back to January 7, 1968, when the Association registered as a labor union with the United States Department of Labor. At that time, Association president Mike
Pyle of the Chicago Bears said, "The Association will take a
militant attitude to protect its members and to undertake all
appropriate action to see that the players' demands are
met." There was dissatisfaction among the players, he said,
over minimum salaries which were "too low," the pension
plan "which was not comparable to the one baseball has
going," and the pre-season pay, which was then ten dollars

per day. What Pyle and company wanted were (1) minimum salaries of $15,000 per player, (2) an additional $100,-000 from each team for the players' benefit fund to augment the $1.3 million currently paid, and (3) a $500 payment for each player for all exhibition games. For their part, the owners hired Theodore W. Kheel, noted New York labor lawyer, and by February the two sides were ready to bargain—fruitlessly, it turned out, because after four meetings in which the owners did little to negotiate, the players broke off further talks. Kheel pleaded poverty. Instead of the $600,000 profit which the Association said each team earned, the average, Kheel claimed, was actually $320,000. In the previous six years, the average player salaries had jumped from $10,708 to $22,500. "That," said Kheel, "compares rather favorably with earnings in other walks of life." The chief clinker in the negotiations was the fact that neither side wanted to include salaries in the discussions. What the players were actually asking were fringe benefits which had the effect of talking dessert when the *pièce de résistance* should have been the topic.

Nothing happened for a week following the rupture. Then, Art Modell, Cleveland Brown owner and president of the National Football League, held out the olive branch. "We continue ready to meet with you at any time," he told the Association representatives, but player demands on pensions and exhibition games, he hinted, jeopardized the ability of eleven of the sixteen clubs to survive. This theme the players rejected and while they talked of striking "unless the owners moved," *The New York Times* reported they agreed to begin negotiations again. After a two-day session in Detroit, the confrontation over pre-season pay and higher minimum salaries was amicably resolved, but there remained the problem of pension allotments, a prickly subject at best. The owners refused to raise their ante by 25 per cent during the 1968 and 1969 seasons or to make further revisions in light of existing conditions. To go beyond that,

they concluded, would be foolhardy considering the scheduled merger of the American and National Leagues by 1970
and the formation of one common pension plan. So when
the owners refused to consider the players' request for a
guaranteed pension funding of $3 million annually by 1970,
a hasty vote of the Association's membership revealed a
twenty-to-one sentiment in favor of striking. Reassured by
this display of confidence, John Gordy of the Detroit Lions,
the Association's new president, told the players not to report for training and the owners immediately struck back by
announcing the camps would not open. It was the first
player strike in professional football. Prophetically, William
N. Wallace of *The New York Times* wrote, "Even if the
strike is settled today, or tomorrow, as it should be, pro
football will be marked. The players, newly organized in a
union structure, will have achieved their goals under the
duress of a strike. Precedent has been set and the players
know forever that the next time they are to sign a contract
with the owners—in 1970—all they must do is carry their
demands to the end, that being a strike." Not so farsighted
were the angry owners and players who found harsh words
to belabor each other. Deacon Jones of the Los Angeles
Rams quipped testily; "It's about time the players shared in
the rewards. We are the ones taking the punishment out on
the field, not the owners."

Mackey's own club president, Carroll Rosenbloom, countered with a fiery blast. "Suspend operations," he shouted.
"Cancel the 1968 season." It began to look as though emotion would devour reason with the future of pro football
perilously balanced. At the penultimate moment both sides
providentially had the good sense to begin negotiating once
more. The owners offered this time to increase their pension
contributions from $900,000 to $1,125,000 in 1968 and to
$1,350,000 in 1969, but Gordy turned thumbs down. "Base-
ball's projected benefits would be 100 per cent above those
of football," he said. But from the owners' viewpoint, what

got under Modell's skin was that "despite granting 21 demands to the players," the sole reason for the impasse was
the question "of granting pension benefits in 1968 to players
who, on the average, would not be eligible to receive such
benefits until the year 2000." [5] For five days nothing happened. Finally, on July 14, after a five-hour-twenty-three-
minute bargaining session, the two antagonists reached
agreement. The owners promised to sweeten the pension
contribution by a half-million dollars to a total of $3 million,
which was about what the players had originally demanded
and the owners castigated as ruinous.

Anyone could see, even at the time of the owner-player
agreement, that 1970 would be the pivotal year in pro football. Not only were the sixteen NFL and the ten AFL teams
to be joined, under the terms of a merger agreement
reached in 1966, but a new alignment, consisting of the
American and National Football Conferences with three divisions each, was about to give pro football a face-lifting. On
top of that, the 1968 player contract would expire in midsummer. A key figure in the game's changing complexion
had been Baltimore's Carroll Rosenbloom. When the NFL
owners—with the biggest stadiums, the most renowned
players and the top television ratings—had balked over
moving into the American League, Rosenbloom was one of
the first to understand the necessity for a complete realign-
ment. He offered to leave even if it hurt. "You know what
you've got and you don't know what you're going to get,"
he said. As it turned out, his Baltimore club landed upright,
becoming part of the East Division of the American Football Conference, along with Boston, Buffalo, Miami, and the
New York Jets.

And so this was the water that had passed under the
bridge when the player representatives and their alternates
descended on New Orleans January 8, 1970, to watch the
Minnesota Vikings play the Kansas City Chiefs in the Super
Bowl and to lay the groundwork for the contract negotia-

tions that were shortly due to begin. Since the twenty-six teams of the NFL and the AFL were merging, it was logical for the players to promote a single bargaining organization to replace the previous two. To lead the new hybrid, a man would need the confidence of both groups, often at odds with each other in the past. Just as the NFL players had assumed a condescending manner toward their AFL counterparts, they now wanted a lion's say in the new Association. Predictably, the AFL players were just as adamant against such a takeover. Whatever the merits or demerits of field performance, they gave up nothing in point of personal privilege. And besides, they mused, "Who won the Colt-Jet game anyway?" Nevertheless, what rankled in the minds of many NFL players was that AFL players had done nothing to aid their cause during the angry negotiations of 1968. What had been won at the cost of a strike now belonged to both camps. Consequently, the president of the new players' group would need to be a person who could cope with the hostility and unite the various factions. John Gordy had re-signed and Jack Kemp of the Buffalo Bills, president of the AFL Players Association, was too much an AFL product to qualify with the NFL players. A search began for a new head. Among the list of potential candidates, John Mackey's name stood high. First, he was a member of the Baltimore organization which, with a pedigree in the NFL, was about to join the AFL. This would satisfy the need of juxtaposition to both camps. Second, Mackey was known as an independent personality, a trait the NFL players demanded. "They felt that I would stand tough if it was necessary," Mackey said, explaining their mood. "The NFL was known for its toughness in the same way the AFL was recognized for its diplomacy." Finally, John Mackey possessed the personal popularity, the dynamic quality that made him a natural choice. The Colts had recognized this trait by electing him first their alternate and later their player representative. Thus, his election on January 10 as president of the newly organized National Football Players Association was not un-expected by those intimate with the decision. "It was a tough job, though," says Mackey. "I had the AFL, who thought one way, on one side and the NFL, who thought another way, on the other side. There was still that chilli-ness among AFL and NFL players, and I did not know what had gone on during the 1968 negotiations. Conse-quently, it was hard being president and chief negotiator in the same year with so little time to adjust."

The previous collective bargaining agreement ran out just three weeks after he took office. Despite some effort to ne-gotiate, the first week of July passed without a contract and talk of a second strike arose. The issues were about what they had been two years before: increased pensions, fringe-benefit improvements, and a larger share of the pre-season game purse. When no agreement was reached, the players instructed their members not to report to training camp, and as before, the owners decided to bar experienced play-ers from their camps. To enliven the controversy still fur-ther, the players then called on the College All-Star squad to give up playing the world champion Kansas City Chiefs on July 31. "We're not trying to hurt the Chicago *Tribune* charity," a Players Association spokesman said, "but if the Chiefs can't practice, the All-Stars shouldn't." By now, Mackey was in the thick of the struggle, and not answering his telephone when reporters called. In Baltimore, among Colt enthusiasts, his stock began to fall. "Naturally," said a reporter for the Baltimore *Sun*, "the man in the street who makes $7,500 a year can't see it either. All he knows is that players in the NFL average about 30 grand a year, have plenty of money to spend on the road and pretty decent working conditions. If that is bad, he would like some of it." But the fans were largely unaware of the complexity of the negotiations which had to take place in a new environment, with twenty-six club owners and hundreds of additional players involved. "There's no way the players could ever win this thing in the press," Mackey confided. Furthermore, he went on to a *Sun* reporter, "I'm not worried about winning it in the press. All I want is a fair shake, and we haven't been getting that."

At the beginning of serious negotiations, the owners were not organized to confront Mackey and the players' attorney, Alan Miller. They didn't understand that the Association president had determined when he took the job not "to get taken in by some smooth talk. I gave up all my off-season work, took courses in labor law, surrounded myself with the smartest people I could find and did my homework. When I went into the negotiations, our side knew exactly where the pie was cut in all phases. We prepared ourselves thoroughly." It came as a shock, therefore, for Mackey to discover the owners were not equally prepared. If he had been an owner, he would have hired someone to negotiate rather than to handle it himself. As it was, the owners made such statements as "We're not going to do anything," "We don't have to do anything," "We can do anything we want to do," which were inadmissible. "In labor law, you know, there are certain things an employer must do and there are certain things that an employee can't do," he said, explaining the owners' attitude. But the owners found this too formal for their tastes. With some few exceptions, they thought it would be a breeze, just "walk in and have a drink and sign a contract."

The first snag to hit the negotiations was owner insistence that the pay ceiling for pre-season games remain undisturbed, contending the issue was resolved in 1968 when the players agreeed not to seek another raise for such games. Mackey told them that it had "expired with the collective-bargaining contract," but they refused to believe him. They were sold on the idea of perpetuity, and many months were spent just arguing the point. From the outset, he insisted that the way to negotiate was to sit down and reach an agreement without the lawyers. After you make your decision, "you bring them back and have it put in legal language. The whole issue could be solved in less than two hours," Mackey went on, explaining how it was with his own employer Carroll Rosenbloom. "We would have gotten it over fast," he said. "All the small things he would automatically concede. 'You can have this, this, and this,' he would say of a long list of items. It doesn't make sense to hassle and haggle over whether or not you're going to get an extra penny for meal money or whether you're going to get one ticket or two tickets for an away game. It's a lot of wasted conversation, dialogue that could be spent talking about something more meaningful, the hard core, the meat of the thing. I think the most important thing in negotiating is to know how far to push and when you've gone as far as you can, to say 'That's it!' "

The one image Mackey personified throughout was determination. "He has one speed—full," said teammate Curry. He stood his ground even when the other side began feeding stories to the press to embarrass the Association and downgrade him personally. When Mackey pointed out that pro football's pensions were inferior to those in baseball and hockey, the owners let the rumor drop. It would require an increase in ticket prices, thereby hoping to arouse popular opinion against the players. "We've never asked the owner to raise the ticket prices," Mackey countered, the *Sun* reported. "That was their own suggestion of what they'd have to do to meet our demands and they're trying to pin it on us." At another point in the negotiations, while the subject of players' personal appearance was under discussion, one owner looked up and happened to note Mackey dressed in a purple jump suit. "Why do you wear that purple suit?" he inquired.

"Why are you wearing white socks?" Mackey retorted with asperity.

"Because I like them," the owner answered, not desiring to be questioned.

"I like my purple suit," Mackey said, quietly ending the exchange.[6]

But just as all roads lead to Rome, all discussions eventually led to the question of pension payments, as they had in 1968. The owners agreed to increase their allotment from $2.8 million to $4.5 million a year, but the players said no. They sought a contribution that would average $6.45 million over the next four years—a sum, one owner said, that could mean that half the teams would operate in the red. After all the arguments had proved fruitless, the players proposed to place the impasse before the Federal Mediation and Conciliation Service in Washington. This the owners accepted, but the initial pass to get both parties before the arbitration board failed. The owners were convinced that Washington's political climate would aid the players and insisted upon meeting somewhere other than the capital, perhaps Philadelphia. Mackey weighed the pros and cons, said yes, and agreed to work around the clock, if necessary, in cooperation with Gilbert J. Sedin and Ralph C. Patterson, the government's representatives.

In the meantime, not hearing that the conference had been shifted to Philadelphia, the Association's player representatives descended upon Washington, establishing headquarters on the ninth floor of the Hilton in anticipation of the meetings with the federal mediators. They hung up a red-white-and-blue sign that said *Employees of the National Football League and Its 26 Franchises. On Strike. Please Do Not Patronize* and waited for the consultations to begin. It was trying enough to have the negotiating site shifted to Philadelphia, with the loss of their leader, but far worse was the knowledge that out in Kansas City, the players' strike was reaching crisis proportions. What would be the outcome of a break in the Association's façade? Mackey understood why there were many fringe players who were worried. The strike might finish their careers. He knew, too, the Chiefs, as world champions, deserved to play the All-Stars, but to end the strike on that note might be to lose everything. Hank Stram, coach of the Chiefs, had said it would take five days to get ready for the game, meaning a decision by July 25. Since there was still time to say yes or no, Mackey felt safe about leaving Washington for the bargaining in Philadelphia. In his absence a call came through from Jim Tyrer, the Chiefs' player representative, and Len Dawson, the star quarterback, saying there was overwhelming sentiment among the players to play the game. At that, headquarters panicked, and in Mackey's name gave permission to go ahead with the game.

Mackey was handed the news while huddled in negotiation, and as soon as the discussions were ended raced back to Washington, arriving at three o'clock in the morning, worn, weary, and exhausted. "What do you think?" they asked him uneasily as he entered the room. Mackey had to make an instant decision. If he answered negatively, he would jeopardize his authority—which Mal Kennedy, the players' business director, credited with so far holding the thirteen hundred players together. He couldn't afford the risk. The only course open, he decided, was to plug into the Chiefs and wish them well. "Go ahead," he said, as soon as he was able to reach their spokesmen. "Good luck, and I hope you beat the All-Stars." Tyrer helped him across the abyss by making it crystal-clear the Chiefs' appearance in the All-Star game was not a "lever" in the negotiations with the owners, but a "sincere effort to maintain tradition." They would disband after the game, if the bargaining was still in process. So the danger of a player collapse subsided, leaving Mackey still in control. "I've been here for ten days," said Bill Curry, impressed by the denouement, "and I'll tell you one thing I've learned: John Mackey is going to be a great, great leader of something for the rest of his life. He can't get off the hook after this. He just has too much leadership ability." [7] Despite this, Mackey had reservations concerning what might happen in another crisis. He decided to delay his return to Philadelphia for three days, in case his hand was needed at the helm in Washington.

When he arrived, he found progress in the City of Brotherly Love at a standstill. After a hectic day of bargaining, the owners broke off further negotiations and retired to New York to talk among themselves. Again, as so often in the past, the discussions were unable to solve the thorny pension issue. Reflecting the employer viewpoint, Leonard Tose, owner of the Philadelphia Eagles, said he could not understand why young men with the best years ahead of them could be so concerned with pensions. Tose, a thirty-year veteran of the trucking wars, which included negotiations with the Teamsters, said, "We never have a strike over pensions. You have a strike over what the other fellow is taking home, what's in his paycheck [but] I can't imagine a guy 25 years old worrying over what he is going to collect at age 55." This was a different ball game all right, and the owners, experienced in other lines, had not understood the difference. After Mackey announced to the press he was sorry the owners had come to Philadelphia "not knowing what their position was," he returned to Washington to make a report to the Association members.

What bothered the players was not only the unwillingness of the owners to continue uninterrupted bargaining until an agreement had been reached, but also the continued circulation through the press of unfounded facts. "The things that have gotten into the newspapers and on the air about us have been incredible," said Curry. "The owners issue a statement and every word of it is printed or makes the network news. We issue a statement and all they say is, 'The players issued a rebuttal.'" The worst information involved the pension figures. "Even our members, the players around the country," Curry went on, "call us and say, 'Hey, I just read in the papers what we've been offered, why don't we accept it right now?' And then we have to tell them that's not what we've been offered at all. The money the

owners have offered us—$18 million over the next four years
—is not as much as it sounds. There are no past service benefits. The plan wouldn't include retired players. We want
everybody included. There is no provision for partial disability and no widows' benefits and no provision for an increase in our major medical plan. We don't have optical or
dental benefits." This was precisely Mackey's view. "The figures you see are wrong," he said.

Now that the first scheduled pre-season game was but a
week away, the plight of the owners was becoming desperate. They had to count on the income of these games to
keep their figures out of the red and time was running out.
Without players in training camp, all could be lost. They
gambled on opening them to any experienced player who
wished to report, but the plan fizzled. Less than two dozen
of the 1300 players involved broke ranks. For some it was
principle, for others the fear of reprisal. "There are a lot of
people in pro football," said Pat Matson of the Cincinnati
Bengals, "who know how to make injuries happen, if you
know what I mean." [8] With the balance of power unchanged and negotiations in a deep-freeze stalemate, only
one course remained. That was to enlist the support of
Commissioner Pete Rozelle, who informed both sides of his
"availability" and, unknown to the public, was already moving.

On Friday night, July 31, the day following the owners'
abortive effort to break the strike, Rozelle invited Mackey
and Alan Miller, the players' attorney, to his Sutton Place
apartment in New York City. Together the three watched
the Chiefs—College All-Star game and shared quips. Mackey
discovered that Rozelle had a disarming side to him that he
had never appreciated. He learned that Rozelle was not
"holding back," as he had suspected up to then. When the
Commissioner moved cautiously, it was because he had to
deal with twenty-six owners, known for their stubbornness,
and you had to think of their problems as well as those of

the players. The stern question was "not so much the decision, but the timing," and Mackey was about to receive a
demonstration of Rozelle's timing.

On Saturday, August 1, the Commissioner lined up his
ducks and summoned the owners to a conference the following day at 12:30 P.M. in his wood-paneled office on the
twelfth floor at 410 Park Avenue. In order to field all developments, the players' delegation, headed by Mackey, flew in
from Washington and occupied quarters at the nearby City
Squire Motel, waiting for the nod from Rozelle. At 1:30 P.M.
the players received the word, and joined the owners, each
faction occupying separate rooms. At long last, after weeks
of frustrating effort, both sides were prepared for the nitty-
gritty. The talks droned on into the evening and early
morning hours with shirtsleeve bargaining all the way. At
midnight the air conditioning automatically went off and a
haze settled overhead. The only one to retain unruffled
composure was Rozelle, who moved from one group to another, helping to hammer out the differences, recounted
The New York Times. "Look at him in that blue jacket," one
of the owners joked. "And how the hell does he keep that
tie on?" One by one a dozen of the owners drifted upstairs
to Rozelle's private office on the thirteenth floor. There,
stretched out on sofas, chairs, and even the beige rug, they
slept, awakened only by the intermittent snoring of Sid Gill-
man, the San Diego Chargers' general manager.

On and on the negotiations ground for twenty-two con-
secutive hours until a settlement was finally reached in what
could best be described as "an unhappy but a relieved atmosphere." Asked to state his reaction to the outcome,
Mackey wearily replied, "There wasn't any winner. We
have an agreement, that's the important thing." In a strik-
ingly similar vein, one anonymous owner sighed, "I'm not
happy with the settlement, but it's done and I didn't think it
was possible. I'm just exhausted." It was a four-year contract, assuring peace until 1974, with the owners agreeing to

a $19.1-million package, an $11-million increase based on 1969 levels. For the first time, the players obtained disability, widows' benefits, maternity and dental benefits.

While the owner-player quarrel was now at an end, the effect of the strike and the settlement lingered on. The public knew that its favorite sport had been threatened with suspension during 1970 because of the inability of the players and owners to agree on a contract. In addition, their emotions were stimulated by the media's reporting primarily the owners' arguments and emphasizing the salaries and working conditions the players demanded. Goaded by such reports, it was relatively easy for the prejudiced to conclude that the difficulty arose from a tiny group of arbitrary players, headed by John Mackey, a black. This was more than their white egos would swallow and they waited for a chance to embarrass Mackey. It came in the season's opener against the Kansas City Chiefs. "It was the first time I'd ever been booed in my life," Mackey sighed. When it happened a second time a month later against the Boston Patriots, loyal teammates jumped to his defense. "John Mackey," said Curry, "was elected by his peers to do a most thankless job. He received no pay, worked long hours and put up with a lot of abuse. He doesn't deserve the boos of the fans. He did an outstanding job negotiating for us and the players are grateful. The owners also respected the job he did and the businesslike way he conducted himself." A white Georgian, Curry knew what was welling up inside the minds of Mackey's tormentors. They were refusing to accept—yet—the sight of a black American with the power to suspend or terminate a game they cherished.

For Mackey the cure to white racism was "to get involved," to learn about other people's backgrounds. "You have to accept the fact that a person is black and has his own way of thinking. It's based on how he was raised and the things that formed his life. You shouldn't feel that all your friends must be like you—one of the problems with

Baltimore is that most people live in ghettos and think that whatever is happening in their particular ghetto is happening all over the world. You have 'little Italy,' you have 'Poland town,' you have a Jewish neighborhood, you have a white neighborhood, you have a black city and people just don't get together to know people. I'd just like people to know people, to accept them for whatever they are. You don't have to agree with everything they do, everything they say and you might not even want them for your friends after you meet them, but at least you give them a chance."

In Mackey's view, the process of racial and ethnic understanding has to begin before children reach school age. "They don't learn prejudice in the schools," he says pointedly. "They develop it at home so the integration of neighborhoods should precede the integration of the school system. If you integrate neighborhoods, you'll find out how people live and you will know them on a different level. You have to live with people to know people. You can't take them out of an isolated area, throw them into an integrated school and then try to correct the problem. That doesn't really correct the problem because they return to their isolated situation." Believing this, Mackey, his wife, and their three children decided to live in Pikesville, an integrated suburb of Baltimore.

Away from football, Mackey has now joined that growing group of black athlete-entrepreneurs. He is president and board chairman of John Mackey Enterprises, which grosses $2.5 million a year, largely through wholesale food distribution. Mackey Enterprises is already on the capitalistic road to becoming a conglomerate. Along the way, he is developing his own guidelines for success. "When you buy a company," he says, "buy management along with it. And then you motivate the employees by holding out a little 'cookie' by which they will receive X amount of shares of this or that—bonuses, you know—depending upon their earnings.

You don't buy a company unless you can secure the old management for at least five years."

So Mackey, only twenty-nine, has arrived. He has parlayed a strong personality and a superb athletic skill to reach the pinnacle of pro football. Whatever obstacles there were because of color, he has brilliantly overcome. In the words of his former coach, Ben Schwartzwalder, he "has proven that color doesn't matter. It's what you are that really counts."

Alvin F. Poussaint ══════════════

A product of New York's East Harlem, Alvin F. Poussaint was born May 15, 1934. The beginning was humble enough but not exactly what one associates with the Upper East Side of Manhattan Island. In the first place, the great deterioration that struck East Harlem after World War II had not begun. There were still large Italian enclaves, a scattering of Irish, Puerto Ricans, and blacks; a certain homogeneity reigned, and the social fabric seemed impervious to the trauma of the fifties and sixties. And, as though this stability were not in itself unique for urban blacks, young Poussaint was one of eight children, in a family closely regulated by two watchful parents.

The forebears of the elder Poussaint had come to the United States from French-dominated Haiti during the nineteenth century and, after some years in the South, had emigrated to New York City. Their descendant was a devout Catholic and saw to it that the Church's influence extended to his children. A printer by trade, he had operated his own shop on Third Avenue, which specialized in promoting community affairs. When times grew harsh, he gave up the business and hired out as a linotypist, eventually becoming a typographer. Poussaint's influence on his son was like a hand hidden from view. Young Alvin knew it was there if the need arose, but for the most part it remained out of sight. Recalling the indirect effect of the paternal role, he could say later, "I always knew that he supported me, particularly in education. If I took that route, he would support me as much as he possibly could."

In contrast to this rather formal relationship, Alvin's mother was a warm personality, a full-time housewife who never worked outside the home. Because of this, she always had ample time for her eight children, to whom she was devoted. "It gave me a certain security while I was growing up," the younger Poussaint admits, speaking of their affinity.

Outside the home, other influences began to pile up: school, teachers, friends. The pupils at his elementary school in East Harlem were mostly black—root and branch of his own culture, and therefore without the experience or knowledge to affect his. But he did come under the influence of teachers who perceived his academic skills and encouraged Alvin to use them.

Moreover, when Poussaint was nine years old, an attack of rheumatic fever hospitalized him for six months and curtailed his physical activity for months after. To fill the vacuum, he became a voracious reader, devouring everything he could get his hands on. Added to that "I had a sister-in-law," he recalls, "who was very interested in encouraging me in school and listening to me talk and giving me books to read. Consequently, I became sort of academically focused."

With such stimulation, the response was not unexpected. By the time Poussaint completed junior high school, he knew he had an aptitude for science and mathematics, and decided to compete for a place in one of New York's special high schools. His matriculation in prestigious Peter Stuyvesant High School in downtown Manhattan opened a new world that was farther from East Harlem than the ten miles which separated the two. For the first time he was in a school "with nearly all white kids, and just a few blacks."

The excitement and the challenge of being with other bright students swept him along to a delta of new activity. "I was very active in school, wanted to learn everything about everything. A lot of things I just took up on my own. I taught myself to play the clarinet, the saxophone and flute. I started writing, too. I became associate editor of the literary magazine and received the creative writing award upon graduation."

Each day, however, he had to return to the environment surrounding the Poussaint home on 101st Street between Park and Lexington avenues, and by the early fifties East Harlem was becoming the center of the drug culture, particularly among blacks. A lot of his friends turned to drugs, and Poussaint doesn't really know why he didn't except that he was always terrified of it. "The idea of being 'hooked' on something frightened me," he says, "and I used to feel sorry for the kids who were and had to spend all their time worrying about getting a shot. Every so often one of them would die or if they didn't die from an overdose, he would end up in jail for stealing, and it didn't seem worth whatever he was getting from it to participate in it although there was a lot of pressure in the community on the kids to become drug addicts."

One interruption in this two-dimensional world occurred summers when young Poussaint went to a so-called progressive camp in upstate New York. It was one of the rewards of having a father on the Board of Directors of the 135th Street YMCA. In his role as chairman of the Boys Department, the elder Poussaint had received free scholarships to the camp in the hope of attracting black youth. And what was more natural than to give one to Alvin? This, too, was a new world composed mostly of Jewish middle-class youngsters. Because a lot of the campers hadn't known blacks, there was some evidence of discrimination, but the camp itself tried hard to promote interracial harmony. "It opened up a whole new vista," Poussaint says, looking back.

In the spring of 1952, Poussaint, barely eighteen, graduated from Stuyvesant, determined to enter college. His natural inquisitiveness was not yet weaned and he yearned for
more of the milk of knowledge. He looked longingly at Yale
University, which had approved his application, but father
Poussaint said no. He was certain it would cost more money
to go away to school, and furthermore, he was a trifle skeptical of what might happen to his son in a strange location,
divorced from his ever-watchful eye. Consequently, he insisted that Alvin remain in New York; faced with this edict,
Poussaint enrolled at Columbia. Despite initial misgivings,
he liked the university although he had to study harder
than at any previous time in his life because of the intense
scholastic competition. "I was always studying," he says of
that period; "my time was fully devoted to activities around
the school." There were so many papers and other things to
write that his creative ambitions became stifled. "I may
have written some short stories or fiddled around with some
poetry or something, but I didn't write for any formal publication."

The one objection he had to Columbia was feeling "very
out of place. Even though it was nominally open, it was not
at all open socially. Social situations were awkward, there
being a prevalent feeling among whites that blacks
shouldn't come to social events. They didn't expect you to
show up at the dance." Accordingly, Poussaint was not
overly surprised when a couple of white friends who had
asked him to their homes reneged on the invitation at the
request of their parents. "I resented it," he said, commenting
on their bigotry, "but I wasn't surprised by it. I didn't mull
over it very long for I had had incidents of that type all
along, one time or another. You knew there were limitations
to how far you could go with white people and how far they
would go out to you, so you accepted it."

Long before graduation, Poussaint knew what he wanted
from life. In fact, the seed had germinated while he was bed-

ridden with rheumatic fever. That long experience had
made him familiar with hospital life and the people who inhabited the world of medicine. He liked the doctor-nurse
camaraderie, and the possibility of becoming part of the
medical team. As a result, he applied to the Cornell Medical
School and the fall of 1956 found him studying medicine at
New York Hospital on East 68th street in the ward in which
he was born twenty-two years before. If anything, Poussaint
now felt more isolated, for he was the only black American
in a class of eighty-six students. There was one black in each
of the three classes ahead of him, but they were from foreign countries. Now, more than ever, he could feel the crisp
sting of white prejudice. Indirectly, he was told of certain
professors "who would never have a black intern in their
surgery program." Since they obviously hadn't, it was hard
not to believe such tales. Poussaint concluded that it was
not only a sign of white racism but a commentary on black
ability as well. "I think some of the professors genuinely
doubted whether blacks could do certain things, which was
a kind of white supremacy syndrome."

From all this, Poussaint was developing a deep interest in
the emotional ills arising from racial pressures. From camp
to university to medical school, he had witnessed a series of
white slurs that had no basis in reality. They were simple fig-
ments of white imagination turned hard by continual usage.
Unless determined efforts were made to root out the prejudice, a whole nation would continue to be weighed down
by the syndrome he had seen among the faculty. Blacks
would suffer more openly than whites, but no one, regardless of color, would completely escape the hand of racism.
Thus committed, Poussaint decided to concentrate on psychiatry, and his application for internship was accepted by
the Neuropsychiatric Institute of the University of California at Los Angeles.

His four years at UCLA were a rerun of the four spent at
Cornell—only more so. There was the same racial prudery

that abounded in New York, the same hesitation to invite a
person of black skin to white social gatherings. The authorities even went so far as to ask the white nurses if they had
any objection to working with a black intern or taking his
orders. Certain doctors at the Institute told him to decline
invitations to professors' houses. They were no more than
pro forma inducements and should be read as such. Despite
such impediments, Poussaint impressed his personality and
his skill for the first time on a white-oriented structure. In
his last year at UCLA he was selected chief resident, in
charge of the intern training program.

Moreover, by graduation time a lot of racial water had
passed beneath the bridge. The sit-ins of the early sixties
were by now history. So were Birmingham and Selma, and
Watts was but a few blocks and a few months away. Feeling
as he did and deeply conscious of the affronts he had swal-
lowed as a university student, a medical neophyte, and now
an intern, he was eager to join the civil rights fray. For a
number of reasons, the path led predictably to Jackson, Mississippi, at that point the center for Student Nonviolent
Coordinating Committee activity. Bob Moses, the famed
SNCC leader, asked Poussaint to join him. The two had
been classmates at Peter Stuyvesant. Also penned to the invitation was Poussaint's sister's name. And when they told
the UCLA graduate that they needed a director for the
Medical Committee for Human Rights, Poussaint gave them
assurance he would provide a backup for medical services.

At the time Jackson resembled an armed camp. Because
of SNCC activity, it almost had "the air of a war." Anyone
connected with SNCC invariably carried with him the fear
of arrest or murder at the hands of the police. It was indeed
a time for taking stock of the causes for this black-white impasse that threatened to blow up the community.

Poussaint thought back to the day in 1619 when a Dutch
frigate landed twenty black slaves in Jamestown. By analyz-
ing what had happened since, he saw how their descendants

had been methodically dehumanized by white slavemasters. In the process "families were broken up, the Negro male was completely emasculated, and the Negro woman was systematically sexually exploited and vilely degraded." [1] In order to make degradation permanent, whites had resorted to all manner of deviltry to fix the mood of subservience. "The more acquiescent the Negro was," Poussaint concluded, "the more he was rewarded within the plantation culture. Those who bowed and scraped for the white boss and denied their aggressive feelings were promoted to 'house nigger' and 'good nigger.'" Out of such mental deflation, nothing would arise but generations of docile "Uncle Toms." One could not even survive without submitting to the emotional torture.

The imbalance between the races was fortified by a system that treated blacks as children and whites as the community's only adults. "It was sickening for me," Poussaint wrote later, "to hear a Southern white dime-store clerk address a Negro minister with a doctoral degree as 'Jimmy,' while he obsequiously called her 'Miss Jane.' If the Negro minister rejected these social mores he would probably be harassed, punished or in some way 'disciplined.'" Poussaint himself was no stranger to such white supremacy. He told of leaving his Jackson office one day with his Negro secretary only to be hailed by a white policeman yelling, "Hey, boy! Come here!" Somewhat bothered, he retorted: "'I'm no boy!' He then rushed at me, inflamed, and stood towering over me, snorting, 'What d'ja say, boy?' Quickly he frisked me and demanded, 'What's your name, boy?' Frightened, I replied, 'Dr. Poussaint. I'm a physician!' He angrily chuckled and hissed, 'What's your first name, boy?' When I hesitated he assumed a threatening stance and clenched his fists. As my heart palpitated, I muttered in profound humiliation, 'Alvin.'

"He continued his psychological brutality, bellowing, 'Alvin, the next time I call you, you come right away, you hear? You hear?' I hesitated. 'You hear me, boy?' My voice trembling with helplessness, but following my instincts of self-preservation, I murmured, 'Yes, sir.' Now fully satisfied that I had performed and acquiesced to my 'boy status,' he dismissed me with, 'Now, boy, go on and get out of here or next time we'll take you for a little ride down to the station house.' "

Infuriated by the incident, Poussaint realized the law had momentarily ripped away his manhood before a woman "for whom I, a 'man,' was supposed to be the 'protector.' In addition, this had occurred on a public street for all the local black people to witness, reminding them that no black man was as good as any white man. All of us—doctor, lawyer, postman, field hand and shoeshine boy—had been psychologically 'put in our place.' "

The thought made him skeptical of the widely held theory that blacks could become peer members of American life if they would only take pride in their blackness, instead of indulging in self-hate. "No amount of self-love," he reasoned, going back to his confrontation with the policeman, "could have salvaged my pride or preserved my integrity. In fact, the slightest show of self-respect or resistance might have cost me my life. The self-hate that I felt at that time was generated by the fact that I and my people were completely helpless and powerless to destroy that white bigot and all that he represented. Suppose I had decided, as a man should, to be forceful? What crippling price would I have paid for a few moments of assertive manhood? What was I to do with my rage?"

Frustrated and humiliated, Poussaint began to tick off the tragedies of white suppression. Because of the loss of "assertiveness, self-confidence, and the willingness to risk failure," blacks had not wanted to initiate business ventures on their own. "A castrated human being is not likely to be inclined in any of these ways," he declared.

The same debility, arising from white domination, underlined the poor scholastic record of black youngsters, particularly the males, who were found on investigation to achieve less in elementary school than females of the same age. The systematic crushing of the former, to prevent their filling the role "upheld as masculine for the rest of American youth," Poussaint viewed as the primary reason. To undergird his point, he brought out a study which showed that "even when Negroes are given objective evidence of equal mental ability in a relatively brief interracial contact, they tend to feel inadequate and to orient compliantly toward whites." [2] It was all part of the matriarchal system which whites had imposed upon blacks to make certain that white males could not compete with black males, on any level.

This led to a double legal standard, one for whites, the other for blacks. Poussaint had only to look about to see that "if a black man rapes a white woman, he may get the electric chair, that when a white man kills a black man or rapes a black woman, he gets off lightly, especially if he is a policeman." Even worse was the unconcern in the white community over blacks committing crimes against blacks. "It's only niggers cutting each other up," they blithely said.[3]

An additional irritation, Poussaint discovered, was the way whites thought nothing of placing their feet on black necks and challenging them to make good under the "Protestant ethic myth of hard work" as they had. For the few who did succeed in crossing the line, the final blow was the realization that "American society did not really allow the most 'successful' Negro to overcome the stigma of being black." Never did this emerge more clearly, Poussaint thought, than during the urban riots when "doctors and lawyers with 'personal acceptability' were as vulnerable to police abuse and fire as the ghetto youth dressed in hand-me-downs." [4]

In view of all this, what happened in Jackson was fairly predictable. The SNCC campaign had begun as a traditional civil rights movement of non-violence, in the format of Martin Luther King. Northern liberalism applauded the spectacle of self-effacement, and in the summer of 1964 long lists of white college students trooped south to aid the cause of racial equality, expecting to be received with open arms by grateful blacks. Those who had preceded them in the early sixties were often seen joining hands with blacks and singing "Black and white together, we shall overcome." But a transformed milieu, formed by the anger and rage of generations, awaited their arrival. Black youths were finding it more and more difficult to work with whites. Poussaint could report, after talking to more than a hundred black volunteers, the conviction that "most of the whites who came down were either just white racists of another variety or that they had psychological 'hang-ups' centered around black people." [5] It seemed as though they weren't there a week before they wanted to take over and talk instead of listen.

There were several specific bones that caught in the black throats. One was the condescending attitude of white paternalism, what Poussaint dubbed "the 'White African Queen' and 'Tarzan' complexes." [6] A black project leader who saw it said of the whites, "They always boss you around and act as if you don't have any sense." This was particularly galling to the black leaders because they were anxious to develop black leadership that would fashion a new life for black people.

Sadly enough, much white endeavor suffered from a lack of rapport inside the black neighborhoods. Poussaint picked up the story of some white students believing they "could identify better with the local black people if they—the whites—were dirty and unkempt" for this, they assumed, was a way of "getting down to the level of the people." Such efforts, of course, raised their stock in the black community like a lead balloon. In other ways, too, the effort to please the local black populations proved equally unsuccessful. A number of whites, wanting to appear relaxed among the blacks, actually repulsed them. Native black Mississippians refused to believe they would exhibit such behavior "back home with their own kind," and concluded they must be a bunch of "misfits, beatniks, leftovers, white trash, sluts, etc.," who were rejects of their own society.

In addition, there were some whites the blacks accused of holding a martyr complex. They saw a trip to Mississippi and a part in the SNCC summer project as promising huge dividends among their friends at home. "They come down here to get beaten," said one SNCC official, "and then they can go back to their homes in the North and act like martyrs and become big wheels." What contributed to this irritation was the mass media that often blew up white experiences to the neglect of black deeds. "I'm not going on any more demonstrations and get my head 'whupped,'" said one embittered black, "so that some white kid can get his picture in the paper." Another complained, "We've been getting beaten up for years trying to integrate lunch counters, movies, and so on, and nobody has ever paid any attention or wrote about us. But these white SOBs come down here for a few months and get all the publicity. Everybody talks about how brave and courageous *they* are. What about us?" [7]

But as trying as these various abrasives were, the chief black jeremiad was the running sexual battle with white civil rights workers. "The Negro girls were often resentful and jealous of the attention which Negro men showed to the white girls, and vice versa," Dr. Poussaint revealed. "To a lesser degree, the Negro males were resentful of white males who showed an interest in Negro girls. They accused them of wanting to continue the racist exploitation of black women." [8] In an atmosphere as charged as Mississippi, such interracial encounters were ticking time bombs. No one knew what might happen if Southern whites, panicked by the fear of miscegenation, went on a rampage. Black residents were all too aware of such a possibility and resented the white workers "for unnecessarily making survival more

difficult for them." In many incidents, the problem—
Poussaint found—was a desire on the part of white volunteers to "prove they were not racially prejudiced by having
intense social relations with black people." According to the
psychiatrist, "when black girls were discussing white girls a
remark that became popular was 'I think all these white
girls down here sat up North dreaming about being raped
by some big black Negro and came down here to see what
it was like!'" Not unexpectedly, such fiery rifts ended in explosive scenes between the racial protagonists. Poussaint
noted that "so much energy was expended by both black
males and females in discussing the problems created by
white girls in particular that on many days little project
work was accomplished."

Small wonder that a twenty-two-year-old black worker
from Greenwood could sum up his reaction to the 1964 project for Dr. Poussaint as follows: "I don't know any 'different' kinds of white folks because all of them are racist at
heart, even those in the movement. I could say that some of
them are worse than the white segregationist because they
are out here feeling sorry for the 'poor colored folks' and
they are doing nothing more than satisfying their own needs
by being nice to the Negroes. I made a lot of mistakes in my
life, and one of the greatest was to think the whites in the
movement were different from other whites. There is no difference. They just do it in different ways. Everything I
learned, I got from Negroes. Whites didn't do anything on
my project but raise hell and sleep around and do all sorts
of other things that kept hell going. We didn't get any work
done because we used all our energy fighting them. I feel
that they should go and try to help their folks and stay
away from the black community because all they're doing is
screwing up the minds of the local people. They came down
here and started talking about all that could happen and
they went away, leaving the local people with a lot of hope
and nothing else. They went away themselves feeling they

had saved those poor Negroes but they hadn't. It would have been better, in a way, if they had never come down." [9]

Under such circumstances, what could be more natural than a dramatic growth of black power? Blacks, wanting above all a chance to work out their own destinies, searched for ways to release their rage and frustration. It was the anger of young blacks which began the sit-in demonstrations and encouraged white students to go south; it was also the anger of young blacks that brought the civil rights movement to an end before liberal Northern whites or older Southern blacks realized what was happening. By the summer of 1965, black SNCC workers were becoming militantly hostile to the few white workers who remained in the South. Poussaint found that he was prescribing hundreds of tranquilizers for what he could only describe as acute attacks of rage. While this new mood was developing, the media continued to concentrate on the exploits of Martin Luther King, Jr. During the previous March, King had reached his high-water mark at Selma with a vast outpouring of blacks and whites working together. It was "the largest gathering of ministers since the Council of Trent," [10] said one, and the effect of the march from Selma to Montgomery, protesting the restrictions on black voting in Dallas County, Alabama, had led to passage of the Voting Rights Act of 1965, the most significant civil rights measure to pass the Congress. Yet, less than six months later, the militant mood which had swept the SNCC outposts in Mississippi blew across the streets of Watts, the Negro district of Los Angeles. When King visited the riot-torn area, he was treated more as an impostor than a hero. At a gathering of some three hundred militants, he was taunted with sarcasm and interruptions. " 'We must join hands . . . ,' he began. Someone yelled, 'And burn!' Undaunted, King continued, 'You are all God's children. There will be a better tomorrow. . . .' But the crowd expectorated on non-violence. A Black Muslim roared, 'Get out of here, Dr. King! We don't want you!' " [11]

From the vantage point of the seventies, it is hard to be-lieve that white America, reflected by the press, could not see what was transpiring, that the civil rights movement had passed its watershed. Even a year later, when James Mere-dith initiated his now-famous march through Mississippi, the press was as eye-shy as before. The predominantly white reporters who followed the march refused to recognize the changed mood. "I remember," said Poussaint, recalling his part in the march, "that many were frightened and resentful that they were assigned to this 'senseless and foolish march.' They were angry with the leaders and other demonstrators who were ultimately responsible for their predicament." It was partially out of antagonism and partially out of a search for something dynamic that caused these scribes to empha-size Stokely Carmichael's call for "black power." The SNCC leader was good copy, especially when painted in ominous hues. A white society that had applauded non-violence, be-cause it was no threat to the *status quo,* now grimaced at the possibility of blacks grabbing power. To some it was the same old story of white inability to comprehend even-handed racial prerogatives. Almost two centuries before, a coterie of the most enlightened whites on American soil had proclaimed the equality of man in the Declaration of Inde-pendence, but by implication applied it only to white men —for the chief architect, Thomas Jefferson, while "trem-bling" at the thought of human bondage, had retained his slaves. Poussaint saw the same inconsistency in the relation-ship between white men and red men as between whites and blacks. "When the white man wiped out a camp of In-dians," he said, "it was called a 'victory.' When the Indians wiped out a camp of whites, it was called a 'massacre.'" [12] And, Poussaint went on to point out, this was no historical accident for the same measure of racism existed today in Congress. Unhesitatingly, members of the House could vote to unseat black Adam Clayton Powell for official misconduct while turning a deaf ear to appeals for unseating white Mississippi congressmen who had been elected illegally in 1964 because black voters were denied the right to vote.

For Dr. Poussaint, the psychiatrist, who had returned North in mid-1966 to take an assistant professorship at Tufts University School of Medicine, the spectacle was most provocative, for hitherto the American black had kept his emotional gnawing to himself. As DuBois had written in the *Souls of Black Folk*, "an American, a Negro; two souls, two thoughts, two unreconciled strivings; two warring ideals in one dark body, whose dogged strength alone keeps it from being torn asunder." The juxtaposition of the two, now forcibly changed, prompted Dr. Poussaint to note six different personalities emerging from the black community, some low-key non-aggressive, some directly or indirectly aggressive:

1. "The cool ones." In this category one would find the original Dick Gregorys, the ones Poussaint called "the compensatory happy-go-lucky" type. They were apt to joke and needle the whites a bit in contrast to their former obeisance. Knowing that "soul food" was gauche to most whites, they delighted in eating chitterlings, neck bones, and watermelons. Cognizant also of white distaste for tonsorial forgetfulness, they liked to let their hair grow *au naturel*. All this was done to tweak the white conscience without going to the length of crossing swords.

2. "The achievers." This type was trying to create an imposing image with its own hands. It was not "happy-go-lucky," it was not whimsical, it was striving to find a place inside the system. While labeled Uncle Tom by the more militant blacks, these men and women, for the most part college-educated, were bent on getting from the system their share of its benefits without letting the system control them, as it had their fathers and mothers. The Bonds, the Chisholms, the Conyers, the Mackeys, the Whartons, the Gibsons, the Brimmers belonged to this list. Their success was their militancy.

3. "The conformists." Black citizens, mostly middle-class, who formerly had gained their release by remaining Uncle Toms and hoping for a crumb of white recognition. The greatest compliment these people could receive, Poussaint wrote, was to be told by whites "You don't act like all the other Negroes," or "You don't seem Negro to me." [13] Their most lofty achievement—*à la* the white Protestant ethic—was to drive a status Cadillac. But their underpinnings were jarring loose as the wave of black militancy shook their community, and they discovered that "white acceptance" was no longer a sign of merit but a reminder of guilt. "Many blacks," Poussaint reported, "who were previously anxious to be one of a few Negroes at a cocktail party, now reported that they were declining invitations from whites for social functions where they were to be representative 'token' blacks." [14] It was one of the several openings in a formerly solid racial wall through which one glimpsed the new Negro thinking more of his reputation with black brothers than with whites.

4. "The aggressors." Never overly impressed by whites, this group at the first scent of black power flocked to the action where they could compete directly with whites. Muhammed Ali (né Cassius Clay) was typical of their type of release. Like Ali, they resented association with the white man's problems, declined to serve in Vietnam, and short of violence behaved in an anti-white manner.

5. "The sublimates." This group of vicarious activists was anxious to vituperate the white man, to make him aware of his disenchantment with whiteness. Their heroes, wrote Poussaint, were "Congressman Adam Clayton Powell and Malcolm X, who were both willing to 'tell the white man like it is' and did so, for a while at least, with apparent impunity." [15] Such an army of "invisible men" was hardly a burr under the white saddle, but it did serve as a spur for detecting the path of black antagonism.

6. "The militants." The best example of this group was, of

course, the Black Panthers, organized in Oakland during October 1966 by Huey P. Newton and Bobby Seale. Its ten-point program called for, among other things, the destruction of American capitalism, an end to the Vietnam war, and the release of black prisoners who had been sentenced to prison, not by black peers but by unsympathetic whites. The Panthers, not large in number but united in their opposition to the white power structure (symbolized by the police, whom they dubbed "pigs"), were a seething bed of revolutionary tinder. Their presence in the urban centers of the U.S. had prompted FBI director J. Edgar Hoover to call them the country's "most dangerous and violent-prone of all extremist groups." And whether one believed Hoover's definition of "dangerous," the Panthers certainly reflected Poussaint's description of this type of objector, a "chronic resentment and stubbornness toward white people—a chip on the shoulder." [16]

Reviewing these various categories, Poussaint was struck with the fact that their image—with the exception of the "achievers"—was almost wholly negative toward white men and women. Prior to the civil rights movement, they had hidden their rage and frustrations out of fear for white reprisals. Once the racial bars began falling, the black majority spread out in several directions trying to find its place in a new environment. "First, I was hung up on whites," said the Reverend Jesse L. Jackson, national director of Operation Breadbasket, thumbing through his experience, "then I went through an anti-white, pro-black period, and now whites being around don't threaten me because I have self-confidence. I don't need to waste time worrying about them and their reaction to me." [17]

Poussaint wondered how such "self-confidence" could be instilled in Negroes. He saw clearly that American blacks could wander forever through a wilderness of nonentity, lacking the inner strength to cope with whites. His work at Tufts and, after mid-1969, as associate dean and associate professor of psychiatry at Harvard Medical School, was piling up source material for developing conclusions.

For this reason, during an interview with him, I asked what he thought black students should do to obtain both a feeling of black identity and a peer attitude in the presence of whites—the *sine qua non* of black self-confidence. His answer was a call for separatism to gain identity and some form of integration to assure equality with whites. The caveat, Dr. Poussaint pointed out, was the great difficulty of creating black identity on an integrated campus or of establishing black self-assurance in a separated atmosphere. The two had to be delicately placed in balance.

To illustrate the point, the doctor could recall saying that blacks "have to learn that 'black is beautiful.' It's also important for every black to see successful black institutions. I think that if we are to undo the 'white-is-right' conditioning of the black mind, we must have counter-programs that legitimize blackness. Whites still have undue psychological control over our minds. For instance, one white person can walk into a group of two hundred blacks and change the whole character of the meeting. Some blacks are intimidated. Others begin directing their remarks to the white person as if to seek his approval. Still others become so angry they can't think straight. Therefore, the presence of that one white can interfere with the free communication and development of black people." [18] And yet, he went on to say, "an integrated college is one of the ways that blacks can begin to find out how to work with whites," something extremely important "since most of us are going to be dealing with them in the real world." The problem of the all-black school—the separated school—is that, particularly in the South, "there is still a strong influence on blacks that makes them feel inferior to whites," and unless counter steps are sought, they can hardly expect to gain self-confidence.

Being a psychiatrist as well as now a professor of medicine, Poussaint took up the familiar subject of discrimination

against black participation in the professions, another example of white assault on Negro self-confidence. The size of
the black membership in the American Psychiatric Association, for instance, was clearly typical. With about 11.5 per
cent of the U.S. population, Negroes constituted only 2.2
per cent of the total APA enrollment. Not only was this a
plaintive commentary on the tiny black enrollment in American medical schools, it also pointed up the minuscule influence of blacks on medical decisions. Poussaint, along with
other black psychiatrists, had already concluded that the
only way to shift the balance within the APA was to initiate
a black caucus—which was done during the 1969 annual
convention in Miami.

As a result, he said, "We achieved a lot of things. For one,
we became organized. We got the APA to begin to include
blacks on more and more committees. We got them to appoint blacks to different positions, to different boards where
they had never been before. We got a black vice-president
of the association—the first one in the association's history
[Dr. Charles Prudhomme, staff psychiatrist at Howard
University]. We got a commitment to look into all the training programs, to insure that psychiatrists are learning more
about blacks and other minority groups in their training.
We got an assurance from the Association that they would
appoint a black psychiatrist to work in the central office in
Washington. We got a commitment from the National Institute of Mental Health to organize a center to look at racism
and minority group problems. We stimulated other activities with the mass media, partly through individual acts,
and also through group action. It was a very positive role
we served and I think we probably could not have accomplished it without organizing through the black caucus to
focus attention on it."

The full salutary effect of the caucus only became evident
in 1970 when the NIMH announced plans for a unit within
the institute to "deal exclusively with the mental problems

of minority groups," which the black psychiatrists said had "their basis in white racism." According to Dr. Prudhomme, "One of the reasons for setting this up is because the black community is sick and tired of whites coming in and poking around conducting studies. The [black] attitude is 'go study yourself.' The plan, then, is to study matters heretofore done exclusively by whites . . . a lot of myths have been propagated that way. We hope to do better. . . . Also, the work done by blacks in psychiatry, psychology and medicine has gone overlooked up to now. It should be pulled together. It's time for ghetto psychology to be studied by products of the ghetto. Most articles on the ghetto are written by whites." Dr. Poussaint was one of three psychiatrists, named by the caucus, to head the center once it began operations.

As to filling the gap in the number of black physicians in the U.S., Dr. Poussaint is happily optimistic. "The number of black physicians, compared with whites, is increasing," he states. "More blacks are entering medical school than ever before; as a matter of fact, I am told this year's freshman class at Cornell contains ten blacks," a 1000-per cent improvement over his 1952 class. In his view, medical discrimination is declining and in a number of schools there is no discrimination whatever, with authorities "making a special effort to take in black students, even to work with them so that they get the type of background which enables them to succeed." [19]

The one sour note in this widening effort to build black self-esteem in the medical profession came from outside academe—from political throats that condemned the practice of compensatory training. In the winter of 1970, no less a person than the Vice-President of the United States, Spiro T. Agnew, challenged the concept of open admissions designed to help those with inferior high school records to obtain college and graduate degrees—i.e., minority groups. Dr. Poussaint bristled at this, saying the Vice-President implied that "minority group students are now or will be accepted to medical school without being qualified, that minority group students might practice medicine in America without meeting established standards. Such a suggestion casts a veil of suspicion on every black medical student in America [for] long established licensing procedures require every doctor in America, minority or majority, to pass a state or national test before he is allowed to practice medicine." He went on to add that "the purpose of the recruitment of minority group medical students is to overcome the widely held belief that minority group students would not be accepted at predominantly white schools." What troubled Dr. Poussaint most was the suspicion that here again a white leader was discrediting the black effort to achieve equality and to that extent undermining the capacity to cross the abyss. "The question a responsible Vice-President should pose," he said, "is: 'When next you are sick, will you be able to find a doctor?' " [20] By doing that, Mr. Agnew would disabuse any thought of being partial to whites.

It was this state of imbalance, however, that continued to haunt the psychiatrist. Whether you looked at education or medicine—the two fields in which he was intimately associated—or in a broader sense at the white economy, everywhere he looked he saw evidence of white supremacy, the unwillingness to share equally with blacks. Any effort to establish a class of black entrepreneurs, for example, faced the most formidable obstacles. Black capitalism was no more than a dream as long as funds with which to turn the wheels were unavailable. In Dr. Poussaint's mind, this was the "biggest thing" holding back black ownership from getting a piece of the economy. "Blacks just don't have any capital," he said. Second, because of white insistence on maintaining a dominant role in industry, as in every other function, "blacks have never had the opportunity psychologically or otherwise to gain the types of experiences and even psychological disposition to run the show." They have maintained a "slave mentality," never learning to be self-assertive around whites. Accordingly, the record of black participation in industry is worse than with other ethnic groups. "The most obvious explanation for this," the Harvard dean asserts, "[and one missed by Nathan Glazer and Pat Moynihan in their *Beyond the Melting Pot*] is that central to the entrepreneurial spirit is assertiveness, self-confidence and the willingness to risk failure in an innovative venture. A castrated human being is not likely to be inclined in any of these ways." [21]

Furthermore, Dr. Poussaint maintains, with the present mores extant, it makes little difference to white society whether a black entrepreneur is successful or not. He is still black. "We should all know by now," he says, explaining his viewpoint, "that American society does not really allow the most 'successful' Negro to overcome the basic stigma of being black. After many years of striving and 'proving themselves,' most blacks have to face the painful realization that whatever 'personal acceptability' they achieve among one white group is not necessarily transferable to another. The sad fact remains that one can be a 'responsible community leader' in Brooklyn and be regarded 'a nigger' in Long Island or Mississippi."

But completely apart from black capitalism and the black's current inability to dent a capitalistic economy controlled by whites, Dr. Poussaint is skeptical of the system itself, what he calls the "capitalistic Protestant ethic." [22] "We have moved," he tells, "from a mentality of myself—to my family—to my block—to my community—to my people—to my nation. This progression is an indication of the great psychological growth of black people." [23] On the other hand, the core emphasis of the Anglo-Saxon ethic is the individual. "It is too individualistic and too focused on the self," says Dr. Poussaint. "What black people need is a sense of helping each other, a sense of community, of pulling others along, and not just being concerned about one's self. I would want to replace the capitalistic Protestant ethic with an ethic that was focused more on the growth of a community or a growth of a people than on an individual person getting a job or becoming rich, for frequently it seems to force a sense of disunity among blacks instead of a sense of togetherness."

Also, the system itself does not allocate to blacks their fair share of the nation's bounty, in the Poussaint view. "Blacks seem to wind up at the low end of the totem pole. It doesn't seem to work for them," he declares. "I can't say that capitalism has to be changed completely, but I think it has to be modified to make it more equitable. At some point, we're going to have to face the question whether it makes sense for some individuals to get three hundred million dollars a year while others earn two thousand." The Harvard dean makes no pretense of being a professional economist, with morsels of wisdom on greater or lesser governmental control, but he fully understands how the unions were able to get a "fair shake" for their members through organization. If a large segment of the population without such protection (for example the blacks) still get the short end of the stick and the private capitalistic economy fails to right the imbalance, "then," says Dr. Poussaint, "I see no hope but for the government to step in and do something to balance the distribution of goods."

Since such an eminent authority as the National Advisory Commission on Civil Disorders (the Kerner Commission) held in 1968 that white racism is the chief spring supporting black unrest in the U.S., it was rather natural during the interview with the Harvard psychiatrist to inquire "What can whites do to rid themselves of white racism?"

"Well," he replied, taking time to weigh his words, "that's a difficult one, because I think that before you can rid yourself of anything, you have to recognize that you have it."

"Then, how do you recognize it?" I went on.

"Many whites don't recognize that they have it, or don't

want to recognize that they have it," he responded. "It's a very hard thing to educate them on this subject. There are some people who feel that you can't. But one of the ways to change this is to indoctrinate white people in a different way from the beginning so they won't develop as racists."

"How do you do that?"

"The media would be very important," he answered. "Instead of seeing only Step'n Fetchit or Rochester on TV, blacks should be in all roles so that children see and take things for granted. You could do this in the schools and in the communities as well if the latter would open their doors and let blacks in. You see, that's a problem. One of the best ways for people to become prejudiced and bigoted is not to have blacks around. If they're not around, you can really develop fantasies about how awful they are. But white children playing with black children, black children playing with white children, these things help to do away with some of the attitudes, particularly if the action occurs early in life."

In all this, it is Dr. Poussaint's view that if prejudice is to be eliminated, a heavy burden rests on the white press. Until white reporters, editors, and publishers "investigate their own feelings of white superiority and unconscious racism," they will never report black news accurately and objectively.[24]

On this score, I asked him whether he thought any progress was being made in the way white writers reported news of black citizens.

"A little bit," he answered. "Not much yet. I think some. I think it's less biased than it used to be."

"Do you have any incidents in mind to show this?"

"Where it's less biased?" he inquired, turning the question over in his mind before answering. "I think you don't see all of the 'innuendo words,'" he went on to say. "You don't read about 'so-called black militants,' or 'self-styled black revolutionists,' you know, the type of adjectives that tend to cast a negative tone on whomever they're describing. I don't see that as much."

"But what about white racism?" I broke in. "Is it declining?"

"I think in some ways, yes," he said. "I think that white racism in the United States is probably less oppressive than it used to be. There's no doubt about that, but a whole lot still exists and is impeding the country from becoming healthy."

"Do you foresee, in your wildest moments, a period—say —twenty, thirty, or even fifty years hence that white racism will be the relic of another age?" I asked.

"No, no I don't see it happening that soon."

"How long do you think it will take?" I pursued, pressing the point.

"I think it may take a long time, if ever, because I can't see it being resolved even in the context of the United States. South Africa will still be there, affecting people and affecting the United States and U.S. policies. There is also Vietnam and the other Asian countries which have become a problem."

Moreover, another reason for the persistence of white racism, in his view, is the animosity this feeling engenders among blacks. "They simply don't want to put up with the psychological arrogance of whites," Dr. Poussaint remarked.[25] Referring to this, I asked him "Is so-called black racism, in your opinion, a reaction to white racism?"

"Yes," he replied, "I guess black racism could exist independently of any whites, but in the United States black racism is mostly in response to white racism. Even when Black Muslims—who are known for their black racism—talk about whites, they usually speak about what whites have done to blacks and because they allegedly oppress, exploit, murder, and kill they are white devils—it's all reactive, you see.

They don't come on saying whites are inferior. Their approach is that whites are bad people."

"So if we want to get rid of black racism, the place to start is with white racism?" I put in.

"That's what I think, because for a long time blacks have really wanted to get into the system and be part of it," he replied, "and because they were rejected and kicked around, they developed their own counter reactions."

"Do you think underneath it all, then, that blacks want to be part of the system?" I went on.

"Well, the polls show that that's what most blacks still want."

"You subscribe to that theory, then?"

"I think probably most blacks still want to be a part of the system, but perhaps in a new way. I think there is less wanting to be assimilated into it. Now I think they would like to be pluralistically integrated into it. We have to allow for a lot of different ways for blacks and other groups fitting into a society which we have always had. There have been Italian enclaves and Irish enclaves and still are, right here in Boston. They still function and the residents go out into the dominant society."

At that point our conversation led rather naturally into the question of integration versus separation, and the viability of each for achieving better racial relations. Would it be better, for instance, to emphasize one or the other or a combination of both? What was Dr. Poussaint's view of this?

As he sees it, there is no panacea plan open to blacks. "I think some black people might want to stay in their own enclave, some integrate with whites, and some leave the country, which is happening too." Certainly, many black families shy from becoming involved in any integrated program which invites white abuse. "Suppose, for example, a black family should move into Belmont [a Boston suburb] and most of the families are bigoted, and things happen to the

kids?" he asked rhetorically. There is also the further conviction on his part that despite the desire to become a part
of the white system, blacks still like to be with those who
share similar concerns. The first priority for whites, Dr.
Poussaint points out, may be peace in Vietnam, whereas for
blacks it is survival in the U.S.

Of far greater immediacy to him than a discussion about
integration is what blacks should be contributing to solve
their ills. "We can blame many of our present conditions on
whites and we would be largely right. We could say that
blacks destroy other blacks because this white-oriented society is a violent one. We could say that our self-dislike is
the result of racism and thus rationalize taking it out on
each other. We could say that because we are powerless we
are more competitive and jealous of each other's success,
that's why we fight each other. We could say that poverty
and slums provide a fertile soil for the growth of the less de-
sirable elements in human nature, and that's why we rob
each other. We could speak of a white-controlled law and
judiciary which discriminate against blacks and encourage
black criminality, and argue that those are the reasons we
kill each other. All of these indictments, in some degree,
would be correct." [26] But this would do nothing to aid black
Americans. It would, in fact, fire their depression and hostility toward white society, ending in further degradation and
a further denial of the self-confidence needed to compete
with whites. What blacks need is to draw upon the inner
strength which enabled them to survive the past four
hundred years and find new ways to "walk tall"!

Andrew F. Brimmer

¶ In white U.S. there is nothing particularly unique in the rise of a successful economist. The doors of opportunity are open from the university campus to the inner sanctum of the power structures on Wall Street or in Washington. Given intelligence, training, and a boost here and there, the path is relatively soft underfooot.

But with the black youth who is held back, first by a segregated society and then by a prejudiced political and economic world, the one who survives *is* unique, particularly if he began in the Old South, as Andrew Felton Brimmer did.

Brimmer was born on September 13, 1926, in Newellton, a tiny village of a thousand persons (60 per cent Negro) in northeastern Louisiana. It was a time when Jim Crow walked the highways by day and the Ku Klux Klan by night. As Roy Wilkins pointed out, it was a year when the Democratic Party, reflecting the national mood, permitted Negroes to watch the National convention in one-state-removed Houston "behind a chicken-wire fence!"

The Brimmer family, like so many black families of the period, was closely knit. Andrew and Vellar, his wife, had three sons and two daughters, of whom young Andrew was the fourth. Until the Great Depression stuck its long fingers into the farm economy, the elder Brimmer was a tenant farmer, tilling the plantation of Tensas Parish near the Mississippi River. As the financial tendons began to tighten, Brimmer concluded he had had enough. He found a job with a local grain elevator and somehow survived the onslaught.

At the recession's lowest point, young Andrew began his education. While all schools felt the pinch, the blow fell with special severity on Southern Negro institutions. Across the South, for every seven dollars spent on white pupils only two dollars went to educate blacks. In Louisiana, the Negro school year was forty days shorter than the comparable schedule for whites. It was a common belief that "to educate a Negro youngster was to ruin a good farm hand."

Despite the fiscal and social handicaps, Brimmer applied his energies, and in the process discovered the value of education and the cost of segregation. The former convinced him of the need for high school and the latter required a thirteen-mile bus trip to Tensas Parish Training School because the Newellton High School was *de jure* white. When he graduated in the spring of 1944, he was the lone male to receive a diploma.

Meanwhile, he had learned the value of hard work. To general-store owner John Quigless of Newellton, where Brimmer clerked, he was an "in spite of" individual—"That's the best way I can describe that boy; he worked for us two years, after school and on Saturdays. He just didn't let anything get him down. I can't remember any specific incident; he was only a teen-ager. But he was smart, and had a retentive mind. We never had to tell him anything but once; he could adapt well to any situation." [1]

Brimmer was ambitious and already knew that white response to black aspirations at that time was as touchy as a cactus needle. Like many members of his family before him, the seventeen-year-old Tensas graduate decided to forage north in search of greener pastures. There were relatives in Detroit and Chicago, but he determined to join a married sister in Bremerton, Washington, whose husband worked at the Bremerton Navy Yard, turning out warships for Uncle Sam. He arrived there on Independence Day and soon had a job as electrician's helper in the shipyard.

The work was temporary. Brimmer knew the draft would take him after his eighteenth birthday in September, but in the interim he yearned to learn more. This could be a hedge for the day he would be finished with military service. Since he had always dreamed of journalism as a career, what was more natural than to take two evening courses—English composition and literature and international relations—at Olympic Junior College?

As it turned out, he rode the fascinating wave of higher education for the next ten months, enjoying a previously unknown stimulus. Then the military axe fell. He was sent to infantry school at Fort McClellan, Alabama, for training as a paratrooper, but by that time World War II was grinding to a close and Private Brimmer found himself transferred to the Ordnance Corps. In November he was assigned to the 645th Ordnance Company in Hawaii, and before his discharge a year later at Fort Lewis, Washington, he had risen through the ranks to acting first sergeant. At last he was free to follow his educational bents. By combining his personal savings with moneys granted under the educational provisions of the GI Bill of Rights, Brimmer was able to enroll at the University of Washington at Seattle in January 1947. Still convinced his career lay in writing, he decided to concentrate on journalism and, adding a pinch of theory to a pinch of the practical, took a job as assistant editor of a weekly newspaper, the Seattle *Dispatch*. As the months passed, he began to see how white prejudice was preventing black Americans from advancing in the fourth estate. Moreover, other ambiguities troubled him about life in the United States, and when a faculty adviser suggested, at the end of his sophomore year, that journalism was unpromising for a Negro, Brimmer agreed. He turned to economics, a discipline he found increasingly fascinating. One year later he had his baccalaureate degree.

Indeed, Brimmer's appetite for economics was insatiable. Within months he was back at Washington, armed with a fellowship from the John Hay Whitney Foundation, anxious to complete his master's degree in economics. For a dissertation, he probed the economics of fair employment, an indication of his growing concern for the economic plight of U.S. minorities. Five years had passed since he left Louisiana, but time and distance could not erase the memory of white discrimination. He was beginning to see, more clearly than ever, how intricately the fortunes of black people were tied to an economic system dominated by racism.

His years at the University of Washington ended, Brimmer decided to further his economic horizons abroad. A Fulbright scholarship enabled him to spend a year in India, studying the Indian economy at the Delhi School of Economics and the University of Bombay. The experience provided material on his return for two publications—one on India's industrial organization and the other an analysis of that country's entrepreneurship. By the end of the school year, he had reached two conclusions: the teaching of economics was his forte and, to do so, he needed a doctorate.

He let out his nets, and when he pulled them in, there were tuition-paid offers from four institutions, Harvard being his choice because of its educational rank. His three years there were filled with the challenge of studying under such renowned professors as Hansen, John Williams, Haberler, Galbraith, and Gerschenkron, among others. They were also filled with the joy of meeting Doris Millicent Scott, a graduate student at Radcliffe, and marrying her in 1953. In the same year, he took a position as research assistant at the Center for International Studies at the Massachusetts Institute of Technology and followed this the next year by teaching money and banking and the principles of economics at Harvard.

When he left in June 1955 to serve as an economist with the Federal Reserve Bank of New York, he was already intimate with America's polarized worlds—black poverty and white capital. But while he had personally experienced the dulling effect of Southern poverty, his knowledge of the other world was chiefly academic. New York changed this. His milieu now included the world's foremost banking institutions, and as he delved into such problems as capital, labor, and management his mind took on a more practical cast. The head of the research department, the man to whom Brimmer reported, recalled how "most of the young people I had around would come up with radical ideas for solving all the Fed's problems. Andy was not one of them." [2] Midway in his three-year tenure, he spent four months in the African Sudan as part of a three-man team, advising the government on the establishment of a central banking system. In addition, he continued to work on his doctoral thesis, an in-depth study of life insurance companies, and upon completing the task in 1957, received a Ph.D. from Harvard.

The following year, intent on returning to the classroom, Brimmer left the New York Fed to accept the post of assistant chairman of the economics department at Michigan State University. It was a time when numerous instructors were joining the faculty; his assignment was to locate them in roles where they could give the curriculum a new look, no easy charge for a thirty-two-year-old black who had not had time to learn the inner machinations of campus politics. He found himself lined up against the department's old guard, who refused to budge and had the power to disregard his changes. In the end, his adversaries succeeded in taking away his administrative job, blue-penciling a promotion and keeping him from tenure. That was more buffeting than Dr. Brimmer would accept, and in July 1961 he moved to the Wharton School of Finance and Commerce, University of Pennsylvania, as assistant professor of finance.

As it happened, the shift was a boon. It gave Brimmer a

chance to wash out the experience in East Lansing and brought his name to the attention of the Kennedy administration, which was on the lookout for bright young blacks to staff the Washington hierarchy.

Wharton's dean, Willis Winn, tells how popular his new professor became with Southern students. The faculty made the assignment, not knowing whether he could perform well with those from below the Mason-Dixon line. Not only did Dr. Brimmer exhibit a keen humor, but he was asked to supervise their theses. "He was the best teacher we ever had," the group agreed.

While this was unfolding onstage, offers began arriving in the wings, inviting him to Washington. Such diverse organizations as HHFA, AID, State, and Commerce made offers. President Kennedy's informants, many of whom were Harvard graduates, knew of Brimmer's work in Cambridge, New York, and East Lansing. Besides, it was now possible to fatten his dossier with complimentary words from Dean Winn. For some months, however, his reply was invariably negative on the reasonable theory that he shouldn't leave shortly after assuming the job in Philadelphia. But in the spring of 1963 the pressure became too strong. Winn gave him a leave of absence to accept a Kennedy appointment as Deputy Assistant Secretary for Economic Policy Review in the Commerce Department.

Within two months of his arrival, Dr. Brimmer was busy digging up testimony in support of the government's effort to bar racial discrimination in interstate commerce. There was evidence, he found, of Negroes having to travel "dangerously long distances on the highways before finding lodging." Armed with these data, he appeared beside Under Secretary Franklin D. Roosevelt, Jr., before the Senate Commerce Committee to back the Department's plea for adoption of Title 11 of the Civil Rights Act of 1964. When this legislation, "the most far-reaching and comprehensive law in support of racial equality ever enacted by Congress," finally reached the congressional hurdle, protagonists for the legislation relied heavily on Brimmer's research. Later still, the U.S. Supreme Court cited the Roosevelt-Brimmer presentation in declaring Title 11—the public accommodations section—constitutional

Dr. Brimmer's part in the civil rights victory was one of the first demonstrations of his usefulness as an economist working for black equality. He made no excuses for his low-key effort, explaining it wasn't "because I don't have a deep commitment, but because I'm simply not a popular leader. If I got up and tried to lead a demonstration no one would follow." He had said the Negro revolution should be looked at as two sides of the same coin, first the need for legislation with which to act and second, the use of such authority to accomplish social and economic advances. "It is the work of preparing for the second state that I can best serve." [3] But it would be wrong to infer from this practical attitude that his "deep commitment" didn't occasionally surface with emotion, as the following story testifies: He was asked by an industrial spokesman in the course of a lecture on economics "Why it was that so many Negroes would rather receive welfare than work for a living?" Dr. Brimmer bristled. "When I go to work in the morning, I see a lot of buses going downtown full of white faces, and I assume they're going to work. But I also see buses going out to the suburbs, and they're filled with black faces. They don't live out there, so I assume they're going to work, too. The wages we pay for domestic help aren't much different from what they'd get from welfare, are they? No, I can't accept your thesis." [4]

By January 1965 Lyndon B. Johnson was so impressed by Dr. Brimmer's work that he promoted him to Assistant Secretary of Commerce for Economic Affairs and a month later handed him the ticklish job of reducing U.S. gold drain abroad through voluntary action by American companies. Crisscrossing the country as a self-styled "traveling salesman in behalf of the voluntary program," Dr. Brimmer called on companies to go easy on overseas investments in marginal projects and, where possible, to borrow abroad. Using a small staff of Department economists and secretaries, he spent hours conferring with top executives of many of the nation's largest corporations, sifting out their overseas commitments. To give the presentation greater specificity, Dr. Brimmer took the data of the Commerce Department's Bureau of International Commerce (which separated export-import statistics by commodities and countries) and from the Balance of Payments Division in the Office of Business Economics he got figures to show dollar outflow into foreign investments. His plea was a request for voluntary cooperation to avoid the pitfalls of mandatory regulations. "It's not just because this is the line the President took," an insider was heard to say. "Andy has developed a great appreciation for markets and their relatively free functioning, and he really does want interference in them kept to a minimum." By fall, the program was not only beginning to take hold but also to accomplish some salutary side effects. Dr. Brimmer was coming to know the business mind as no professor could; businessmen, for their part, were finding him a welcome addition to the "body politic." "He listens to what you say and holds a pretty good balance between bending too much with opinion and being too inflexible," one said.[5] His most difficult problem was to ward off criticism of U.S. policy. Detractors argued that the federal government was among the worst offenders, contributing to the deficit with its military and economic aid expenditures. How could he ask for their help, they implied, if his own employer refused to level with industry? Dr. Brimmer's reply was that without such expenditures, it would be unsafe for American companies to invest abroad. At year's end, the balance of payment figures showed tremendous improvement. From a deficit of $2.8 billion in 1965 they had dropped to $1.3 billion in 1966, and admiring employees at Commerce were writing in honor of their boss' achievement a rollicking octet titled "Brimmer über Alles--or the Commerce Fighting Song," sung to "It Came upon a Midnight Clear":

> Hooray for Andy, the people's choice,
> For Arthur S. Flemming's Award—°
> He raised his balance of payments voice,
> To hoist the corporate petard.
> All hail, to Andy, hooray! hooray!
> For Connor's °° all-gracious aide.
> "Invest Abroad" in stillness lies
> Since Andy's stopped the parade.°°°

This departmental ode was empirical proof of a new mood inside Commerce since Dr. Brimmer's arrival thirty-two months before. Quietly he had changed its former self-pity and in the process fashioned a vibrant personality of his own. Before Brimmer, the Department's economists had the queasy feeling that they were fall guys for the Council of Economic Advisers, the Fed, and the Treasury. They perspired over the statistics while the others took the credit. "We have had a new sense of usefulness under Brimmer," declared George Jaszi, director of Commerce's Office of Business Economics, pointing to the rise in morale.[6]

The lift could be traced to two facets in Brimmer's character. Whatever aversion he had to uninhibited gregariousness, he was—in private conversation among the employees —a warm, thoughtful individual who came through "with the disarmingly warm inflections of less-educated Negroes." Second, he was not work shy. At Commerce he gained the reputation for being a seven-day-a-week man who often stayed at his desk until nine or later at night. So habitual

---

° Award honoring outstanding young men in the federal government who are under 40.

°° Secretary of Commerce John T. Connor.

°°° Words by Lawrence C. McQuade, music by E. Allan Poe.

were his long hours that he once forgot and called a friend at 10:30 P.M. to offer him a job. With a top man showing that kind of industry and enthusiasm, departmental underlings found it hard not to follow suit.

In fact, the upgrading caught the eye of President Johnson, who saw in his protégé the kind of man he wanted to advance—self-made, down-to-earth, a believer in personal persuasion to produce a consensus. Johnson was fond of blacks who worked *with* the system, not *against* it, and Dr. Brimmer was that kind of individual. When Watts exploded in the summer of 1965, the President appointed Brimmer to a task force that investigated the riot. With typical thoroughness Brimmer ordered the Census Bureau to conduct a special survey of the deterioration in South Los Angeles. When the figures were compiled, they showed one of every ten male workers out of work at a time the national figure for non-white males had dropped to 6 per cent. In housing, the same sorry pattern was discernible. In South Los Angeles the proportion of dilapidated units increased from 3 per cent in 1960 to 5 per cent in 1965, while the proportion of deteriorating units in Watts rose from 15 to 28 per cent. "The trouble in Watts," the Assistant Secretary concluded, "is that it is a sort of way-station in the Negro migration from the South. Those who can get out do it as fast as possible. The only people who are left are those who simply can't get a decent job." [7]

Six months after Watts, the President again had reason to measure Dr. Brimmer's potential. The Federal Reserve Board by a split (4–3) decision voted to raise the nation's discount rate to an anti-inflationary 4.5 per cent against Johnson's wishes. Angry words rose from the White House and the President reserved his special pique for Fed Chairman William McChesney Martin. He argued that the monetary decisions of the Federal Reserve Board should have been geared to the fiscal decisions of the administration so that both could work together to combat inflation. A delay of one month, when the President's budgetary message was due, would have sufficed, he thought.

On the face of it, the President's logic was plausible, but beneath the surface a war of philosophy raged, and a struggle for economic power. Martin, a former president of the New York Stock Exchange, had become a Board fixture since his appointment in 1951 by former President Harry S Truman. During his first decade of Board membership, Martin was the unchallenged leader. A businessman, he was surrounded by conservative businessmen. But beginning with John F. Kennedy, the complexion had changed. Successively, three economists—George W. Mitchell, J. Dewey Daane, and Sherman J. Maisel—were appointed, two by Kennedy, one by Johnson. The only hard-core support that remained was Charles N. Shepardson, a former dean of agriculture at Texas A & M, and C. Canby Balderston—both Eisenhower appointees. Balderston's appointment was due to expire on February 28, giving Johnson the long-awaited opportunity to fill the Board with men whose leanings were liberal. His problem was Martin, a person of such impeccable credentials in the business community that Kennedy had retained him. As the President saw it, he had to soften the Board's hard core without risking the enmity of Martin's supporters. Also, since the rumor was abroad that the Chairman would resign if Johnson appointed an easy-money man to replace Balderston, the President had to proceed with extreme caution. What he needed was someone near the middle of the road, close enough to his philosophy to be sympathetic to social problems but not far enough left to prompt Martin's resignation—a swing man, so to speak, who would not attempt to embarrass the Chairman.

The President summoned Martin to the White House for a face-to-face conference. Why not find a businessman, preferably Republican, to take Balderston's place, the Fed Chairman asked? This would balance the professional economists and make the Board more representative. Johnson delayed, but to satisfy Martin ordered emissaries into the field in search of a businessman. In the back of his mind, however, a different plan was taking shape. Instead of a businessman, the rationale went, if only a person could be found, politically liberal, with the practical insights to pass for a businessman, how could Martin refuse?

As his mind fingered the invisible list of possible choices, it came to rest on the name Brimmer. This could be the man he wanted. First, he was a student of economics with a Ph.D. from Harvard who had taught on some of the country's most prestigious campuses. He was articulate and widely known as the author of a large volume, *Life Insurance Companies in the Capital Market,* written while he was at Michigan State. The study that went into this work showed him a Neo-Keynesian with faith in the government's ability to control the currency through judicious shifts in the credit and interest rates. "I came away from that study," Dr. Brimmer had said, "with the conviction that monetary policy works." Yet there was another side to his fiscal habit. He was known on Wall Street as the man who had spent three years during the middle fifties working with the Federal Reserve Bank of New York. As one associate put it, "he developed a certain loyalty to the system, an affinity for the Federal Reserve way of thinking." Then, too, in the past year he had performed outstandingly in turning back the deficit on the balance of payments. "The more I dealt with him," said one top business leader, "the more I came to respect him, though I cannot say we always agreed." Finally, the fact that Dr. Brimmer was a Negro gave the President a certain leverage. Indeed, declared *The Wall Street Journal,* "The President had Martin in a box. If he resigned, it would look as though he didn't want a Negro on the board."

Armed with this list of arguments, Johnson proceeded to confer again with the Fed Chairman and, now convinced the day was his, named Dr. Brimmer to the Board with befitting praise. The decision had been taken, the President said, "after long and thoughtful consultation." Others with whom Johnson talked were also agreed on the choice. "He is a man of wide professional experience and great personal integrity," the President said, "a man of moderation, whose brilliance is combined with a sense of fair play that I believe will enable him to serve with distinction in this new and important assignment."

Martin moved in quickly with approving words to remove any suspicion that he opposed the appointment. "Mr. Brimmer," he said, "achieved a very commendable record as a member of the economic research staff of the Federal Reserve Bank of New York during the nineteen-fifties, and I believe that he can be counted upon to build further upon that record in his service as a member of the Board, especially in view of the experience he has gained as Assistant Secretary of Commerce in working on the difficult problem of the nation's balance of payments." To which the President presumably added "Amen." Outside the Washington family, *Newsweek* commented, "a typical Johnsonian strike —artful, expedient, and surprising." In a different vein, former colleague Walter Adams, of Michigan State, saw the appointment as well-earned. "Andrew Brimmer," he was quoted as saying, "would have achieved high success 'in spite of' his race, and regardless if 'his skin were red, white, green or purple.'" [8] The nominee himself greeted the news on a pragmatic key. Was color a help or a hindrance, he was asked? "How can anyone answer that?" he smiled. "Who knows what went through the President's mind? Many people in business, banking and in Washington knew me. I wasn't a mystery to anybody." [9]

During the week that followed, he was quizzed by members of the Senate Banking Committee who were anxious to find out what allegiances he had. "I would like to feel I would be a member of an institution," he told Democratic Senator William Proxmire of Wisconsin. "I wouldn't want to feel that I'd be anybody's man," he went on, with obvious reference to President Johnson and Chairman Martin. He said he would neither be joining a bloc nor escaping a bloc. "I would like to feel I would exercise a genuine independence of judgment." Would this be the attitude of a man "beholden to no one and who would act in the public·interest," Republican Senator Strom Thurmond of South Carolina inquired?

"It certainly would be, Senator." Dr. Brimmer answered.

Other questions were raised regarding his monetary guidelines and the Board's role. Again he steered an unruffled course, disarming the conservatives with talk about the Board as something of a financial "court" and reassuring the liberals with an advocacy for "increasing the channels of communication" between the Board and the administration. This was in line with what his friends had been saying. "I think Brimmer would be darn careful about voting to raise the discount rate," especially if the Board's action might stimulate an outburst at the White House, said one, and another added, "He's not wildly liberal, he's right down the road with Walter Heller and Gardner Ackley" (President Johnson's former and current chiefs of CEA). The vote for confirmation, after listening to the testimony, was unanimous. Democratic Senator Paul H. Douglas of Illinois found him "extraordinarily well qualified," and Republican Senator Wallace Bennett of Utah, chimed in, "I am going to be very happy to vote for you."

Six days later, Dr. Brimmer took the oath of office in the East Room of the White House before three hundred officials, friends, his wife, and their seven-year-old daughter Esther. A smiling LBJ used the occasion to express his pleasure with the appointment and his high regard for Dr. Brimmer, whose achievements in life, he said, "are his own." Alluding to his fiscal qualifications, the President recalled how some had said that "not one man in 100,000 really understands the complexity of high finance and monetary policy, [but] Dr. Andrew Brimmer is one that, I believe, does understand it." He expected his appointee not "to be an easy-money man or a tight-money man [but a] right-money man, one who, I believe, will carefully and cautiously and intelligently evaluate the Nation's needs and the needs of all of its people and recommend the policies which . . . will best serve the national interest." Finally, the presidential charge: "We must continue to sustain high employment without inflation. . . . We must meet the heavy demands of our military and economic effort in Vietnam without losing our momentum for social progress here at home."

The Board's ability to take affirmative action depends primarily on its responsibility for the nation's monetary policy which automatically affects interest rates and the supply of credit in the economy. The discount rate which the Board had raised in December from 4 to 4.5 per cent was now, by general admission, a salutary step and had in fact taken the heat off the administration for not raising taxes to counter the rising tide of inflation. By the time Dr. Brimmer joined the Fed, the economic strains of prolonging the 1964–1965 economic boom, shackled to the deficit financing of the Vietnam war, were again filling the nation's money centers with apprehension. What would the Board do in the absence of continued reluctance by the President to suggest a rise in taxes?

There was no way that Dr. Brimmer could escape the pressure. Not only was he aware of White House pressure against any cooling of the economy that might threaten the "high employment" the President demanded, he also knew, as a student of banking, that inflation could destroy the U.S. economy. And hovering in the back of his mind, as the first Negro member of the Board, was the question of what effect his decisions could have on the future of American blacks. The latter, *The Wall Street Journal* pointed out, was "bound to count heavily when he must weigh the issues of higher interest rates or inflation, easier credit or slower economic growth—questions on which he could well cast the Board's tie-breaking vote." Nevertheless, Dr. Brimmer had assured members of the Senate Banking Committee that he would not be "anybody's man" and—Johnson or no Johnson—when the time came to raise interest rates to their highest level in thirty-five years, he went along with the rest of the Board.

In fact, the more he thought about it, the more critical he became of the administration's refusal to carry its fair share of the battle against inflation by raising taxes. Speaking to members of the business and financial community in Boston on July 18, he came out flatly for new taxes to curtail the overheated boom. If the administration was gun-shy over the political effect of additional taxation, it could accomplish the same objective by reducing the tax credits that industry enjoyed. Suspension of a 1962 law giving business a 7 per cent write-off of new capital expenditures would produce a larger income tax yield. Coupled with this proposal was a suggestion that the banks show restraint. He accused them of making too many business loans, a policy that was, he said, "endangering the health of the banking system and the economy as a whole." Why, he hinted, couldn't the banks say no to these appeals and, if necessary, place the blame on the Federal Reserve Board?

By midsummer, it was abundantly clear that the Fed was fighting a losing contest. Whatever progress had been made in cooling the economy was being negated by the easy-money policies of the federal government and the commercial banks. On Wall Street, for the first time since the 1933 bank holiday, there was talk of panic. The Board now had to decide whether a higher discount rate would check the inflation. Spokesmen from the district Federal Reserve banks said it had to be done. On August 23, as the crisis reached its height, the Board's Open Market Committee met to evaluate the situation. The twelve-man body, made up of Board members and presidents of the Federal Reserve Bank of New York and four of the eleven remaining Federal Reserve banks serving in rotation, split three ways—those who "wanted the screws tightened still further," those who wanted action triggered to new declines, and those who feared what a "screw tightening" would do to the heated economy. The result was a bar to Fed action and an acknowledgment by the majority that, in their opinion, manipulation of the discount rate had its limitations as a monetary weapon, that other forces had to be used to solve the crisis. Finally, on August 30, the administration took the hint, and a week later the President ordered the industrial tax credit suspended, as Dr. Brimmer had been urging. As the weeks passed, the Board eased its restrictions on bank reserves and the economic fever momentarily subsided. When certain members of the financial community accused the Board of "financial brinkmanship" prior to the August squeeze, Dr. Brimmer publicly took issue. Speaking in November to members of the Arizona Bankers Association, he refuted the idea of a financial panic. "If market pressures had been moving to precipitate a panic situation, the Federal Reserve would not have hesitated to inject whatever amount of bank reserves may have been required to avoid it," he said.

At the time Dr. Brimmer was initially tapped for membership on the Board, there were friends who wondered if he would continue to interest himself in studies showing the economic progress of U.S. Negroes. "His great advantage," said a Commerce colleague, "had been as an economist, working on Negro problems, and none of us wanted to see that lost." That it clearly hasn't vanished is one of the signal hopes in the Negro Revolution, for no one could occupy a better seat to study the economics of black America than a member of the Federal Reserve Board. As Brimmer has humorously observed, "I was speaking before a Negro group when one man rose to comment that the Federal Reserve Bank is one example where we have more than our proportionate share—one in seven."

As Dr. Brimmer looks into the crystal ball of black hopes, he sees education as the vital link in the advancement of Negroes. Much progress is evident, but higher objectives are needed. Pointing to Census Bureau statistics, he shows how "in 1957, the median years of schooling for non-white men (who were eighteen years of age and over and in the labor force) were 8.0 years, compared with 11.5 years for white men—a gap of 3.5 years. By 1967, the median for non-white men had risen to 10.2 years, while the median for white men had climbed to 12.3 years. Thus in a decade, the differential shrank to 2.1 years, or by three-fifths. Among non-white women, the median years of schooling rose over the period from 8.9 years to 11.5 years; for white women, the rise was from 12.2 years to 12.4 years. In this case, the differential was cut by more than two-thirds, from 3.3 years to 0.9 years."

Converting such figures into improved black earning capacity, however, finds Dr. Brimmer less sanguine. According to the Census Bureau, in 1959 Negro men with one year or more of college had a median income 97.8 per cent that of whites with eight years or less of elementary education. By 1967 the ratio had risen to 124.2 per cent, demonstrating that Negroes at the college level earned one-quarter more than whites with only an eighth-grade achievement, and to 133.5 per cent for blacks with a baccalaureate degree—or one-third more, a testament to racial discrimination.

Moreover, it is the accumulation of past deficiencies, as Dr. Brimmer points out, that victimizes the black. Because black parents are less educated and earn less, their children are caught in the same cycle of lower educational expectations. As a 1968 study undertaken by the American Council on Education showed, "roughly 55 per cent of the black students' fathers, compared with 26 per cent of other students' fathers, had not graduated from high school. . . . Over one-third (35 per cent) of the black students' fathers were employed in unskilled or semi-skilled occupations, against less than 12 per cent for the fathers of white students. . . . Income of the black students' families was substantially below that of other students' families. Nearly three-fifths (56 per cent) of the black students and one-seventh (14 per cent) of the non-black students reported their parents' yearly income as under $6000. Only 6 per cent of the black students, compared with one-fourth of the white students, reported parental family income of $10,000 or more. . . . Black students (especially at predominantly white four-year colleges) were relying heavily on loans, scholarships, and grants—rather than primarily on family support—to finance their first year of college."

Even more embarrassing for those blacks who hurdle such obstacles to embark on a college career is to find that they are less qualified scholastically than their white counterparts. On this, the ACE study revealed that "black students seem to have done less well in high school than non-black students. Over two-fifths of the black students (42 per cent) and less than one-third of the white students (31 per cent) reported average grades below B−. About 6 per cent of the black students and almost 14 per cent of the other students reported high school grades of A− or better. . . . Black students were proportionately less likely than white students to be a member of a scholastic honor society, win recognition in the National Merit Program, or publish an original writing. . . ."

The issue, as this makes painfully clear, is the racial imbalance. "Personally," says Dr. Brimmer, "I think the only way to compensate is for blacks to do remedial work in areas such as mathematics, reading and writing skills, physical sciences, and foreign languages, where the need seems to be greatest. Only by bringing black students up to par in these and similar fields can the colleges create the necessary foundations on which these students can build a substantive education."

For this reason, the Fed Board member frowns at mention of the rising demand for "black studies" and similar programs coupled with requests for separate departments, manned by blacks, and segregated on-campus dormitories.

"It would be a tragic mistake," he says, "for Negro students to waste their college years languishing in 'black studies' and similar sheltered workshops which do little or nothing to prepare them to meet the vigorous competition for employment opportunities in the post-college world." [10] Understandably, Dr. Brimmer's chief objection to the growth of "black studies" is the manner in which it threatens his dream of an integrated society, not the possibility of teaching black contributions to American life. He contends, for instance, that the "typical college curriculum ... has devoted very little to Negro history in America. Most forward-looking administrators are responding. These demands are surprising many faculties, who find themselves in conflict between the need to maintain traditional academic standards and the need for quick exposure." But this development, as part of the total instructional tableau, is quite apart from the militant desire to support what he calls "a new cult of incompetence—which 'black studies' can only assure. We should get on with meeting the real challenge of education today: the preparation of disadvantaged young people to take their place in an open and integrated society."

No economist—black or white—is more familiar than Dr. Brimmer with the kind of ghetto economy spawned by white racism, its limitations and its inability to absorb blacks. He is convinced, through personal study, that separatism in the economic world is as deplorable as on the college campus. As long as it exists, blacks cannot expect to get their share of the national income.

What has been the consequence to date of economic discrimination? "In general," Dr. Brimmer says, "the effects are similar to those produced in international trade when a high tariff wall is erected between two countries: separate markets prevail in the two areas for items subject to tariff control. For the Negro community in the United States, the greatest barrier imposed by segregation is not in the market

of goods—to which they generally have relatively open
access—but in the market for personal services (such as bar-
ber and beauty shops and funeral services) and in public accommodations (such as hotels and restaurants). Consequently a protected market has evolved for the provision of
these services within the Negro community."

As one might expect, viewing this barrier, "Negro professionals are highly concentrated in fields such as medicine,
education and religion—all hedged in by segregation—but
all of which also enjoy a protected market. In occupations
which are dependent upon unprotected national markets,
Negroes are conspicuously absent. For example, in 1960 (the
latest year for which comprehensive Census data is available) engineers, scientists, and technicians comprised only 3.8
per cent of all Negroes classified as professional, technical,
and managerial; the corresponding figure for whites is 10.5
per cent.

"In business also Negroes are concentrated in enterprises
serving the protected Negro market. Life insurance provides
probably the best example. Beginning in the 1880's, the
major life insurance companies either stopped selling policies to Negroes or did so on the basis of different actuarial
tables which greatly increased the cost of protection to Negroes. The result was the creation of an environment where
Negro life insurance companies were able to grow and pros-
per. In enterprises that sold to a more general public, such
as hardware and department stores, Negroes made little
headway."

But since the mid-fifties, the process of desegregation has
wrought immense changes. Like Joshua crumbling the walls
of Jericho, the civil rights camp has begun the disintegra-
tion of the walls of segregation. For the first time, ghetto
business is not simply the province of those who depend
upon the separatist barrier. The milieu, to be sure, is colonial, surrounded by an affluent white mother country, but if
blacks are to demonstrate fiscal competitiveness in the

changing environment, now is the time, black chauvinists argue, to promote black ownership of community facilities, known by its protagonists as "black capitalism." In this economic objective they are disputed by Dr. Brimmer.

First, he contends, the ghetto is "a poor economic environment for business investment." Its residents in 1968 earned 66 per cent of white median incomes and their unemployment rate was twice that of those on the outside. "Moreover," says Dr. Brimmer, "economic advancement within the Negro community may not improve profit prospects of Negro-owned businesses. Instead, it may accelerate the competition from national firms seeking to serve the expanding Negro market."

A second obstacle, from Dr. Brimmer's viewpoint, is the profit limitation of "black capitalism." "Negro-owned businesses," he says, "tend to be small in terms of sales, employment and profits, and heavily concentrated in personal services and retailing." [11] A 1969 seven-city survey of 564 black-owned businesses, undertaken by the National Business League, pointed out the fact that a typical black entrepreneur "averaged only 2.2 full-time employees, 1.1 part-time employees, had a mean gross income of only $19,147, and a mean net profit of only $3,430." Furthermore, profit figures inside the ghetto are being threatened by the tremendous incidence of crime. This may run as high as $3 billion a year, representing "almost 10 per cent of Negroes' aggregate family income in 1969, compared with five per cent for the economy as a whole."

Third, says Dr. Brimmer, "the attempt to expand small-scale, Negro-owned businesses is running against a strong national trend." This is particularly true with food stores, which constitute the largest black retail outlet. While the fifteen-year period between 1948 and 1963 saw a rapid growth in the number of retail establishments with sales over $1 million, the number with receipts under $20,000 declined by 160,000, and when compared to their total receipts dropped "from an insignificant 3.8 per cent in 1948 to a microscopic 1.5 per cent in 1963." From such statistics Dr. Brimmer concludes that "a much larger fraction of the total food budget is being spent in supermarkets rather than in small grocery stores," a situation obviously detrimental to black ownership.

A fourth reason for Dr. Brimmer's dour view of "black capitalism" is that self-employment in the ghetto is an economic mirage. The salaries one receives in "managerial positions or as craftsmen are roughly one-third to two-thirds higher than the rewards of self-employment in the same occupations." To illustrate, Dr. Brimmer disclosed that "in 1958 a self-employed male in retail trade had median earnings equal to 69.8 per cent of the earnings of a salaried manager; in 1963 the ratio had declined to 65.1 per cent, and by 1968 it had declined further to 63.8 per cent. On the basis of this historical evidence, self-employment in retail trade is not a promising choice for a future career."

Dr. Brimmer's *coup de grâce* is his claim that "black capitalism" falls short as an employer. "If 'black capitalism' were even moderately successful over the next decade," he said, "it would lead to the creation of between 550,000 and 885,-000 jobs. If it achieved even the most optimistic expectations, the new jobs created would account for only slightly more than half of the growth in the Negro labor force. So, in 1980, black capitalists would be able to supply no more than 13 per cent (and in actuality probably a much smaller proportion) of the jobs Negroes would need."

"Hopefully," he adds, "as the fallacy of black capitalism withers away, the emerging opportunities for genuine participation in business" will be seen more clearly. "Such efforts should be mainly outside the ghetto, and they must be in the expanding sectors of the economy if they are to have any chance of surviving."[12]

The echo of these allegations before the American Economic Association had hardly died when Dr. Brimmer was being challenged by black economist Dunbar S. McLaurin for "being defined out of existence by the white economy." Brimmer had carefully defined "black capitalism" as being black entrepreneurship in the ghetto, not black participation in ownership outside the walls in open competition with whites or in joint ownership with them, but the distinction was lost. Ten days later, a group of eight prominent Negro businessmen descended on Washington to challenge the Brimmer thesis. Dempsey J. Travis of Chicago, president of the United Mortgage Bankers of America, ridiculed Dr. Brimmer for having "never met a payroll in his life. If we agreed with Dr. Brimmer on black business, there would not be 50 black mortgage banks."[13] The same Mr. Travis, ten months before, in an address titled "Is Black Capitalism Dead?," had conceded, according to *The New York Times,* "that the number of Negro-owned commercial banks, for example, had declined to 20 in 19 cities from 49 in 38 cities in 1929. . . . When you think of the number of people involved, we've actually gone backwards, since the nineteen-twenties."

At the same Washington meeting, Dr. William R. Hudgins of New York, president of the Freedom National Bank in Harlem, had joined the chorus of protest. "Prior to organization of this black-controlled bank five years ago," he declared, "less than 5 per cent of the business ownership in Harlem was indigenous. A 1968 survey showed that 38 per cent of the Harlem businesses were locally owned. If there had been no Freedom National Bank, there would not have been this upward motivation. We must have leadership from our business community. If there is no business, then there is no leadership." He seemed to have forgotten how, ten months before, on the same platform with Travis, he had disclosed that affluent black people were holding back their support from the Freedom Bank. "The brothers are coming," he said, "but they're coming pretty damn slow."

Nor were blacks the only ones to jump on Dr. Brimmer

for raising objections to the concept of "black capitalism." The Nixon administration was deeply involved in promoting the concept. During the 1968 campaign, the Republican standard-bearer had labeled it "a bridge to human dignity," and promised the black community that he would put dollars where his mouth was. Negroes would get "a piece of the action," as he put it. He gave Secretary of Commerce Maurice H. Stans the job of implementation, but since there were 116 federal programs, administered by twenty different departments and agencies, already involved in helping new industries and since the President gave Stans no additional authority and no money, the program was clearly "dead-headed."

The White House had no comment on Brimmer's views, but Arthur McZier, minority spokesman for the Small Business Administration, commented that "Brimmer didn't really know what the programs were." For the first five months of fiscal 1970, said McZier, SBA loans to black capitalists were up 15 per cent for the corresponding period in 1969. When told what McZier had said, Dr. Brimmer remained unimpressed. He told a *Newsweek* correspondent that it was "irrelevant. Whether it's being tried or not, I am saying it should not be tried."

It was not that Dr. Brimmer was unaware of the black community's profile. He understood the desire for recognition all too well. Even on the subject of "black capitalism," which called for separatism, he said he knew how it had evolved, for black America was a large country in its own right. "If Negroes in the United States—numbering 22 million strong—constituted a separate country, they would be the twenty-sixth ranking nation in the world—slightly smaller than Argentina and slightly larger than Canada. They would be the third largest black nation, outranked only by Nigeria and Ethiopia. They would have an aggregate personal income of close to $35 billion, and income per head would be about $1600. Excluding the United States, only fourteen countries (none in Africa) would have per capita income at or above this figure."

The real fact, he went on, is that however roseate this view of black hegemony, it is only a mirage, for with Negroes distributed in every state in the Union, they do *not* constitute a separate nation. Taken as a whole, and "casting aside all illusions," he added, "one can see readily that the true economic strength of the Negro community is distressingly feeble." Not only do they earn on the average three-fifths as much as whites, but by other standards they are much poorer. For instance, their share of corporate wealth, reflected in stock ownership, is far less. A 1967 survey, sponsored by the U.S. Office of Economic Opportunity, found that Negro families owned about $200 million in stocks; this represented roughly $38 a family and only 1.3 per cent of all assets owned by Negro families. It also represented only 0.14 per cent of the total owned by all American families. In contrast, white families had average stock holdings of $2,603, accounting for one-sixth of their total assets.

"These data on asset accumulation," Dr. Brimmer concluded, "are simply the most glaring evidence of the pervasive weakness which distinguishes the Negro's economic position in the United States. At the same time, they have about two-thirds as many years of schooling as whites; they represent one-fifth of the poverty and own only two per cent of the wealth accumulated by American families."

It is necessary to keep these statistics firmly in mind, he went on, "because they make unmistakably clear the dangerous nonsense which lies at the core of separatism. They also define the nature and magnitude of the task which confronts us. Thus, our fundamental economic objective should be the closing of these gaps between the black and white communities as rapidly as possible." In the Brimmer view, the closing of certain gaps is primarily a black responsibility; in the case of others, the support of the white community is crucial.

Blacks, for example, have to realize that an automated society has few openings for unskilled and semi-skilled labor. Tomorrow's jobs are for those who have the educational levels to qualify, which means increasing the number of black high school and college graduates. While the record of blacks completing high school is rising in comparison with white students, the chasm between the number of whites and blacks finishing college is widening.

In October 1960 the Census Bureau estimated that the gap between black and white high school graduates entering the labor market was twenty-five percentage points. Eight years later, the schism had dropped to four points. But the figures for higher education told a different story. Between 1950 and 1968 the number of black college graduates rose from 2 per cent to approximately 4.25 per cent, compared with a white increase from 6.5 per cent to about 11 per cent. Accordingly, an original advantage of 4.5 percentage points increase to 6.75 points.

"This should be a matter of concern to all of us," declares Dr. Brimmer, "because the limited number of Negro college graduates is one of the major obstacles to increased participation of Negroes in the professional and managerial occupations. In 1968, fewer than half a million Negroes had completed four or more years of college.

The educational deficiency is the chief reason why, in Dr. Brimmer's words, the median black is still "anchored in those positions requiring little skill and offering few opportunities for advancement." On the other hand, it is evident that the 1960s was a period of considerable gap-closing for blacks who were qualified to compete with whites. Between 1960 and 1969, for instance, the percentage increase for blacks in professional and technical positions was two and a half times the rate for whites, and during the same period the increase for black managers, officials, and proprietors (the second-highest-paid group) was almost four times as rapid. Moreover, at the bottom of the totem pole, black advances outran white gains. As Dr. Brimmer points out, "In the 1960s, non-white workers left low-paying jobs in agriculture and household service at a rate of two to three times faster than did white workers." [14] But, he added, "beneath these over-all improvements, another—and disturbing—trend is also evident; within the Negro community, there appears to be a deepening schism between the able and the less able, between the well-prepared and those with few skills."

It is a case of wheels within wheels, for outwardly the economic progress of black America is advancing proportionately faster than for whites. Statistics compiled by the U.S. Department of Commerce, Bureau of the Census, show that in 1959 the median income of black families was 54 per cent of that earned by whites, and by 1968 63 per cent. The reason for the "deepening schism" among Negro families, despite their over-all economic advance, is the structure of black society itself, the distribution of children and the high number of female-headed households.

Not only does the average black family tend to be substantially larger than its white counterpart, but black children are unevenly divided. Compared with white families, the average black husband-wife family is .76 members larger and the female-headed family 1.26 members larger. And the latter is growing rapidly: between 1959 and 1968 the number increased by 24 per cent, and the family members under eighteen rose by a frightening 35 per cent. During the same period there was, says Dr. Brimmer, "an *absolute increase* of 609 thousand non-white family members eighteen or less classified as poor living in a female-headed family." Poverty, the Social Security Administration says, is the correlation between income and food costs. In 1968, an urban family of four was so classified if its total income was less than $3553. Using the yardstick, Dr. Brimmer points out that "While the 22 million Negroes constituted only 11 per cent of the country's total population in 1968, the 2.3 million poor children in non-white families headed by females represented 52 per cent of all such children."

To make these poverty figures more alarming, the Bureau of the Census reports that while blacks in stable patriarchal families are moving out of the poverty classification at about the same rate as whites, the opposite is true for matriarchal families whose incomes remain too low to escape. "In my judgment," warns Dr. Brimmer, "this deepening schism within the black community should interest us as much as the real progress that has been made by Negroes as a group." [15]

A further gap he hopes to close is the black lag in understanding the American economic system. Because of racial discrimination, Dr. Brimmer points out, "Negroes have had little contact with the world of economics, business and finance," and until this changes, they are poorly equipped to plot meaningful progress in their enclaves. "With few exceptions, they have not had an opportunity to acquire the familiarity with production, financing, marketing and other economic processes which determine the structure of the American economy and condition its performance." Out of 50,000 professional economists in the U.S., Negroes account for probably less than 2 per cent of the total.

Blacks have had little interest, moreover, in the day-to-day operation of the business world, as illustrated by an *Ebony* survey of its readers, which disclosed that 99.6 per cent do *not* read *Dun's Review;* 99.5 per cent do *not* read *Barron's;* 98.6 per cent do *not* read *Forbes;* 98.2 per cent do *not* read *Business Week;* 97.2 per cent do *not* read *Business Management;* 96.2 per cent do *not* read *Fortune.* Furthermore, it seems that only 1.4 per cent of the households reading *Nation's Business*—and only 1.9 per cent of those reading *The Wall Street Journal*—are black.

This deficiency in trying to attack black economic problems is in marked contrast, the Federal Reserve Board member thinks, to the civil rights movement of the 1950s,

when the effort to desegregate the schools, bar job discrimi-
nations, open up modes of public accommodations, and pass
open-housing legislation was undertaken by experts in the
field of law and politics. Today blacks are trying to solve
problems in the economic sphere for which they have had
scant training. "In my opinion," Dr. Brimmer declares,
"there is an urgent need to remedy this deficit in the economic intelligence of the black community." Unfortunately,
there is no evidence that black students are accepting the
admonition. As a matter of fact, Dr. Brimmer asserts, they
apparently do not see the relevance of economics to such
problems as poverty, discrimination in employment, and the
control and improvement of black enclaves in urban areas.

"In my judgment," he goes on, "if one is to make a successful attack on this range of issues, he must acquire at
least a good working knowledge of the economic roots from
which many of these obstacles spring." Otherwise, it is impossible to test "glamorous—but ill-conceived—schemes . . .
in the crucible of rigorous economic reasoning," as they
ought to be.[16]

While filling the gaps in education, in poverty, in economic know-how is something for blacks to achieve, white
business leaders share the responsibility. "They, too," says
Dr. Brimmer, "ought to refocus their sights on the essential
task of providing expanding opportunities for full participation by Negroes and other minority groups in the mainstream of the economy." Some, hopefully, are taking off
their coats, rolling up their sleeves, and going to work, but
others, Dr. Brimmer thinks, "are allowing themselves to be
associated with activities—which can only serve to foster racial division and separatism." To illustrate this Dr. Brimmer
cites the hypothetical example of an automobile manufacturer who gives a new-car franchise to a Negro to replace a
dealership in the ghetto previously owned by a white
man.[17] Yet this actually happened in Detroit during 1969,
when Nathan Conyers, brother of U.S. Rep. John Conyers,

Jr., took over Hettche Motor Sales, the oldest Ford dealership in the city, situated in the West Side, where much of
the rioting had occurred two years earlier.

"Why, one may ask, do I find efforts of this type disturbing?" Dr. Brimmer asks. "The answer is clear: they represent wrong choices favoring separatism over better choices
favoring participation in an integrated society. All of us
could agree that the presence of so few Negroes and other
minority group members among new-car dealers is deplorable. Thus, steps to correct the situation are certainly merito-
rious. On the other hand, was the transfer of a franchise
from a white man to a black man in the ghetto the best way
to draw Negroes into this segment of the automobile industry? I think not. Vacancies occur in dealerships outside the
ghetto, so why did the company not choose that route? Instead, the choice the manufacturer made pushed us another
step in the direction of separatism and away from an open
economy."

On the subject of economic integration, Dr. Brimmer reserves his most severe criticism for white banks which out of
decent motives arrive at wrong conclusions on ghetto financing and out of wrong motives arrive at wrong conclusions
on the use of black personnel in their institutions. As to the
first charge, Dr. Brimmer says the commercial bank which
failed to open a branch in a ghetto area did so with the
"very best intentions: it did not want to aggravate racial
tensions by seeming to foreclose the opportunities for a
group of local businessmen and professionals who later announced plans to launch a black-owned bank," but in doing
so, it added to "the racial divisions from which we are already suffering."

On the problem of using black personnel in white-controlled banks, there has been a "substantial improvement
over what the situation was a few years ago," Dr. Brimmer
says. But a survey conducted by the Federal Reserve Board
of its twelve districts shows that "none of the large banks

had Negroes serving on their boards of directors" and "less than a dozen" in positions of responsibility (vice-president and above).[18] "Black people," he emphasizes, *"must get inside* the corporate structure to learn how basic decisions are made and how genuine economic power is exercised." On this the fault is white prejudice and its inability, to date, to take black America into its confidence. "As a rule," the Fed governor contends, "most bank directors (particularly in the largest institutions) are not included on boards because they have substantial ownership of the banks' stock. Instead, they are included because they represent large customers (or potential customers), have a wide network of useful contacts (sometimes political), or help project a good image in its community." Accordingly, "qualified" representatives can and must be found in the black community.

This gap has to be filled if the concept of an integrated economy is to flourish. The fact that white leadership has failed to understand this is one of the chief reasons for the growth of a separate black economy, led by black-owned ghetto banks. Since 1963, eleven such banks have gained a start, and in Dr. Brimmer's words "operate at a substantial disadvantage in terms of both operating costs and efficiency." They earn "one-quarter to one-third" as much as the nation's banks generally. "Because of this combination of handicaps," Dr. Brimmer emphasizes, their multiplication should not be encouraged as a means of stimulating economic development in the black community, a statement that immediately drew fire from Owen Funderburg, president of the black-owned Gateway National Bank of St. Louis. Funderburg contended that the Fed governor was not "black oriented and had only a limited knowledge of problems in the ghetto." [19]

Dr. Brimmer let the comment pass, but soon afterward, in a speech to the American Economic Association, he suggested alternatives for stimulating the ghetto economy. Let the large commercial banks, with millions in capital, partici-

pate through a "new vehicle," established by the federal
government, that would permit them to invest in urban development through the purchase of equities in small and
medium-size businesses. A precedent already existed for this
under a section of the Federal Reserve Act of 1919 that allowed member banks to invest in international corporations
chartered by the Federal Reserve Board. Dr. Brimmer advised: "If American banks are thus enabled to assist indirectly in the equity financing of businesses abroad, in my
opinion, there is no logical reason why they should not be
permitted to do likewise in the United States." To be effective, they should have a minimum capitalization of $150,000.
While this was perhaps not the best—or only—vehicle
"through which commercial banks could enlarge their contribution to urban development," he went on, "it certainly
appears to be far more promising than reliance on small
banks in the ghetto as vehicles for economic development." [20]

It is this freshness of approach, this refusal to be locked in
orthodox economic postures, that marks Dr. Brimmer. A
conservative in dress, an economist in outlook, and an evan-
gelist for black improvement, he nevertheless mixes his determination with a measure of lightness. As *The Wall Street
Journal* reported in 1967, "When he rolled up to work on a
Saturday afternoon in his wife's sprightly white Mustang
and wearing casual Saturday clothes, an old hand couldn't
help thinking, 'Wow, the Board really is changing.'"

Notes

(*Chief sources other than author's interviews
are indicated below*).

John Conyers, Jr.

1. Avrum Schulzinger, "Conyers: Father and Sons," Detroit Sunday *News Magazine*, March 22, 1970.
2. Simeon Booker, "A New Face in Congress," *Ebony*, January 1965.
3. *Ibid.*
4. *Ibid.*
5. "The People versus the Pentagon," *The Progressive*, June 1969, p. 5.
6. *The New York Times*, June 7, July 18, 1969.
7. *Congressional Record*, October 14, 1969.
8. Detroit *Free Press*, October 31, 1968.
9. *Ibid.*, January 7, 1969.
10. *Ibid.*, February 9, 1969.
11. *The New York Times*, November 5, 1967.
12. *Congressional Record*, October 14, 1969.
13. *Ibid.*
14. *Ibid.*
15. *The New York Times*, June 29, 1967.
16. *Congressional Record*, December 20, 1969.
17. *The New York Times*, December 12, 1969.
18. *Congressional Record*, February 24, 1970.
19. *The Christian Science Monitor*, September 8, 1969.
20. John Conyers, Jr., "Politics and the Black," *Ebony*, August 1969.

Kenneth Allen Gibson

1. Nathan Wright, Jr., *Ready to Riot* (Holt, Rinehart and Winston, 1968), p. 38.

2. *Ibid.*, p. 42.
3. *Ibid.*, p. 8.
4. *Newsweek*, May 25, 1970, p. 63.
5. Marge McCullen, "Newark's Kenneth Gibson: The Man and the Mayor" (Greater Newark Chamber of Commerce, 1970).
6. *Ibid.*
7. *Ibid.*
7. *Ibid.*
8. *Ibid.*
9. *Ibid.*
10. Thomas R. Brooks, "Newark," *Atlantic*, August 1969.
11. *Ibid.*
12. *The New York Times*, December 21, 1970.
13. "Newark."
14. *The New York Times*, January 14, 1970.
15. *New Yorker*, June 27, 1970.
16. "Newark's Kenneth Gibson."
17. *The New York Times*, September 20, 1970.
18. *Ibid.*, July 6, 1970.
19. *Business Week*, August 15, 1970, p. 23.

Clifton Reginald Wharton, Jr.

1. Clifton R. Wharton, Jr., "Agriculture in Developing Nations," remarks before the Agricultural Technology Institute commencement exercises, March 20, 1970.
2. Clifton R. Wharton, Jr., "The Green Revolution: Cornucopia or Pandora's Box?" *Foreign Affairs*, April 1969.
3. Commencement address, Johns Hopkins University, May 26, 1970.
4. "Negro Pace Setter—Dr. Clifton Reginald Wharton, Jr.," *The New York Times*, October 18, 1969.
5. "The Stewardship of Excellence," address to the AAUP, April 23, 1970.

6. "A New Boss Takes Over at Michigan State," *Ebony*, July 1970.

7. East Lansing *State Journal*, September 9, 1969.

8. *The New York Times*, October 18, 1969.

9. Mary Kelly, "Wharton Reflects on Job Preparation," *The Christian Science Monitor*, October 20, 1969.

10. Detroit *News*, October 17, 1969.

11. *MSU Faculty News*, October 21, 1969.

12. Detroit *News*, October 24, 1969.

13. East Lansing *State Journal*, December 13, 1970.

14. William T. Noble, "The Unusual Man Who Will Run MSU," Detroit *News Magazine*, December 14, 1969.

15. *Michigan State News*, January 21, 1970.

16. Robert Berg, "MSU's Black Prexy Maintains His Calm in First Six Months," Detroit Sunday *News*, July 5, 1970.

17. "The Evolutionary Challenges to Black Profiles: Changing Patterns in Black Intellectual Leadership," remarks before the 12th Annual Scoutleaders Recognition Dinner, Detroit, February 7, 1970.

18. Quoted in Detroit *News*, April 22, 1970.

19. "Open Admissions and Agnew," *Saturday Review*, May 16, 1970.

20. Commencement address, MSU, May 2, 1970.

21. Statement on campus violence and the Indochina war, May 5, 1970.

22. *Michigan State News*, June 5, 1970.

Shirley Chisholm

1. David English, *Divided They Stand* (Prentice-Hall, 1969), p. 146.

2. *Ibid.*, p. 147.

3. *Ibid.*, p. 148.

4. Susan Brownmiller, "This Is Fighting Shirley Chisholm," *The New York Times Magazine*, April 13, 1969.

5. *Divided They Stand*, p. 149.

6. *Ibid.*, p. 150.
7. "This Is Fighting Shirley Chisholm."
8. *Divided They Stand*, p. 151.
9. *Ibid.*, pp. 151–52.
10. Quoted in *Divided They Stand*, p. 152.
11. "This Is Fighting Shirley Chisholm."
12. *Ibid.*
13. *Divided They Stand*, p. 153
14. "This Is Fighting Shirley Chisholm."
15. *The New York Times*, March 19, 1968.
16. *Divided They Stand*, p. 153.
17. *The New York Times*, November 7, 1968.
18. *Divided They Stand*, p. 153.
19. *The New York Times*, January 30, 1969.
20. *The New York Times*, May 22, 1970.
21. *Congressional Record*, August 6, 1969.
22. From a speech to the Institute on Man and Science, Rensselaerville, N.Y., August 1, 1969.
23. *The New York Times*, July 21–25, 1969.
24. *Congressional Record*, December 11, 1969.
25. *The New York Times*, March 18, 1970.
26. *The New York Times*, September 18, 1969.
27. *Ibid.*, May 22, 1970.
28. *Ibid.*, April 3, 1970.
29. Chisholm: "On the Washington Scene." (office release) 1969.

Horace Julian Bond

1. *The New York Times Magazine*, April 27, 1969.
2. Douglas Kiker, "Now, From the State that Brought You Lester Maddox," *Playboy*, June 1970.
3. John Neary, "Close-up: Julian Bond, a Militant inside the System," *Life*, November 11, 1968.
4. David Llorens, "Julian Bond," *Ebony*, May 1969.
5. "Close-up: Julian Bond. . . ."

6. *Playboy* article.

7. *The New York Times,* June 18, 1965.

8. *Newsweek,* January 24, 1966.

9. Reese Cleghorn, "Quiet, but Angry, Rebel," *The New York Times Magazine,* October 20, 1968.

10. *Newsweek,* January 24, 1966.

11. *The New York Times,* January 13, 1966.

12. *Nation,* February 7, 1966.

13. *The New York Times,* March 17, 1966.

14. Reese Cleghorn, "No Seat for the Negro Who Won," *New Republic,* January 29, 1966.

15. Quoted in "Close-up: Julian Bond. . . ."

16. *The New York Times Magazine,* April 27, 1969.

17. "Quiet, but Angry, Rebel."

18. *The New York Times Magazine,* April 27, 1969.

19. *The New York Times,* January 4, 1970.

20. *Time,* April 6, 1970.

21. *Ibid.*

22. *The New York Times Magazine,* April 27, 1969.

23. Speech at Auburn (N.Y.) Community College, April 29, 1970.

24. "When Black Power Runs the New Left," September 24, 1967.

25. *The New York Times Magazine,* April 27, 1969.

26. *Ibid.,* August 31, 1969.

27. "Quiet, but Angry, Rebel."

28. *The New York Times,* January 4, 1970.

John Mackey

1. George Vecsey, "John Mackey's Great Escape," *Sport,* August 1968.

2. *Ibid.*

3. John C. Schmidt, "How Many Men Can Do All Mackey Does at One Position?," Baltimore Sunday *Sun Magazine,* September 27, 1964.

4. *Newsday*, October 21, 1961.
5. *The New York Times*, July 9, 1968.
6. *Ibid.*, July 22, 1970.
7. Bill Tanton, "Pro Gridders Tired of Thrashing in Press," Baltimore *Sun*, July 27, 1970.
8. *The New York Times*, August 1, 1970.

Alvin F. Poussaint

1. Alvin F. Poussaint, "A Negro Psychiatrist Explains the Negro Psyche," *The New York Times Magazine*, August 20, 1970.
2. Irwin Katz and Lawrence Benjamin, "Effects of White Authoritarianism in Biracial Work Groups," *Journal of Abnormal and Social Psychology*, 61:448 (1960).
3. Alvin F. Poussaint, "Why Blacks Kill Blacks," *Ebony*, October 1970.
4. Alvin F. Poussaint, "A Psychiatrist Looks at Black Power," *Ebony*, March 1969.
5. Alvin F. Poussaint, "Black Power," *Ebony*, August 1967.
6. *The New York Times*, May 13, 1967.
7. "Black Power."
8. *The New York Times*, May 13, 1967.
9. "Black Power."
10. George R. Metcalf, *Black Profiles* (McGraw-Hill, 1968), p. 38.
11. *Ibid.*, p. 45.
12. *The New York Times*, November 12, 1967.
13. "A Negro Psychiatrist Explains. . . ."
14. "A Psychiatrist Looks at Black Power."
15. "A Negro Psychiatrist Explains. . . ."
16. *Ibid.*
17. Alvin F. Poussaint, M.D., and the Reverend Jesse L. Jackson, "A Dialogue on Separatism," *Ebony*, August 1970, p. 68.
18. *Ibid.*, p. 64.

19. *The New York Times,* June 21, 1970.
20. *Ibid.,* February 14, 1970.
21. "A Negro Psychiatrist Explains...," p. 58.
22. "A Psychiatrist Looks at Black Power," p. 146.
23. "A Dialogue on Separatism," p. 64.
24. *The New York Times,* November 12, 1967.
25. "A Dialogue on Separatism," p. 64.
26. "Why Blacks Kill Blacks," p. 148..

Andrew F. Brimmer

1. Mary Alice Fontnot, "Andrew Brimmer of Newellton Influences U.S. Monetary Policy," Baton Rouge Sunday *Advocate,* November 16, 1969.
2. "A Mediator Moves into the Fed," *Business Week,* March 5, 1966.
3. *Ibid.*
4. *The Wall Street Journal,* March 3, 1966.
5. *Ibid.*
6. "A Mediator Moves into the Fed."
7. *Ibid.*
8. "Andrew Brimmer of Newellton Influences U.S. Monetary Policy."
9. Al Rothenberg, "Black Banker," *Look,* October 21, 1969.
10. "Education and the Economic Advancement of Minority Groups in the United States," address by Dr. Brimmer to the annual convention of Phi Epsilon Pi fraternity, Miami Beach, August 28, 1969.
11. Andrew F. Brimmer and Henry S. Terrell, "The Economic Potential of Black Capitalism," from a paper presented at the 82d annual meeting of the American Economic Assembly, N.Y.C., December 29, 1969.
12. *Ibid.*
13. *The New York Times,* January 7, 1970.
14. Brimmer, "Economic Integration and the Progress of the Negro Community," *Ebony,* August 1970.

15. "Economic Progress of Negroes in the United States: The Deepening Schism," Founders' Day convocation address by Dr. Brimmer at Tuskegee Institute, March 22, 1970.
16. "An Economic Agenda for Black Americans," Charter Day convocation address by Dr. Brimmer at Atlanta University, October 16, 1970.
17. "Education and the Economic Advancement of Minority Groups. . . ."
18. *Ibid.*
19. *The New York Times,* January 8, 1970.
20. "The Black Banks: An Assessment of Performance and Prospects," address by Dr. Brimmer to a joint session of the American Finance Association and the American Economic Association, Detroit, December 28, 1970.

George R. Metcalf, a graduate of Princeton University and the Columbia University School of Journalism, is a former State Senator of New York. Between 1951 and 1965 Mr. Metcalf sponsored an outstanding series of bills in the areas of civil rights and public health. He co-sponsored fair housing laws that formed the basis for similar legislation enacted throughout the United States, pioneered health-insurance legislation and co-sponsored New York State's basic law on narcotics addiction. In 1965 Mr. Metcalf withdrew as a candidate for re-election in order to devote more time to writing and to the cause of fighting for racial justice. Currently, in addition to writing, he teaches Black Studies at Auburn Community College.